Muslim/Arab Mediation and Conflict Resolution

Inter- and intraclan conflicts in northern Israel pit hundreds against each other in revenge cycles that take years to resolve and impact the entire community. The Sulha is a Shari'a-based traditional conflict resolution process that works independently of formal legal systems and is widely practiced to manage such conflicts in the north of Israel, as well as throughout the Muslim and Arab worlds.

The Sulha process works by effecting a gradual attitudinal transformation, from a desire for revenge to a willingness to forgive, through restoration of the victim's clan sense of honour. *Muslim/Arab Mediation and Conflict Resolution* examines the process of Sulha, as practiced by the Arab population of northern Israel, where it plays a central role in the maintenance of peace among Muslims, Christians, and Druze alike. It presents detailed analysis of every stage of this at times protracted process. It uses interviews with victims, perpetrators, Sulha practitioners, community leaders, participant observation, and lawyers, along with statistical analysis to examine how Sulha affects people's lives, how various sectors of society impact the practice, and how it coexists with Israel's formal legal system. Furthermore, it examines how Sulha compares to Western dispute resolution processes.

This book offers the first comprehensive exploration of the entire Sulha process, and is a valuable resource for students and scholars of Middle East studies, Islamic studies and conflict resolution.

Doron Pely is Executive Director of the Sulha Research Centre (www.sulha.org) in Shefa'amer, Israel. His research explores Muslim/Arab dispute resolution practices, and conflict and justice in multi-cultural environments.

Israeli History, Politics and Society
Series Editor: Efraim Karsh
King's College London

This series provides a multidisciplinary examination of all aspects of Israeli history, politics and society, and serves as a means of communication between the various communities interested in Israel: academics, policy-makers, practitioners, journalists and the informed public.

1 **Peace in the Middle East**
   The challenge for Israel
   Edited by Efraim Karsh

2 **The Shaping of Israeli Identity**
   Myth, memory and trauma
   Edited by Robert Wistrich and David Ohana

3 **Between War and Peace**
   Dilemmas of Israeli security
   Edited by Efraim Karsh

4 **US–Israeli Relations at the Crossroads**
   Edited by Gabriel Sheffer

5 **Revisiting the Yom Kippur War**
   Edited by P. R. Kumaraswamy

6 **Israel**
   The dynamics of change and continuity
   Edited by David Levi-Faur, Gabriel Sheffer and David Vogel

7 **In Search of Identity**
   Jewish aspects in Israeli culture
   Edited by Dan Urian and Efraim Karsh

8 **Israel at the Polls, 1996**
   Edited by Daniel J. Elazar and Shmuel Sandler

9 **From Rabin to Netanyahu**
   Israel's troubled agenda
   Edited by Efraim Karsh

10 **Fabricating Israeli History**
    The 'New Historians,' second revised edition
    Efraim Karsh

11 **Divided against Zion**
    Anti-Zionist opposition in Britain to a Jewish state in Palestine, 1945–1948
    Rory Miller

12 **Peacemaking in a Divided Society**
    Israel after Rabin
    Edited by Sasson Sofer

13 **A Twenty-Year Retrospective of Egyptian–Israeli Relations**
Peace in spite of everything
Ephraim Dowek

14 **Global Politics**
Essays in honor of David Vital
Edited by Abraham Ben-Zvi and Aharon Klieman

15 **Parties, Elections and Cleavages**
Israel in comparative and theoretical perspective
Edited by Reuven Y. Hazan and Moshe Maor

16 **Israel at the Polls, 1999**
Edited by Daniel J. Elazar and M Ben Mollov

17 **Public Policy in Israel**
Edited by David Nachmias and Gila Menahem

18 **Developments in Israeli Public Administration**
Edited by Moshe Maor

19 **Israeli Diplomacy and the Quest for Peace**
Mordechai Gazit

20 **Israeli–Romanian Relations at the End of Ceauceşcu's Era**
Yosef Govrin

21 **John F Kennedy and the Politics of Arms Sales to Israel**
Abraham Ben-Zvi

22 **Green Crescent over Nazareth**
The displacement of Christians by Muslims in the Holy Land
Raphael Israeli

23 **Jerusalem Divided**
The Armistice Region, 1947–1967
Raphael Israeli

24 **Decision on Palestine Deferred**
America, Britain and wartime diplomacy, 1939–1945
Monty Noam Penkower

25 **A Dissenting Democracy**
The Israeli movement 'Peace Now'
Magnus Norell

26 **British, Israel and Anglo-Jewry 1947–1957**
Natan Aridan

27 **Israeli Identity**
In search of a successor to the pioneer, tsabar and settler
Lilly Weissbrod

28 **The Israeli Palestinians**
An Arab minority in the Jewish state
Edited by Alexander Bligh

29 **Israel, the Hashemites and the Palestinians**
The fateful triangle
Edited by Efraim Karsh and P. R. Kumaraswamy

30 **The Last Days in Israel**
Abraham Diskin

31 **War in Palestine, 1948**
Strategy and diplomacy
David Tal

32 **Rethinking the Middle East**
Efraim Karsh

33 **Ben-Gurion against the Knesset**
Giora Goldberg

34 **Trapped Fools**
Thirty years of Israeli policy in the territories
Schlomo Gazit

35 **Israel's Quest for Recognition and Acceptance in Asia**
Garrison state diplomacy
Jacob Abadi

36 **H. V. Evatt and the Establishment of Israel**
The undercover Zionist
Daniel Mandel

37 **Navigating Perilous Waters**
An Israeli strategy for peace and security
Ephraim Sneh

38 **Lyndon B. Johnson and the Politics of Arms Sales to Israel**
In the shadow of the hawk
Abraham Ben-Zvi

39 **Israel at the Polls, 2003**
Edited by Shmuel Sandler, Ben M. Mollov and Jonathan Rynhold

40 **Between Capital and Land**
The Jewish National Fund's finances and land-purchase priorities in Palestine, 1939–1945
Eric Engel Tuten

41 **Israeli Democracy at the Crossroads**
Raphael Cohen-Almagor

42 **Israeli Institutions at the Crossroads**
Raphael Cohen-Almagor

43 **The Israeli–Palestine Peace Negotiations, 1999–2001**
Within reach
Gilead Sher

44 **Ben-Gurion's Political Struggles, 1963–67**
A lion in winter
Zaki Shalom

45 **Ben-Gurion, Zionism and American Jewry**
1948–1963
Ariel Feldestein

46 **The Origins of the American–Israeli Alliance**
The Jordanian factor
Abraham Ben-Zvi

47 **The Harp and the Shield of David**
Ireland, Zionism and the state of Israel
Shulamit Eliash

48 **Israel's National Security**
Issues and challenges since the Yom Kippur War
Efraim Inbar

49 **The Rise of Israel**
A history of a revolutionary state
Jonathan Adelman

50 **Israel and the Family of Nations**
The Jewish nation-state and human rights
Alexander Yakobson and Amnon Rubinstein

51 **Secularism and Religion in Jewish–Israeli Politics**
Traditionists and modernity
Yaacov Yadgar

52 **Israel's National Security Law**
Political dynamics and historical development
Amichai Cohen and Stuart A. Cohen

53 **Politics of Memory**
The Israeli underground's struggle for inclusion in the national pantheon and military commemoralization
Udi Lebel

54 **Moment in Palestine in the Arab/Israeli War of 1948**
On the Israeli home front
Moshe Naor

55 **Britain's Moment in Palestine**
Retrospect and perspectives, 1917–1948
Michael J. Cohen

56 **Israel and the Palestinian Refugee Issue**
The formulation of policy, 1948–1956
Jacob Tovy

57 **Jihad in Palestine**
Political Islam and the Israeli–Palestine conflict
Shaul Bartal

58 **Ralph Bunche and the Arab–Israeli Conflict**
Mediation and the UN, 1947–1949
Elad Ben-Dror

59 **Muslim/Arab Mediation and Conflict Resolution**
Understanding Sulha
Doron Pely

Israel: The First Hundred Years (Mini Series)
edited by Efraim Karsh

1 Israel's Transition from Community to State, edited by Efraim Karsh
2 From War to Peace? edited by Efraim Karsh
3 Politics and Society since 1948, edited by Efraim Karsh
4 Israel in the International Arena, edited by Efraim Karsh
5 Israel in the Next Century, edited by Efraim Karsh

Muslim/Arab Mediation and Conflict Resolution
Understanding Sulha

Doron Pely

LONDON AND NEW YORK

First published 2016 by Routledge

2 Park Square, Milton Park, Abingdon, Oxfordshire OX14 4RN
711 Third Avenue, New York, NY 10017

Routledge is an imprint of the Taylor & Francis Group, an informa business

First issued in paperback 2018

Copyright © 2016 Doron Pely

The right of Doron Pely to be identified as author of this work has been asserted by him in accordance with sections 77 and 78 of the Copyright, Designs and Patents Act 1988.

All rights reserved. No part of this book may be reprinted or reproduced or utilised in any form or by any electronic, mechanical, or other means, now known or hereafter invented, including photocopying and recording, or in any information storage or retrieval system, without permission in writing from the publishers.

Notice:
Product or corporate names may be trademarks or registered trademarks, and are used only for identification and explanation without intent to infringe.

British Library Cataloguing-in-Publication Data
A catalogue record for this book is available from the British Library

Library of Congress Cataloging-in-Publication Data
Names: Pely, Doron, 1953– author.
Title: Muslim/Arab mediation and conflict resolution : understanding sulha / Doron Pely.
Description: New York, NY : Routledge, [2016] | Series: Israeli history, politics and society ; v. 59 | Includes bibliographical references and index.
Identifiers: LCCN 2015039808 | ISBN 9781138185326 (hbk : alk. paper)
Subjects: LCSH: Compromise (Islamic law)—Israel. | Mediation—Israel. | Dispute resolution (Islamic law)
Classification: LCC KBP817.2 .P45 2016 | DDC 347/.16709—dc23
LC record available at http://lccn.loc.gov/2015039808

ISBN: 978-1-138-18532-6 (hbk)
ISBN: 978-1-138-61463-5 (pbk)

Typeset in Times New Roman
by Apex CoVantage, LLC

To Galina and Adam

Contents

List of figures	xiv
List of tables	xv
Foreword	xvi
Acknowledgements	xviii

Introduction   1

Sulha: essence and characteristics   1
Sulha in the literature   3
How Sulha works   5
Methodology   6

1 Sulha in Muslim jurisprudence and customary justice   10

Primary sources of Muslim jurisprudence   11
Islam's (Sunni) major schools of law   15
The evolution of Muslim customary justice   17
Tahkim *(Arbitration)*   19
Sulha (Settlement)   24

2 The theoretical foundations of Sulha   35

What is conflict?   35
Muslim/Arab vs. Western conflict resolution perspectives   36
Sulha and conflict resolution theories   39
Where do we go from here?   49
Re-integrative honouring concept   49

3 Honour, revenge and forgiveness in Sulha   54

About honour   55
Revenge and forgiveness   60

xii *Contents*

> *About revenge   61*
> *About forgiveness   66*
> *Forgiveness and reconciliation   68*
> *The interplay of honour, revenge and forgiveness in Sulha   70*

4   Sulha: structure and characteristics   76

> *Re-integrative honouring concept (RHC)   77*
> *RHC survey   77*
> *Assumptions   79*
> *Sulha stages   80*

5   Sulha and gender   128

> *Conflict and patriarchy   128*
> *The impact of interclan conflicts on women   129*
> *The impact of women on Sulha   131*

6   Sulha and Western ADR   138

> *Western and Muslim/Arab conflict resolution assumptions   139*
> *Sulha mediation elements vs. Western-style ADR mediation elements   141*
> *Arbitration elements in Sulha and Western-style ADR   143*
> *Confidentiality, venting and neutrality in Sulha and Western ADR   144*

7   Sulha and Israel's legal system   153

> *The differences between the Sulha and Israel's legal system   153*
> *Sulha and the courts   154*
> *Is the Sulha agreement admissible evidence?   157*
> *How do the Sulha and Israel's formal legal system complement each other?   159*
> *Sulha's place within Israel's judiciary system: a quantitative perspective   161*
> *Discussion   167*

8   Sulha case study   174

> *Murder in A'eblin   174*
> *Dispute's origin   174*
> *Who started the Sulha process and why?   176*

What did the Sulha Committee do immediately after the dispute started? 177
What did the perpetrator's clan do/say? 177
What did the victim's clan do/say? 179
How did the Sulha process start? 179
Was there a Hudna? How long? How many times was it extended? 179
How did the Jaha's deliberations proceed? 179
What tools did the Jaha use during the process? 181
The Sulha ceremony 181

Conclusions 186

Findings and new insights 186
Possible directions for future research 187

Appendices 191
Bibliography 199
Index 211

Figures

2.1	Maslow's hierarchy of needs	44
2.2	Sulha's hierarchy of needs	45
4.1	Stage 1: depicted averages – victim's clan	83
4.2	Stage 2: depicted averages – victim's clan	87
4.3	Stage 3: depicted averages – victim's clan	93
4.4	Stage 4: depicted averages – victim's clan	97
4.5	Stage 5: depicted averages – victim's clan	103
4.6	Stage 6: depicted averages – victim's clan	109
4.7	Stage 7: depicted averages – victim's clan	117
8.1	Getting ready for the Sulha ceremony	175
8.2	The killer's family approaching the Sulha site	178
8.3	Victim's brother returns the blood money	180
8.4	Christian clergy ties a knot in the Sulha flag	182
A.1	Photograph of a Sulha agreement	192
C.1	General map of Israel	198
C.2	Map of research region (northern Israel)	198

Tables

4.1	Stage 1: descriptive statistics – victim's clan	83
4.2	Stage 2: descriptive statistics – victim's clan	87
4.3	Stage 3: descriptive statistics – victim's clan	92
4.4	Stage 4: descriptive statistics – victim's clan	97
4.5	Stage 5: descriptive statistics – victim's clan	102
4.6	Stage 6: descriptive statistics – victim's clan	109
4.7	Stage 7: descriptive statistics – victim's clan	116
4.8	Descriptive statistics (averages): victim's clan – all stages, all variables	119
4.9	T test analysis: desire to avenge – all Sulha stages	120
4.10	T test analysis: willingness to forgive – all Sulha stages	122
4.11	T test analysis: sense of damage to honour – all Sulha stages	122
4.12	T test analysis – revenge, forgiveness, honour – start and end of Sulha process	123
7.1	Tabulation of quantitative data and analysis for courts' Sulha-related decisions	164

Foreword

I don't really remember anymore why I decided to write my master's thesis on Sulha. But I did. At the time, I was living in Amherst, Massachusetts, and studying for my MA in dispute resolution at the University of Massachusetts, Boston.

When I went to Israel on a business trip, I asked around casually about Sulha, which is practiced by the Arab community in Israel, and the wife of my business partner at the time gave me a number of a man she said "was a professional Sulha maker"; the name was Faraj Khneifes. I called without much hope, and somehow ended up talking with Faraj's brother. He gave me another number and encouraged me to call. I did. The voice on the other side of the line was immediately friendly and welcoming. "Come Friday," he said. "We'll have breakfast and go meet some Sulha makers."

I showed up Friday morning. Faraj was getting dressed; his wife and children welcomed me, and we chatted awkwardly as we all waited for Faraj. He finally appeared after about 30 minutes, greeted me like a long-lost relative and, nudging me forward towards the front door, declared: "Let's go eat!" I trudged after him, quite uncertain about what was going to happen next. We walked about 300 yards and entered an enclosed compound swarming with hundreds of men (the women had a separate compound) and laid out with tables and chairs capable of feeding many people. "A relative is getting married today," Faraj explained as we dove into a long greeting line, full of people and faces I'd never seen before.

I took my cue from Faraj and shook the hands of all the greeters. Faraj introduced me as "someone interested in Sulha". They all nodded, smiled and welcomed me as if my presence there was self-evident. Faraj dragged me to a vacant chair, introduced me to my immediate neighbours, sat me down and said "Eat a good breakfast; I have to help serve."

I had a fantastic breakfast; some of the dishes were familiar; others completely new to me. The noise level was astounding, and the heat built up, even under the blue tarp. Everyone was having a good time. Faraj scampered around, ushering newcomers to vacant seats, and serving them fresh portions of food. Dozens of other men – old and young – were doing the same thing, all with enthusiasm I forgot existed.

After the meal, I washed my hands at the especially set, open-air, communal wash-point, glancing left and right at distinguished elderly gentlemen, who rinsed their false teeth purposefully and flashed toothless grins of greeting at me. We were on top of a hill, in front of a vista stretching all the way to the Lebanese border. I felt a kin sense of happiness and anticipation, the kind one feels as one embarks on a long-anticipated journey.

After the extended breakfast, we got into Faraj's car and drove to the nearby Arab village of Nahef to the home of Sheikh Ihye Abul Rani (Abu Mohammad), the aging, but incredibly alert and eloquent head of the Sulha Committee for northern Israel. The sheikh greeted me with a smile and a warm handshake, seated me next to him in the seating room where there were a dozen Sulha committee members, inquired politely about me and my interest in Sulha and welcomed me publically, saying he would do what he could to help. At the time, I did not understand the full meaning of what took place that afternoon in Nahef; only much later I understood that I had been vetted and passed. I was in.

The next two summers I arrived in Israel in early June and spent nearly two months chasing Faraj and the Sulha Committee across the northern part of Israel, visiting dozens of conflict spots. Initially, I understood very little of what was taking place around me. Confused, bewildered, sometimes alarmed, I scribbled on every piece of paper I could find, asked incessant questions, tasking the patience of dozens of people as I tried to understand what I was witnessing. At the end of two summers, I had enough material to write my master's thesis on the relationship between Sulha and Israel's formal legal system.

As I was thanking Faraj before returning to Amherst, he casually suggested: "Come back, live with us for a while and get to really learn about Sulha." I wasn't sure how such a thing could happen, but the idea intrigued me, and upon returning to the United States, I broached the subject with my wife, gingerly and without much hope. She did not contemplate the matter for more than four seconds and answered. "Great idea; I'm game."

So my wife and I moved from the United States to the town of Shefa'amer, near Nazareth, in the Lower Galilee region of Israel, where we lived for two and a half years – a sole Jewish couple among 40,000 Arabs – Muslims, Druze and Christians. Our house was next door to Faraj's, separated by two lemon and one pomegranate trees. Many times, as he barged out of his house, hurrying to attend to some new or evolving conflict, I would shout to him, "Hey, Faraj, what's happening?" and he would answer: "Hurry up, let's go!" And off we would go, me asking questions to try to understand what was about to happen, he driving skilfully through the winding roads, answering my questions and all the time talking on the phone, organizing, getting the latest news, gathering other members of the Sulha Committee, brainstorming with colleagues.

This book is essentially the story of these years in Shefa'amer.

Acknowledgements

I want to thank Mr. Faraj Khneifes, son of the late Sheikh Saleh Khneifes, for welcoming me to his life, his family, his community and the proceedings of the Sulha Committee – without which none of this journey of learning and discovery would have been even remotely possible.

I also want to thank Faraj's family, the entire Khneifes clan, our neighbours in Shefa'amer and actually all the residents of this crowded and lively town, who welcomed us – total strangers – into their midst with unbelievable warmth and kindness, listened to my broken Arabic with patience and endurance and shared their lives with a generosity I have never experienced before. Special thanks to Said who wrapped us in friendship and practical help, and who taught me (and still does) priceless lessons about every imaginable subject.

I remain deeply indebted and grateful to all the members of the Sulha Committee, who were willing to share with me their wisdom and experience, to Professor David Matz, of UMASS Boston, who patiently re-oriented me from conflict to conflict resolution, and Professor Efraim Karsh, of King's College, London, who guided me expertly on the sometimes bumpy road to completing my doctoral dissertation – the basis for this book.

And most of all, I'd like to express my thanks to those members of the Arab community of northern Israel, who, graciously, and with incredible generosity of spirit, allowed me to witness their lives at times of agony, disaster, despair and pain, but also in times of hope and rejoicing – as they struggled, each in her and his own unique way, to cope with loss, anger, frustration and mourning. I learned a lot, am still learning and will never cease to wonder at how complex and wonderful life is.

Introduction

Sulha: essence and characteristics

Inter- and intraclan conflicts in northern Israel's Arab community pit dozens, hundreds, at times thousands of people against each other in revenge and counter-revenge cycles that may take years to resolve. Such conflicts affect everybody in the community, both within and outside the disputing clans. Members of the perpetrator's clan may be exiled from their place of residence for short or extended durations, or even permanently.[1] Members of the victim's clan may embark on revenge attacks that cause additional casualties and physical damage to the perpetrator's clan, thus plunging entire communities into a maelstrom of fear, anxiety, anticipation of violence and unrelated casualties. In the words of Faraj Khneifes, a veteran Sulha maker: 'A rash act of revenge can ruin not only the victim's life and that of his family but also the lives of the avenger's entire family'.[2]

The only dispute management and resolution tool currently available to deal with such disputes is the Sulha (Settlement in Arabic):[3] a ubiquitous, Shari'a-based traditional inter- and intraclan restorative justice, conflict[4] management and resolution process that takes place independently of national and/or local formal legal systems and is widely practiced, with variations, throughout the Muslim and Arab worlds. In the words of Aseel Rahimi, a Legal Fellow at the American Bar Association Gulf Rule of Law Initiative: 'Sulh is the preferred result and process in any form of conflict resolution'.[5]

This book examines the process of Sulha as practiced by the Arab population of northern Israel,[6] where the vast majority of Israeli Arabs live,[7] and where it plays a central role in the maintenance of peace among Muslims, Christians and Druze alike[8] – alongside the state's formal legal system.

There is broad consensus among researchers and practitioners of Muslim customary justice that the Sulha is highly successful in facilitating reconciliation between and among disputing clans. Khneifes says that '[f]or the past 40 years, there have been three or four Sulha agreements that were broken [by either disputing side]'. He adds that '[i]n general, after the agreement and the ceremony, life goes back to normal, slowly, but visibly'.[9] Gellman and Vuinovich write that the Sulha 'has cultural moral authority to handle grave offences such as murder'.[10] In the words of retired Israeli Supreme Court Justice Sheikh Abdel Rahman

Zuabi, a Muslim Arab who lives in northern Israel: 'Without Sulha, the country, or rather its Arab part, will descend into chaos'.[11] Professor Musa Abu Ramadan, an expert on Islamic law and legal Islamic practise in Israel, views Sulha in similar terms: 'Sulha, as a central part of the region's customary justice mechanism, is crucial to maintaining and repairing communal relations in Israel's Palestinian community'.[12]

The Sulha is anchored in the Qur'an, Islam's holy book, which states that '[t]he recompense of an injury is an injury the like thereof; but whoever forgives and thereby brings about a reestablishment of harmony, his reward is with God; and God loves not the wrongdoers'.[13] Islam is clear about the place of revenge in conflicts, and is equally clear in its choice of forgiveness as the preferred approach to resolving conflicts through reconciliation.

It seems that the Sulha process works by facilitating the Qur'anic prescription, effecting attitudinal transformation of the victim's clan from a desire to avenge to a willingness to forgive. Such transformation takes place through a process of gradual restoration of the victim side's sense of honour. The agreement achieved through the Sulha process is considered binding for disputants, for all generations, past, present and future.[14]

Formal legal systems across the Middle East and the Muslim world usually deal with infractions by individuals, but do not account for the wounds inflicted by conflicts on the community's fabric of life and more specifically on the lives of the extended families (*Hamail* in Arabic) of the disputants.[15] As anthropologist Victor Ayoub posits,

> an individual who resorts to the courts does not solve the problem of the group. Whatever the result of the court action, the need for mediation persists because reconciliation of the disputants continues to be considered important in maintaining the solidarity of the group.[16]

Ramahi provides additional insight into the place of Sulha within Arab culture when she writes: 'Whereas, westerners know the primacy of law, the Arabs know the primacy of interpersonal relationships'.[17]

This is where the Sulha comes in with a view to resolving a variety of conflicts, including murder, physical assault, rape, theft and property conflicts. Its underlying idea is that the neglect of small, relatively less severe feuds will result in their eventual expansion to major conflicts.[18] More broadly, the Sulha's overall purpose – as seen by practitioners, disputants and the community at large – is to mend the conflict-afflicted social fabric of the community by fixing the relations between and among the affected people *and* their relatives. This is based on a view that hurting an individual means hurting the entire community. In the words of three Sulha scholars: 'The Sulh ritual stresses the close link between the psychological and political dimensions of communal life through its recognition that injuries between individuals and groups will fester and expand if not acknowledged, repaired, forgiven and transcended'.[19]

The Sulha is carried out by a Sulha Committee (*Jaha*) comprising a number of dignitaries – men with exceptional standing and clout within the Arab community – who employ diverse mediation and arbitration tools in a process that can range from months to decades.[20]

On the 'mediation side' of the process the Sulha strives to restore the sense of honour of the disputing parties (particularly but not exclusively the victim's clan) in order to restore trust and facilitate a gradual process of reconciliation between them. Through the 'arbitration side' of the process, the Sulha creates both the 'bridging' mechanisms required for guiding (at times even coercing) the disputing clans through difficult periods of stalemate (e.g. major disagreements and/or inability to compromise, accommodate or bring/accept new ideas), as well as the obligatory framework of commitment that forces the disputing clans to stay within the process despite the difficulties and to abide by the decisions of the Sulha Committee.

By way of starting the Sulha process, the disputants' representatives sign a document of authorization (*tafwith*), obliging their clans to fully abide by any decision made by the *Jaha*. The committee then negotiates a temporary truce between the disputants (*hudna*). Afterwards, using shuttle diplomacy, private caucuses and a set of rituals and rites, it attempts to cause the disputants to abandon their traditional proclivity for revenge and to adopt a forgiving posture. Throughout the process both disputants and the *Jaha* leverage honour extensively to manoeuvre, sometimes postpone and ultimately facilitate and maintain a final reconciliation agreement.

Sulha in the literature

Despite the Sulha's ubiquity and centrality in Muslim and Arab cultures, scholarly exploration of the process remains scant. In recent years, there has been a marked increase in the number and quality of Sulha-related research in general, and in the Israeli context in particular, yet scholars have either tended to describe the process in mostly general and descriptive terms,[21] to focus on extremely narrow aspects of its operation[22] or to view it in conjunction with Western arbitration/conflict resolution methods rather than as a distinct process in and of itself – at times with the explicit aim of redressing the perceived Western misrepresentation of Islam as a belligerent religion.[23]

Political scientist Daniel Smith, for example, provides a detailed description of the Sulha but one that lacks rigorous delineation of the process' distinct stages (e.g. recruiting the perpetrator's and victim's clans to the process).[24] Psychologist Susan Nathan provides an accurate description of the Sulha process in northern Israel, yet does it in the most general and impressionistic terms as part of a personal 'travel diary' by a person with limited familiarity with the region, rather than a scholarly study. Elias Jabbour, a seasoned Sulha practitioner, provides a firsthand informative account of the process in northern Israel, yet his narrative is almost purely anecdotal and lacks academic rigour.[25] Even conflict resolution scholar Muhammad Abu Nimer, perhaps the foremost student of the process, stops well short of providing the kind of analysis that will shed fresh light on the Sulha's inner workings.

Part of this absence of detail is due to the fact that many Sulha processes take several years to conclude, requiring an extended presence of the researcher. Furthermore, much of the Sulha process is confidential and closed to the public; only the final ceremony is opened to the public.

Another absent, yet central, element of the Sulha is the fact that it constitutes a unique case of a conflict resolution mechanism that is neither a pure mediating practise (since it includes many arbitrative elements) nor an arbitrative one (since some of its major components contain mediation practices). Most scholars miss this complexity. Thus we have Aseel Ramahi considering Sulha a purely arbitrative practice;[26] Smith, Gellman and Vuinovich discussing Sulha exclusively in the context of mediation; and Abu Nimer using mediation and arbitration interchangeably, as if these are identical practises.[27] As a result, there is no Sulha-related research discussing this distinct mix of mediation and arbitration tools within the process.[28]

Nor do the Sulha's core concepts, notably honour, revenge and forgiveness, receive, in most instances, more than episodic treatment that fails to explain their influence on the process. Thus, for example, Gellman and Vuinovich write about the 'restoration of honour and injustice caused by an imbalance of honour' without explaining why it is so and how this weakness is redressed by the Sulha process.[29] Abu Nimer talks about the necessity 'to deal with the imbalance of honour before compromises on substantive issues can be worked out'[30] yet fails to explain how honour is modified to redress this 'imbalance of honour'.

Sharon Lang links Sulha to the concept of honour (*sharaf*). In her words:

> Sulha is inextricably connected to *sharaf*, and in many ways is about maintaining, restoring, and negotiating respect and reputation. Indeed, it is because Sulha redresses the imbalance of *sharaf* created when one individual attacks another that revenge can be foregone.[31]

Lang proceeds to provide a robust explanation of some of the mechanisms used by the Sulha makers to restore the honour of the victim's clan and facilitate reconciliation, but the description and analysis rely exclusively on mediation-type instruments and totally ignore the considerable arbitrative powers of the *Jaha* and their application within the Sulha process.

One is thus left largely in the dark as to the nature of the interaction between the three concepts (honour, revenge and forgiveness) and the ways and means through which they have come to play such a major role in the process in all its stages: conflict eruption, management and resolution.

All in all, the existing literature tends to treat the Sulha from a folkloristic perspective lacking in-depth analysis of the process itself. It especially fails to demonstrate *how* the application of a judicious mix of mediation and arbitration tools contributes to changing disputants' attitudes; what tools (if any) are used by interveners to effect the desired changes; and how such tools achieve the goal of gradually replacing what is described as an almost unquenchable desire to avenge a perceived collective injury to the clan's honour with a willingness to forgive and move on with life. It is these key pitfalls in the study of the Sulha process, as well as other research lacunae such as the ignored impact of women on the process,[32] that this book seeks to redress.

How Sulha works

We know that the Sulha succeeds in transforming the attitudes of the disputants from a desire to avenge to a willingness to forgive, but we do not know *how exactly* this transformation is achieved. Most explorations focus, for obvious reasons, on the Sulha ceremony – a public event rife with ritual and emotions. Yet there is no study addressing the question of Sulha functionality in its entirety – from the eruption of a conflict through its resolution and beyond, and this is the central question addressed by this book.

Restorative justice theory rests heavily on re-integrative shaming theory (RST). In the words of Nathan Harris and Shadd Maruna, 'The concepts of "shame" and "shaming" occupy a central, if controversial, position within the theoretical understanding of restorative justice'.[33]

This book argues that the efficacy of the Sulha, a communal restorative justice practice, rests on similar underpinnings, with the major exception that the Sulha process does *not* include any shaming of either party to the conflict. On the contrary, it shows that the Sulha's efficacy rests on what can be termed re-integrative honouring concept (RHC) – a novel concept developed by this book. Whereas the RST's prescribed process follows the sequence shaming-acknowledgement-change-restoration, RHC proposes a process comprising the following elements: honouring-acknowledgement-change-restoration.

Using the RHC concept, this book demonstrates how Sulha practitioners gradually restore the sense of honour and dignity of the victim's clan while at the same time maintaining, and if necessary restoring, that of the perpetrator's clan – leading to reconciliation and the reintegration of both clans into a nonbelligerent relationship within the larger community. It also shows that as the clans' sense of honour is sufficiently restored (in their opinion), the victim's clan will gradually become amenable to forgiving the perpetrator's clan, thus facilitating the reconciliation stage of the Sulha (the Sulha ceremony); concurrently, it is shown that when the *Jaha* succeeds in sustaining (and reinforcing) the perpetrator's clan's sense of honour throughout the process, it can bring itself to acknowledge the wrong done to the victim and its clan, to offer an apology and to make amends to the victim's clan, thus completing the enabling restorative justice cycle of honour restoration/maintenance: acknowledgement of responsibility by the perpetrator's clan leading to an apology (and in many cases payment of blood money), to acknowledgement of the option of forgiveness by the victim's clan, to a declaration of the end of the conflict in a public ceremony.

6 *Introduction*

Furthermore, this book shows that the Sulha's success depends on the precise application by the third-party interveners of a finely tuned, diverse set of mediation and arbitration tools timed to achieve reconciliation goals along the following sequence:

- Recruiting the perpetrator's clan – using a mostly arbitrative approach.
- Recruiting the victim's clan – using a mostly mediative approach.
- Establishing a temporary truce – using a mix of mediation and arbitration tools.
- Negotiating with the disputing clans – using mostly mediation practices.
- Determining the Sulha's verdict – using mediation tools in the foreground and arbitration tools in the background.
- Concluding the reconciliation process with a public Sulha ceremony – using mostly mediation applications, with some arbitration tools when/if necessary.

Overall, the book offers a comprehensive and well-rounded discussion that adds to the existing body of knowledge in the field by explaining the ways and means through which the Sulha achieves its goals, something that has not been done before.

Specifically, the book:

- Locates the place of Sulha within Islam and explains the underlying reasons for its abiding and ubiquitous place within Muslim/Arab cultures.
- Underscores the Sulha's uniqueness as an arbitration–mediation conflict resolution mechanism.
- Identifies the Sulha's task-specific stages and the diverse set of tools used by the practitioners in each phase – a key to the process' success.
- Explains the role played by honour, revenge, and forgiveness in the Sulha process and analyses the delicate interaction of these factors by using a new conceptual framework – the Re-integrative Honouring Concept (RHC).
- Demonstrates how women, despite their formal exclusion from the Sulha, exert significant influence on the process and how this influence indirectly accelerates (or delays) progress towards an agreement and directly facilitates the maintenance of the attained agreement and its durability.
- Examines the careful synchronization between the informal Sulha and the state's formal legal system.

Methodology

By way of achieving these goals, the book tracks the shifts in the disputing clans' honour, revenge and forgiveness perceptions as the Sulha process moves from one task-specific stage to the next, from conflict eruption to conflict resolution. It does so through the following steps:

- Locating and describing the Sulha stages.
- Locating and describing the mediation and arbitration tools used in each stage.

- Locating and describing the 'state of honour', 'atate of revenge' and 'atate of forgiveness' of the victim's clan throughout the process.
- Mapping the changes in the aforementioned factors throughout the Sulha process.
- Looking for a correlation between the Sulha stages and the changing phases.

These objectives are pursued through a mix of qualitative and quantitative methods. This approach includes several ethnographic tools, such as interviews, surveys, questionnaires, participant observation, informants' insights and analysis of existing literature, as well as descriptive statistics and basic inferential statistics to examine the reliability of the findings.

Most of the empirical data used in this work were gathered through firsthand field research using the classic ethnographic methods of observation, informal and unstructured interviews and case study analysis.[34] To this end, the author lived in the researched community for almost three years, got to know the members of the *Jaha* well and gained reasonable familiarity with the basic cultural codes, as well as the underlying social, political and economic issues that tend to colour interactions of informants with researchers and consequently insert a bias into the collected data. In many ways, he occupied a space that is probably most accurately described as being somewhere between Morris Freilich's 'marginal native' and Michael Agar's 'professional stranger'.[35]

To ensure data reliability, interviews and questionnaire-filling sessions were carried out with people from multiple clans, in multiple villages and towns, covering multiple conflicts, multiple religious affiliations (and combinations thereof) and socioeconomic groups. The author did not know many of his informants in advance, nor did he select them in any way. They were 'selected' by randomly approaching them or by virtue of being associated with the researched conflicts, which were in turn selected on the basis of the willingness of the disputants to enable access.

Notes

1. Elias Jabbour, *Sulha – Palestinian Traditional Peacemaking Process* (Montreat, NC: House of Hope Publications, 1993), p. 36.
2. Author interview with Faraj Khneifes, 14 June 2009. See also Muhammad Abu-Nimer, 'Conflict Resolution Approaches: Western and Middle Eastern Lessons and Possibilities', *American Journal of Economics and Sociology*, Vol. 55, No. 1 (1996), p. 46.
3. According to *The Encyclopedia of Islam*, the word 'peace' has two distinct terms in Arabic: salaam and sulh. Salaam refers to the abstract notion of peace, whereas sulh refers to the literal act of settlement. Majid Khadduri, 'Sulh', in Clifford Edmund Bosworth, Bernard Lewis and Charles Pellat (eds.), *The Encyclopedia of Islam* (Leiden: Brill, 1997), Vol. 9, pp. 845–46. Anthropologist Sharon Lang provides additional insight into the term sulh. She writes: 'Throughout the Galilee, as in many parts of the Middle East, the Arab population has traditionally practiced a ritualized process of conflict resolution known as Sulh, a term glossed by informants as "reconciliation," "cooperation," or "forgiveness." Regarding the relation of the term sulh to the term sulha, Lang writes: 'Any specific case of sulh is referred to as a sulha, as is the formal public ceremony that marks the culmination of the peace-making negotiations'. Sharon Lang, 'Sulha Peacemaking and the Politics of Persuasion', Journal of Palestine

8 *Introduction*

Studies, Vol. 31, No. 3 (2002), p. 53. However, in the north of Israel, the term Sulha is used by practitioners and disputants alike to denote both the process in general and the ceremony in particular; for example, see the title of Elias Jabbour's book: *Sulha – Palestinian Traditional Peacemaking Process*.

4 This book uses the terms 'conflict' and 'dispute' interchangeably.
5 Aseel Ramahi, 'Sulh: A Crucial Part of Islamic Arbitration', London School of Economics and Political Science Law Department, LSE Law, Society and Economy Working Papers 12/2008, p. 1. Also, see George Irani & Nathan Funk, 'Rituals of Reconciliation – Arab-Islamic Perspectives', *Arab Studies Quarterly*, Vol. 20, No. 4 (1998), p. 53.
6 For the purpose of this study, northern Israel comprises the area from the city of Haifa in the south to the Israeli-Lebanese border in the north, and from the Mediterranean Sea on the West to the Sea of Galilee in the east.
7 More than 60 per cent of Israel's 1.6 million Arab citizens live in this area. The remaining Arab population resides in several contiguous regions (e.g. central Israel and the Negev). About 82 per cent of Israel's Arabs are Sunni Muslims, about 9 per cent are Christians and another 9 per cent are Druze. The author chose to concentrate on the Arab population of northern Israel because they present a large, homogenous group in terms of the way they practice the Sulha, and because the author had access to the Sulha practitioners in this region.
8 The use of Sulha, a Shari'a-based conflict resolution mechanism, by non-Muslim Arab communities is a fascinating sociohistorical phenomenon that deserves separate exploration, but is beyond the scope of this book.
9 Author interview with Khneifes, 2009.
10 Mneesha Gellman & Mandi Vuinovich, 'From Sulha to Salaam: Connecting Local Knowledge With International Negotiations for Lasting Peace in Palestine/Israel', *Conflict Resolution Quarterly*, Vol. 26, No. 2 (2008), p. 130.
11 Interview with author, 12 July 2007. See also Ron Shapiro, 'It's Sulha Time', *Hapraklit* (Hebrew), Vol. 48, No. 2 (2006), p. 436.
12 Interview with author, 29 July 2011.
13 *Qur'an*, 42:40.
14 Gellman & Vuinovich, 'From Sulha to Salaam', p. 136. See also Muhammad Abu-Nimer, 'Conflict Resolution Approaches: Western and Middle Eastern Lessons and Possibilities', *American Journal of Economics and Sociology*, Vol. 55, No. 1 (1996), p. 4; Jabbour, *Sulha*, pp. 31, 57, 60; author interview with Ibrahim M'bada Naum (Abu M'bada), member of the Sulha Committee of northern Israel's Arab community, 13 November 2011; Author interview with Khneifes, 15 July 2011.
15 Abu-Nimer defines the hamula as 'a patronymic extended family composed of five generations descended from a single grandfather'. Muhammad Abu-Nimer, *Nonviolence and Peace Building in Islam: Theory and Practice* (Gainesville: University of Florida Press, 2003), p. 98. *Hamail* is the plural for *hamula*.
16 Victor Ayoub, 'Conflict Resolution and Social Reorganization in a Lebanese Village', *Human Organization*, Vol. 24, No. 1 (1965), p. 13.
17 Ramahi, 'Sulh', p. 2.
18 Author interview with Khneifes, 2007.
19 Abdul Aziz Said, Nathan Funk and Ayse Kadayifci, *Peace and Conflict Resolution in Islam: Precepts and Practice* (Lanham: University Press of America, 2001), p. 182.
20 Thus, for example, the conflict between the Hamud and Rian clans from the Kabul village in northern Israel, which erupted on 7 September 1975 following the murder of three members of the Rian clan, was resolved on 20 March 2008 with the signing of a Sulha agreement. Author interview with Sheikh Abu Riad Ali Shtewe of the Sulha Committee, 16 October 2012.
21 See, for example, Aida Othman, '"And Amicable Settlement Is Best": Sulh and Dispute Resolution in Islamic Law', *Arab Law Quarterly*, Vol. 21, No. 2 (2007), pp. 64–90;

Laurie King-Irani, 'Rituals of Forgiveness and Processes of Empowerment in Lebanon', in William I. Zartman (ed.), Traditional Cures for Modern Conflicts (Boulder: Lynne Rienner, 2000), Chapter 8; Ali H. Qleibo, 'Tribal Methods of Conflict Resolution: The Palestinian Model: Atwa or Sulh Asha'iry', in Jay Rothman (ed.), *Practicing Conflict Resolution in Divided Societies*, Policy Studies, No. 46 (Jerusalem: Leonard Davis Institute, 1993), pp. 57–9.

22 Nurit Tsafrir, 'Arab Customary Law in Israel: Sulha Agreements and Israeli Courts', *Islamic Law and Society*, Vol. 1, No. 13 (2006), pp. 76–98; Shapiro, 'It's Sulha Time'.

23 Said, Funk and Kadayifci (eds.), *Peace and Conflict Resolution in Islam, p. 3*; Paul Salem (ed.), Conflict Resolution in the Arab World: *Selected Essays* (Beirut: American University of Beirut, 1997).

24 Daniel Smith, 'The Rewards of Allah', *Journal of Peace Research*, Vol. 26, No. 4 (1989), pp. 392–93.

25 Susan Nathan, *The Other Side of Israel: My Journey Across the Jewish/Arab Divide* (New York: Random House, 2005); Jabbour, *Sulha*.

26 Ramahi, 'Sulh', p. 13.

27 Gellman and Vuinovich, 'From Sulha to Salaam'; Smith, 'The Rewards of Allah'; Abu-Nimer, *Nonviolence and Peace Building in Islam*, pp. 94, 96–7, 99.

28 For the purpose of this work, the definitions of mediation and arbitration are as follows:

> **Mediation** – a voluntary alternative dispute resolution process, where all parties must consent to participate in good faith and work toward a mutually agreeable resolution, with the facilitating help of a neutral third party. Disputants are not bound to resolve their dispute, although mediated settlements, once reached, can be made binding.
>
> **Arbitration** – an alternative dispute resolution process in which a neutral party (the arbitrator) hears a dispute between two or more disputants, considers the evidence and renders a final decision. Arbitration decisions may be either binding or nonbinding.

29 Gellman and Vuinovich, 'From Sulha to Salaam', pp. 127, 135.

30 Abu-Nimer, *Nonviolence and Peace Building in Islam*, p. 96.

31 Lang, *Sulha Peacemaking*, p. 63.

32 Doron Pely, 'Women in Sulha – Excluded yet Influential: Examining Women's Formal and Informal Role in Traditional Conflict Resolution, Within the Patriarchal Culture of Northern Israel's Arab Community', *International Journal of Conflict Management*, Vol. 22, No. 1 (2011b), pp. 89–104.

33 Nathan Harris and Shadd Maruna, 'Shame, Shaming and Restorative Justice: A Critical Appraisal', in Dennis Sullivan and Larry Tiff (eds.), *Handbook of Restorative Justice* (New York: Routledge, 2006). See also John Braithwaite, *Crime, Shame and Reintegration* (Cambridge: Cambridge University Press, 1989).

34 Tony Whitehead, 'Basic Classical Ethnographic Research Methods: Secondary Data Analysis, Fieldwork, Observation/Participant Observation, and Informal and Semi Structured Interviewing', Ethnographically Informed Community and Cultural Assessment Research Systems (EICCARS) Working Paper Series Source, 2005, www.cusag.umd.edu/documents/WorkingPapers/ClassicalEthnoMethods.pdf (accessed 21 November 2011); Michael Agar, *The Professional Stranger: An Informal Introduction to Ethnography* (San Diego: Academic Press, 1996); David Fetterman, *Ethnography: Step by Step*, 2nd ed. (Newbury Park: Sage Publications, 1998).

35 Morris Freilich, *Marginal Natives: Anthropologists at Work* (New York: Harper & Row, 1970); Agar, *The Professional Stranger*.

1 Sulha in Muslim jurisprudence and customary justice

The speed and scope of the rise of Islam, inextricably bound with the life of its founder the Prophet Muhammad, is nothing short of remarkable by any standard. In the span of 10 years (622–32 CE), following his migration from Mecca to Medina, Muhammad consolidated an administrative, political and theological centre of control that, in the words of historian Montgomery Watt, made him

> not merely undisputed ruler of Medina, Mecca and the surrounding territory, but . . . accepted . . . suzerain by many tribes throughout Arabia. Moreover, within ten years of his death, the state which he created was able to meet in battle and defeat the armies of the two great empires of the Middle East, the Byzantine and Persian, and within a short time to overrun the latter completely. A hundred years after his death the empire of his successors extended from France to India.[1]

The expansion of Islam was accompanied by a parallel expansion of Islamic dispute resolution practices – *Tahkim* and the Sulha, intimately tied to Muhammad's personal experience and practise in his dual role as religious and temporal leader – as 'the basic tenet of civil justice'.[2] For example, the 'Constitution of Medina', written by Muhammad, vividly illustrates the link between the Prophet and these instruments of power when stating: 'If any dispute or controversy likely to cause trouble should arise it must be referred to God and to Muhammad, the apostle of God'.[3] This link will be elaborated later in this chapter, but it suffices to say here that Muhammad was himself a *Tahkim*-practicing *hakam* (arbitrator) – both before and after the founding of Islam – and, more importantly, that even as he practiced arbitration – the main application of *Tahkim*, he expressed a clear preference for Sulha *because* of its dominant mediation element, positioning both practices at the forefront of Muslim dispute resolution – with a preference for Sulha.[4]

Given Muhammad's centrality in the shaping of the nascent Muslim power and the obvious centrality of jurisprudence in the life of communities of all sizes, it is reasonable to assume that an understanding of the origins and evolution of Muslim jurisprudence in general and Sulha, Islam's most ubiquitous customary justice practice in particular, may be helped by gaining an insight into Muhammad's personal preferences and practices in these matters.

Determining the exact origins of Islamic law is a subject of intense scholarly debate. According to historian Wael Hallaq,

> Far more complex than plotting the end-point of the formative period [of Islamic law] is the determination of its beginning. It is no exaggeration to say that of all the major questions in Islamic legal history, the issues involved in studying these beginnings have proved the most challenging.[5]

Moreover, the argument extends beyond the issue of origin to the question of whether and how Islamic jurisprudence incorporated pre-Islamic customary practices as part of its evolution.[6]

It appears that, in a demonstration of the power of cultural cross-fertilization, Islam – as it evolved and expanded rapidly – absorbed pre-Islamic dispute resolution principles, tools and practices, as well as other influences, gradually creating around them a body of 'formal' legal codex (Shari'a)[7] that influenced the evolution of Muslim (as opposed to pre-Islamic) customary practices, which, in turn, influenced Islamic jurisprudence.[8]

The result of these cyclic processes is that in today's Islam, formal and customary applications of the legal process co-exist, draw on each other and often collaborate closely in an attempt to achieve efficiency in conflict resolution and provide a wide spectrum of options that cover both individual and communal disputes. In the words of Barrister Gulam Hyder: 'In the Islamic tradition, regular courts and ADR mechanisms are essentially intertwined'.[9] Israeli Muslim legal scholar Musa Abu Ramadan adds: 'In Islamic jurisprudence, there is a connection between habit and law. Habit actually becomes part of law'.[10] Such a cross-fertilizing, circular relationship between formal and customary law reflects both the historical development of Islam and its special place in the lives of its adherents – as both a religion and a comprehensive system of ethics, law and cultural behaviour.[11]

The insights developed in this chapter provide the background and context needed to explain the task-specific dispute resolution stages that facilitate the practice of the Sulha, the tools that are used within these stages and their impact on the disputants.[12]

Primary sources of Muslim jurisprudence

Islam, and Islamic law by extension, not only defines and regulates relations between humans and the deity, but also contains the only acceptable (by Muslim practitioners) detailed articulation and regulations defining the relations between people and their fellow men and women, including a comprehensive code of ethics and detailed principles of social behaviour.[13]

This inclusive nature extends to Muslim dispute resolution contexts, providing communities, practitioners and disputants alike with a comprehensive set of guidelines, defining the environment and tools within which people can and should manage and resolve their disputes. Consequently, the Shari'a is not a law in the same sense that Western adjudicators perceive it, but rather a comprehensive guide to life, including a complete code of duties and obligations.[14]

The question of Muslim jurisprudence sources is a hotly debated issue. The 'traditionalist' view ascribes the evolution of Islamic law to the simple 'linear' chronology – Allah-Muhammad-Companions-Followers-*Fiqh*[15] – that is accepted by all Muslims as divine in origins.[16] In the words of Islamic law scholar Noel Coulson: 'Law, in classical Islamic theory, is the revealed will of God, a divinely ordained system, preceding and not preceded by the Muslim state, controlling and not controlled by Muslim society'. Coulson proceeds to clarify the divide between history and tradition, noting that Islamic law 'is not considered in the light of any external criteria, or in its relationship to particular epochs or localities' and that because of this unique, history-free perspective, 'the traditional picture of the growth of Islamic law completely lacks the dimension of historical depth'.[17]

Muslim scholars recognize five sources of Muslim jurisprudence: the *Qur'an*, the *Sunna* (habitual practice), *Ijma* (consensus), *Qiyas* (analogy) and *Ijtihad* (independent interpretation by personal effort).[18] According to this outlook, the Qur'an is the first and main source of law, with its revelations constituting the first source of the Shari'a – Islam's legal code. Second in importance stands the Sunna, comprising what Muslims believe to be all of Muhammad's acts and sayings, as well as acts performed by his close associates. Despite being second in hierarchy, the Sunna, in the words of Wael Hallaq, 'contains the bulk of material from which the law is derived'.[19] As will be shown, the direct connection of Muhammad to Muslim customary justice, including his personal preference for Sulha, serves to anchor the place of this institution within Muslim dispute resolution.

The Ijma is the body of collected unanimous opinion and interpretation of the Qur'an by recognized religious authorities and jurists. This is a sanctioning vehicle, used as a base for solving similar legal cases. Sulha interveners make extensive use of a similar method (in terms of its mechanics) as they search for functional (cultural) precedents as part of their deliberative process.[20]

The Qiyas is the body of analogical deductions, comparing the Qur'an to the *Hadith* (sayings of the Prophet) to help apply injunctions to new circumstances. The purpose of this function is to allow Muslim judges and interveners the use of precedence (most resembling to the case in hand) in the absence of clear Qur'anic, Sunna or Ijma guidance.

The Ijtihad consists of deriving rules through intellectual effort, independent of any school of Islamic law. This source of law ceased to operate around the tenth century.[21]

The previously mentioned primary sources of Islamic law are augmented by secondary sources, such as the *Taqlid* (Custom/Tradition) – the practice of following instructions by religious authorities based on their opinion and without comparing the instructions to the written text in the Qur'an.

All Muslims accept two of these sources – the Qur'an and the Sunna – since they are considered products of divine revelation. With respect to the other three sources – Ijma, Qiyas and Ijtihad – the various schools of Islamic jurisprudence (explained later) exhibit diverging approaches and levels of acceptance, based primarily on their attitudes towards the need to strictly adhere to what is accepted as divinely revealed texts (Qur'an and the Sunna), without any additional (human) interpretation.

The chronology mentioned earlier leaves no historical space for 'imported' pre-Islamic influences, be they significant or marginal. To further reinforce the 'divine revelation' argument with respect to the origin of Islamic texts (including legally relevant texts), the Muslim theological argument holds that Muhammad was illiterate and therefore could not 'copy' from other texts. Considering that the Prophet came from a merchant background, it is unlikely that he was completely illiterate, though it is unclear what texts, if any, he was exposed to in his pre-Islamic days.[22]

International law scholar Majid Khadduri sheds light on this 'purism' effort within Islam, writing that 'Muslim jurists took it for granted that since Islamic law was a divinely ordained system, its origin had nothing to do with pre-Islamic law'. But further on, Khadduri asserts that '[t]here is ample evidence to show, however, that Islamic law evolved from Arab customary law'.[23] Indeed, it seems that pre-Muslim customary justice practices already made their transition into Islam in its early phase (during Muhammad's lifetime and the decades attending his death), chiefly through continuous tribal traditions, reinforced by essential support from the Prophet himself.[24]

The non-Muslim perspective on the sources of Islamic law is more diverse in opinion and interpretation, and explores the possible contribution to Muslim jurisprudence of a variety of sources, principally existing pre-Islamic cultures and legal traditions that the nascent Islam came into contact with as it was formulating its own religious and legal foundations. Debate in this area of inquiry is lively and ongoing.

Historian Patricia Crone, for example, brings into focus the potential impact of both Roman and provincial law on the rapidly evolving law during Islam's early years (provincial law is the non-Roman law that local inhabitants practiced in the empire's provinces). She argues that although in principle provincial law should have disappeared with the extension of Roman citizenship to all free people residing within the empire's sphere of influence, it actually survived and 'even came to influence the official law of the land'.[25] It is reasonable to assume that the very same cross-influence process described by Crone took place also with respect to pre-Muslim customary justice, which was the Arabian Peninsula's equivalent of provincial law.

Joseph Schacht, for his part, sees the Qur'anic and Sunna sources as only secondary contributors to the evolution of *Fiqh*. He pinpoints the origin of Islamic jurisprudence to Mesopotamia (today's Iraq) around a hundred years after the founding of Islam (early 700 CE) and ascribes it to Roman and Persian law.[26] This view is disputed vigorously by legal scholar Seymour Vasey-Fitzgerald, who writes: 'There is not a single reference in any Islamic law book to any Roman authority.'[27]

Schacht's view is meaningful and highly controversial, particularly within Muslim legal scholarship, since it puts (and dates) the origins of Islamic law *outside* the Arabian Peninsula – the birthplace of Islam – and places the origins of

Islamic law in a region that was a part of the Persian Empire (and consequently under the influence of the ancient and quite mature Persian jurisprudence) until its conquest by the early Muslims.

There is little disagreement among non-Muslim scholars that Islamic law draws on Jewish and Christian sources. Hallaq writes:

> As a product of a mercantile tribal society, Muhammad was familiar with all the religions and cultures of the Peninsula and of its neighbours, particularly Judaism and Christianity, religions that had many adherents among the major Arab tribes. Medina, to which he was forced to migrate with some followers, had been inhabited by several Jewish tribes.[28]

As an example of such influences, Hallaq points out that

> the "normative way" referred to in verse 5:48 of the Qur'an is represented by the term "*minhaj*", a cognate of the Hebraic word "*minhag*" (the Law). The creation of an Islamic legal parallel here speaks for itself. These verses mark the beginning of substantive legislation in the Qur'an.[29]

Historian Shlomo Dov Goitlein adds that 'the Qur'an contains no less legal material than does the Torah, which is commonly known as "the Law"'.[30]

Crone provides additional explicit support for the perspective supporting the assumption that Muslim law is at least partially based on Jewish roots. She writes:

> Since the order of the subjects in the Mishna and the Muslim law books is related, while in a subject such as ritual purity there is virtual identity of both overall category and substantive provisions, it evidently was not by parthenogenesis that the similarity arose; and it does not take much knowledge of Jewish law to see its influence in the most diverse provisions of Islamic law.[31]

Watt provides an interesting insight into the source and content of early Muslim Qur'anic passages as originating in Jewish and Christian influences on Muhammad and through him on early Muslim legal perspective. As he puts it: 'In later passages the dependence on the Biblical tradition becomes even more marked, for they contain much material from the Old and New testaments'. But Watt concludes that it is likely that both Jewish and Christian influence on Muhammad were of oral rather than written origin. He writes:

> The form of the Biblical material in the Qur'an, however, makes it certain that Muhammad had never read the bible; and it is unlikely that he had ever read any other books. Such knowledge, then, as he had of Judaeo-Christian conceptions must have come to him orally.[32]

Regardless of the specific views, the relevant similarities between Jewish and Muslim legal perspectives revolve around the fact that both religions are based on divine revelation, and that basic and detailed ethical and normative guidelines designed to shape the newly emerging communities of believers were presented in books that were said to be inspired by God (Torah and Qur'an).

From the preponderance of evidence, it is difficult to discern a single dominant source of Islamic jurisprudence, either original (e.g. Qur'an) or external (e.g. Judaism); it appears that the only sustainable perspective has to accommodate a multitude of influences, starting with pre-Muslim but incorporating Roman, Persian and Jewish elements, which were apparently incorporated into Muslim law throughout its formative period, mostly through the simple mechanism of intercultural contact and popular practice.[33]

Islam's (Sunni) major schools of law

Named after their founders, Islam's four major schools of jurisprudence came into being during Islam's first two centuries and reflect differences in regional and doctrinal approaches to legal questions despite their universal acceptance of the Qur'an and the Sunna as the sources of Islam and of Islamic jurisprudence.

The four major schools of Islamic jurisprudence are:[34]

- Comprising about 4 per cent of Muslims, *the Hanbali School* was founded by Ahmad ibn Hanbal (d. 855) and is practiced mainly in Saudi Arabia and Qatar with adherents in Syria and Iraq. It espouses a conservative view of Islam (advocates literal interpretation of the scripts) and rejects, with few exceptions, independent reasoning, reasoning by analogy (Qiyas) and consensus (Ijma).[35] The Hanbalis claim that arbitration has the same effect as a court proceeding; hence the arbitrator shall have the same qualification as a judge, and the award given by him is bound by the parties who chose him.
- *The much larger Hanafi School* (some 31 per cent of Muslims) is the most prominent school of Islamic jurisprudence today with numerous adherents in Iraq, Jordan, Syria, Lebanon, Israel (Arab population), Egypt and Turkey, as well as Russia, India and China.[36] Founded by Nu'man ibn Thabit ibn Zuṭa ibn Marzuban, also known as Imam Abu Ḥanifa (d. 767), it upholds that the nature of arbitration is contractual and is close to agencies and conciliation. Therefore, an arbitrator acts as an agent on behalf of the disputing parties (who appointed him). Since according to this school, arbitration is closer to conciliation, the arbitral award has a lower level of abidingness than that of a court judgment. However, the contractual nature of the agreement would ultimately force the parties to agree to the decision of the arbitrators.
- *The Maliki School* (about 25 per cent of Muslims) was founded by Malik ibn Anas Asbaih (d. 795) and is influential in parts of the Arabian Peninsula (including Kuwait, the United Arab Emirate and parts of Saudi Arabia), Egypt and in North and West Africa. It differs from the other Sunni schools in that it includes legal ruling of the four caliphs that succeeded Muhammad,

and in its preferred methods of prayer.[37] According to the Maliki School, arbitrators can be chosen by any of the parties, and the arbitrator cannot be dismissed or otherwise removed in the middle of the proceedings.

- *The Shafi'i School* (c. 16 per cent of Muslims) was founded by Muhammad ibn Idris Shafi (d. 819) and is influential in Lebanon, Syria, Palestine and Egypt, with adherents in Pakistan and Indonesia. This school incorporates legal inputs from all four sources of Islamic law (Qur'an, Sunna, Ijma and Qiyas) and upholds that arbitration is not like a formal court proceeding and that arbitrators can be changed at any time during the proceedings, as long as this is done before the parties are issued an arbitral award.[38]

To sum up, all schools present a rather rigid position whereby the appointment of a *hakam* must be made by mutual consent of all disputants. They specifically prohibit any third party, even a *Qadi*, from appointing a *hakam* without the consent of the disputants. This ruling aims at ensuring the durability of the process by insisting that all disputants are enfranchised into the process and are not coerced into it.[39] Having said that, according to the Shafi'i, Hanaff and Hanbali schools the disputing parties in a *Tahkim* (arbitration) are allowed to revoke the appointment of the *hakam* (arbitrator) prior to his pronouncement of a verdict, whereas the *hakam* can disqualify himself under similar circumstances. By contrast, the Maliki School of law views the appointment of a *hakam* as irrevocable.

The schools' attitude towards Sulha is that of broad positive acceptance. In the words of Saudi Judge Essam Alsheikh:

> The majority of Islamic jurists share the opinion that the notion of *sulh* is permissible according to the Qur'an, the Sunna . . . Allah the Almighty said: '[m]aking peace is better' (Q4:128). Prophet Muhammad (PBUH) said that *sulh* is permissible between Muslims, except when it makes ill-gotten things permissible or vice versa.[40]

The exception is a situation where the perpetrator's side refuses to accept responsibility for the infraction. In such a case, the Shafi'i School does not accept Sulha as a legitimate mode of dispute resolution because in its opinion it gives the aggressor an unacceptable advantage (that of being able to partake in a reconciliation procedure without taking responsibility). This is one of the main reasons why a Sulha process *must* be started by the perpetrator's clan assuming responsibility for the infraction.[41]

Most Shiite Muslims have a separate school of law – *Jafari* – established largely on the basis of rulings by the sixth Shiite Imam: Jaafar as-Sadiq (702–65 CE). This school differs from the other schools in that it incorporates the Ijtihad (independent interpretation by personal effort), as well as in other aspects such as religious taxation and inheritance.[42] A small percentage of Muslims follow other minority schools, such as the Zaidi and the Ismaili.

The evolution of Muslim customary justice

Within the dispersed, tribal-culture context of pre-Islam's Arabian Peninsula, arbitration (*Tahkim*) and mediation (Sulh) were the primary known available dispute management and resolution tools for situations short of open conflict. There was no alternative formal judicial system. This situation resulted in arbitrators gaining a powerful position within their communities, where they often were people of importance, sometimes even the tribal soothsayers (*kahins*).[43]

Such pre-Islamic interveners often couched their decisions as divine revelations, invoking various deities.[44] This created an important linkage between the deity – both pre- and post-Islam – and dispute resolution, a link that must have been both challenging and useful for Muhammad as he was working to politically and religiously unify the Arabian tribes under the flag of a single revelation.

The challenge was in the presence of a 'competition' (representations of deities other than Allah) for revelation-based arbitration; but at the same time, with such a link (deity-law) already established, Muhammad was left with the formidable (yet more manageable) task of positioning himself and his narrative (Islam) into this existing space and working to cement its primacy as the sole legitimate narrative.

Small wonder, then, that the Qur'an positioned Muhammad explicitly as an arbitrator (*hakam*), stressing that his decisions were not based on any law other than Allah's revelations through the Qur'an,[45] even though the practice predates both Muhammad and Islam.[46]

This control of the nascent Muslim legal system allowed Muhammad to unify the religious and legal systems under one flag (Allah and the revelation through the Qur'an), which remains the essence of Islam's formal and informal legal systems to date.[47]

After his flight to Medina, Muhammad became the highest arbiter in both religious and secular disputes (issues having to do with the daily legal life of the community). There is evidence that he practiced customary law before the founding of Islam, within the context of pre- (and later post-) Islamic arbitration application of *Tahkim*.[48] Furthermore, we can see that despite (or maybe because of) his familiarity with the advantages and shortcomings of arbitration, Muhammad was a strong advocate of settlement (Sulha), specifically because of its mediation components, positioning both practices in the forefront of Muslim dispute resolution – with a preference for Sulha.[49] This link will be further discussed in this chapter, and is key to understanding the Sulha's unique use of mixed arbitration and mediation tools.

Muhammad's dispute resolution background finds a limited expression in the Qur'an, where about 10 per cent of the verses deal with what Western scholars would define as 'legal matters'. But these 'legal' verses are not organized in any systematic way and generally reflect individual treatment of specific problems that Muhammad dealt with in his capacity as arbitrator before Islam. More importantly, it is clear that much of the pre-Islamic customary laws and quasi-legal institutions that existed in pre-Islam Arabia were retained by Islam, subject only to changes that Muhammad decreed. In the words of Muslim jurisprudence scholar David Bonderman, 'no systematic new Islamic legal framework was necessary in the relatively simple society of seventh-century Arabia because the entire pre-Islamic customary laws and institutions were retained, subject only to changes as Muhammad decreed'.[50]

This insight is essential to understanding the evolutionary path of both Islamic jurisprudence and Islamic customary justice practices because it is possible to demonstrate that both practices existed before Islam, were integrated into its formal legal code after its founding, and were later 'exported' through its expansion throughout the world to become central to alternative dispute resolution (ADR) in much of the Muslim world. This demonstrated chronology considerably weakens the 'divine revelation' argument.

Because Muhammad was at the same time an active arbiter and peacemaker, it is reasonable to assume that his daily practice influenced significantly his 'divinely revealed' narrative, feeding the contextual as well as the practical part of his views and instructions in matters of Muslim law.[51]

Muslims see Islamic law as an obligatory set of value-oriented, ethical and practical guidelines, designed to lead the practitioner towards the divine purposes of Allah as expressed in the Qur'an.[52] By comparison, Westerners tend to see Western law as a body of rules and directions (e.g. treaties, legislation, custom, moral and religious commitment) accepted and approved for enforcement by nations, and in general separate from the specific religious dogma.[53]

A unique and significant feature of Islamic ADR is that Islamic law ('formal' law, that is) and Muslim ADR are tightly bound by their common pre-Islamic roots, through practice and, even more importantly, through the fact that Muhammad was both the founder of Islamic law and a practitioner of pre-Muslim (and later Muslim) customary dispute resolution in the form of *Tahkim* and *Sulha*.[54]

Whenever dealing with Muslim jurisprudence, formal or informal, it is important to note that the revelatory foundation of Islamic law ordained a unique position for Islamic jurists, as well as for practitioners of Muslim customary justice: they were never seen as independent actors in the sense that they were not supposed to have created a 'man-made law alongside the divine ordinances'. Islamic jurisprudence is, therefore, in its entirety subordinated to the will of Allah as promulgated through the Qur'an and the Sunna, and its sole aim is to 'see the comprehension and the implementation of the purposes of Allah for Muslim society'.[55]

This point is of prime importance to our understanding of Muslim jurisprudence in general and Muslim ADR in particular because it is reasonable to assume that any legal system based on divine revelation must initially deal with the problem of creating a mechanism that will enable the introduction of new rules (in the postrevelation period).[56] The unique 'cyclical' interrelations between pre-Islamic customary law and Muslim formal and customary law, embodied in the practice attributed to Muhammad both before and after the founding of Islam, provides a convenient platform (and a reasonable explanation) for such introduction of new rules by enabling reliance on existing (pre-Islamic) practices as 'nuclei of crystallization' for the assimilation and development of new rules within the 'formal' framework of the new revelation-based structure.

Bernard Lewis describes the infrastructure that enabled the transition from pre-Islamic to Islamic social structures (including, of course, dispute resolution), writing that '[t]he Umma supplemented rather than supplanted the social usage of pre-Islamic Arabia, and all its ideas were within the structure of tribalism'.[57]

Tahkim (Arbitration)

Islamic law encourages people to seek arbitration whenever they are unable to resolve disputes among themselves,[58] making *Tahkim* a major Muslim alternative dispute resolution practice that has a direct bearing on our discussion. For one thing, the history, evolution and practice of *Tahkim* have affected the evolution of Sulha, empowering it as a practice, and possibly providing it with some of its practical arbitrative tools. Such a linkage may also help explain both the need for and the actual specific application of mixed-use alternative dispute resolution tools by third-party interveners in Sulha. For another thing, the history of *Tahkim* sheds light on both the inter-relations and the resultant unique cross-influences between law and religion in Islam in general, and in Islamic alternative dispute resolution practices in particular.

Tahkim predates Islam; it was incorporated into the rapidly evolving religion and has become a ubiquitous dispute resolution practice within it.[59] In the words of legal scholar Aseel Ramahi, 'arbitration is favoured to adjudication in Islamic jurisprudence'.[60]

The early practice of *Tahkim* included, but was not limited to, commercial, social, religious and political disputes. The arbitrator, much like today's Sulha Committee member, was not a formal occupation, and practicing it depended to a great extent on his perception by the community as a wise, fair, moral and knowledgeable person. As Islam gained prominence throughout the Middle East and beyond, *Tahkim*'s practices were integrated into the Shari'a as both customary and formal law, giving the practice additional formal, as well as moral posture.[61]

However, the current scope of *Tahkim* does not encompass disputes of a *Hudud* nature.[62] Furthermore, it is inapplicable in matters concerning *li'an* (mutual imprecation), *talaq* (divorce), *nasab* (paternity), *fasakh nikah* (judicial abrogation of marriage), emancipation of slaves, *rushd* (adolescence), *safih* (spendthrift), *mafqud al-khabar* (a person whose whereabouts are unknown), *waqf* (endowments) and revenue matters. Such disputes are usually adjudicated by a judge.[63]

Consequently, *Tahkim* is an integral part of today's (and past) legal tradition and procedure (formal and informal) in many Arab and Muslim states, as opposed to Western arbitrative practices that function parallel to (sometimes in conjunction with, but always separate from) the formal legal systems.[64]

20 Sulha in Muslim jurisprudence

There are several reasons for the evolution of arbitration in general and *Tahkim* in particular:

- It provides a method for improving the administration of justice by reducing formalities and procedures (compared with a more formal judicial process), along with a promise (not always realized) of potential reduction in time and cost.
- It provides the means to introduce into the dispute resolution process an expert third-party intervener who may be better informed than judges regarding the specific aspects of the dispute (e.g. an expert in commercial, financial, technical issues).
- It enables the development of substantive law rules that may respond more specifically to the current and exact needs of the user community (e.g. commercial, financial, technical communities). Such rules, because of their specificity and focus, may prove more useful than the more general rules developed by the legislator and applied by the courts.
- The process of arbitration may provide a path to compromise solutions that take into consideration the needs and interests of all involved disputants. Such a process may increase satisfaction (even partial) with the results, reduce resentment and ease return to postconflict normalcy (e.g. re-establishment of commercial, familial or other collaborative relations). This is a particularly attractive feature in a tribal community.
- Arbitration may offer solutions to disputes that do not clearly fall within the purview of the formal courts by applying to the conflict a different (sometimes broader) toolbox.

Legal scholar Walid Abdulrahim locates the source of *Tahkim*'s prominence when he notes that 'Prophet Muhammad was the first arbitrator in Islam.'[65] Muhammad is also associated with the most famous act of arbitration in Islam, whereupon he arbitrated a dispute about determining which Arab tribe would have the honour of placing the Black Stone after the rebuilding of the *Kaaba*. Muhammad's solution was to place the Black Stone in the centre of his outer garment and to instruct each tribe's representative to hold one corner of the garment, thereby enabling the sharing of the task.[66] Such a direct link between the founder of Islam and *Tahkim* as a general practice cannot but help reinforce the posture of this practice within Muslim jurisprudence.

Before and during Islam's early days, *Tahkim* was practiced by a single, two or even more arbitrators, as agreed by the disputants. This flexibility was conducive to facilitating a settlement, but it also created a significant potential for expanded conflict situations (in addition to the original dispute). One such important arbitration-resulting conflict led to the most significant schism in Islam between Sunnis and Shiites (further discussed in this section).[67]

As voluntary *Tahkim* evolved, disputants selected by mutual consent a single individual who acted as arbitrator.[68] Muhammad was instrumental in transitioning *Tahkim* from multi-interveners to a single-intervener practice, mainly because the decisions he rendered were considered to have been divinely guided and therefore did not require additional interveners. But aside from Muhammad's special posture as a sole *hakam*, in many cases, the disputants failed to agree on a single intervener and reverted to a multi*hakam* format, a format that endures today. There are cases where a failure by the two interveners to agree on a verdict leads to the addition of a third *hakam*, who can only add his voice to that of one of the other interveners (each selected by a disputant) in order to break the logjam, create a majority voting block and generate a final decision.[69]

In the transition from the pre-Islamic to the Islamic era, the position of *Tahkim* within Muslim jurisprudence owed much to Muhammad's ability to gain legitimacy both as a political leader and a final arbitrator, the latter being a role that he practiced regularly in his preprophecy period. In Ramahi's words: 'The Prophet Muhammad was chosen as an arbitrator before he became a prophet due to his honesty and trustworthiness and sometimes he was referred to as a *kahin*'[Arabian priest].[70]

Muhammad's unique arbitral posture and his ability to leverage this posture to further his broader goals are demonstrated in the Constitution of Medina (622 AD) that Muslim and non-Muslim residents of Medina, or Yathrib as it was known at the time – Jews, Christians and pagans – signed in an attempt to mitigate a century-old interclan dispute that claimed many lives and disrupted life in Medina.[71]

Twelve of Medina's major clans, including the feuding Aws and Khazraj (pagans), and three Jewish tribes (Banu Nadir, Banu Quraiza and Banu Qainuqa) invited Muhammad to arbitrate the dispute, designating him as chief political administrator and legal authority that had to be referred to in case of conflicts that could not be handled otherwise.

The resultant Constitution of Medina, which regulated inter- and intrarelations between Muslim and non-Muslim subcommunities in Medina, is viewed as the primary document defining the nascent Islamic community and its relationship with the non-Muslim world. By establishing the Medina Muslims – those who had arrived with him from Mecca and his local followers as 'one community (*umma*) to the exclusion of all man', Muhammad demarcated the line between Muslims and all others, framing the starting point for the perceived primacy of Islam (along with its religious legal structure) as the major dispute resolution platform in areas under Muslim control. As historian Efraim Karsh put it: 'The document wisely refrained from specifically abolishing existing tribal structures and practices, yet it broke with tradition by substituting religion for blood as the source of social and political organization'.[72] In practice, both structures (tribalism and religion) seem to co-exist within Muslim customary justice.

Other scholars see the Constitution of Medina alternately as a local proclamation,[73] the founding document of the first Muslim state[74] and even as the first written constitution.[75] Yet regardless of the divergent perspectives on the Constitution of Medina, there is no doubt that it marks the solidifying status of Muhammad as religious, political and legal leader; this position, coupled with Muhammad's continuing activity as an arbitrator, provided him, and through him the institution of *Tahkim*, with a twin grasp – legal and moral – on the rapidly broadening sphere of influence under his control. Bernard Lewis points this out when he writes:

> An important element was certainly his [Muhammad] ability to serve them [the people of Medina] as an arbitrator, and to settle their internal disputes. As well as a new religion, he brought them security and a measure of social discipline.[76]

Tahkim remained a legitimate and powerful practice after Muhammad's death as the caliphs inherited the Prophet's political power and along with it this practise. Having arrived directly from Muhammad, whose source of legitimacy derived directly from Allah, endowed *Tahkim* with the highest level of legitimacy, enabling the caliph to function as a sole *hakam*.[77]

This is not to say that *Tahkim* did not retain some major pre-Muslim features – notably its being to this day a voluntary process, triggered and practiced only by and with the expressed mutual consent of all disputants, as well as by their mutual agreement on the third-party intervener.

Yet having attained the position of 'Chief' Hakam, with its potentially considerable power of arbitrative coercion, Muhammad is still reported to have preferred to resolve disputes by proposing an amicable settlement (Sulha) rather than by imposing an arbitrative-style (*Tahkim*) judgment. As George Sayen put it:

> Sulha gets far more elaborate treatment than tahkim both in the hadith literature and in fiqh treatises that followed in later centuries. Bukhiri . . . devotes an entire chapter to Sulha, which the Prophet apparently found a particularly appropriate method for resolving financial disputes.[78]

Muhammad may have recognized some advantages in the Sulha's unique mixed-mode dispute resolution approach – combining an arbitrator (and his specific tools) with a stated preference and practice toward a mediated solution (along with its mediation tools) – features which will be examined in detail further in this book.

This insight sheds light on the general character of alternative dispute resolution in Islam, and on the particular linkage between and evolution of *Tahkim* (pure arbitration) and Sulha (mixed arbitration and mediation tools) in the clear direction of Sulha. In the words of Ramahi: 'Shari'a has not completely separated sulh and arbitration. Many of the Koranic authorities and hadiths supporting arbitration could also be used as authority for sulh'.[79]

It is interesting to note that *Tahkim* and its special mode of practice in Islam's early days, whereby each side appointed its own arbitrator in the conflict resolution process, was partially responsible for the great schism between Sunni and Shiite Muslims. Twenty-seven years after the death of Muhammad, a dispute erupted between the fourth caliph, Ali ibn Abi Talib, and Mu'awiya ibn Abi Sufian, the governor of Syria. The dispute was brought to *Tahkim* by written agreement between the disputants, stating that each side would nominate its own arbitrator, and that these arbitrators have the authority to set a verdict – given that the verdict adhered strictly to the Qur'an and the Sunna. The arbitrators discussed the dispute and reached a conclusion that both disputants were unfit to rule and that a new caliph ought to be elected by popular vote. Ali's arbitrator announced the decision first. However, Mu'awiya's *hakam* deviated from the agreement, accepting the ruling that Ali was unfit to rule but declaring Mu'awiya fit to rule.

Ali, as the incumbent caliph, disputed the verdict, claiming that the arbitrators deviated from Qur'anic injunctions in their verdict. The dispute thus continued to fester, and Ali's subsequent assassination led to Islam's main schism between Sunni and Shiite Muslims.[80]

The place of arbitration within Muslim/Arab customary justice may also be linked to cultural historical roots associated with the communal aspects of family, clan and tribal hierarchy and politics in that it provides a forceful arbitrative instrument. This instrument basically hands disputants a final perspective regarding legal, ethical and moral guidance, of the kind aimed at instructing people regarding specific disputes, as well as a general guide for their continued lives. Barry Rubin provides one possible insight into this aspect when he quotes the Islamic reformer Muhammad Abdu, who wrote at the turn of the twentieth century that

> [t]he Orient needs a despot who would force those who criticize each other to recognize their mutual worth, parents to be charitable, neighbours to be fair-minded, and people generally to adopt his view of their interests, be it by intimidation or by joyful consent.[81]

Today, *Tahkim* is a central component of the commercial dispute resolution process in many Arab/Muslim countries.[82] For example, in Saudi Arabia, *Tahkim* is a major instrument of commercial dispute resolution between local and foreign companies. There are two different applications of *Tahkim*: specific (for dealing with a currently occurring dispute) and global – a commitment by the parties to a commercial arrangement to arbitrate every dispute that may occur in the future resulting from ongoing commercial relationships.

Both approaches are not problem-free. There are problems of registration, cooperation and enforcement. Even if the parties agree on mandatory universal binding arbitration, when a dispute erupts, they must file a writ of arbitration with the local court – and the document must be signed by all parties to the dispute; otherwise, no official status is accorded.[83]

Also, if one of the disputing parties totally refuses to cooperate (does not respond or participate), it is unclear whether a verdict can be made or enforced.

It is worth mentioning that in Saudi Arabia, an arbitrator must be a Muslim (though not necessarily a Saudi citizen) and that each arbitration verdict must conform with Shari'a and with all existing Saudi statutes.

In addition to all these potential drawbacks, critiques of *Tahkim* view it as a practice burdened by inflated claims.[84]

Tahkim *and Western arbitration*

There are a few basic similarities and differences worth noting between *Tahkim* and Western arbitration:

- In both practises the disputing sides transfer much of the control over the proceedings to the arbitrator(s). This is done both for reasons of expediency and to facilitate the process. *Tahkim* allows the disputants leeway with respect to the choice of arbitrators and their continuing control (that is, disputants in some cases can withdraw consent before a decision is made by the arbitrator). In Western arbitration, once the process starts, it will proceed to a conclusion by the arbitrator. This is seen as an attempt at a more conciliatory posture within *Tahkim*, designed to foster a more cooperative attitude on the part of the disputants.[85]
- Western arbitration exhibits many procedural characteristics found in early stages of court proceedings. *Tahkim* tries to steer away from a courtlike posture, again in the service of fostering more cooperative attitudes between the disputants. Still, the Western arbitrator is not bound by formal (e.g. state) law, and usually tries to decide on narrower grounds, covering the needs and expectations of the disputants and the community they function within. The Muslim arbitrator's primary responsibility is to Muslim law and the community within which the process takes place – bringing the *hakam*'s posture closer to that of a formal judge, despite the procedural attempt to mitigate courtlike behaviour.

Sayen touches on the core difference between Western arbitration and *Tahkim* when he writes:

> At the root of the conceptual conflict between the two procedures is the fact that Islamic Law never developed a distinction between law and equity. If one believes that the law is divinely inspired, the very idea that an alternative kind of justice exists that is more 'just'" in certain cases than the law itself is untenable. Thus, disputes must be resolved either by agreement among the parties or according to the law. It is the end that determines the means used to achieve it. Therefore, unlike arbitration, tahkim never developed an identity separate from conciliation and litigation.[86]

Sulha (Settlement)

Sulha means settlement, negotiation, mediation/conciliation, compromise. In the words of Zahidul Islam: 'Sulh literally means "to cut off a dispute" or "to finish a dispute"'.[87]

The purpose of the Sulha, as seen by the *Jaha* or Sulha Committee (a group of third-party interveners who performs the Sulha process), by the disputants and by the community at large, is to facilitate a transformation of the victimized clan's attitudes from a desire to avenge to a willingness to forgive by restoring their sense of honour, while avoiding damage to the perpetrator's clan's sense of honour. The result of such a process (if successful) is to mend the damaged fabric of the community by repairing the relations between the affected disputants' clans and the community at large. The reconciliation process includes an acknowledgement of responsibility and guilt by the perpetrator's kin group, a willingness to forgive and forgo revenge by the victim's kin group, a payment of a fine ('blood money' in cases involving death and/or injury) and a drive by the community to facilitate the disputants' move toward resolving their dispute.[88]

There is evidence linking the Sulha to early pre-Islamic Semitic writings and later to Christian scriptures, dating from around the first century CE.[89] There is also scant, uncorroborated evidence of women playing a formal role as mediators in some instances in the pre-Islamic Middle East.[90]

Ramahi establishes a link between pre-Islamic customary justice practices and similar customs within the evolving Islam, writing that:

> [t]he adherence to customs continued within Islam. *Al urf wal adah* is a rule that allows the reference to customs and established practices as a legitimate source of law, as long as, they do not contradict with *Sharia* (sic) . . . Many of the rules of conduct practiced before Islam continued to be honoured after the rise of Islam especially customs relating to personal honour, hospitality and courage. The Prophet also encouraged such values as kindness, mercy and justice, which developed the earlier customs and practices of the region . . . Thus, many of the positive tribal customs were incorporated into Islamic teaching and jurisprudence.[91]

In line with this perspective, the Sulha's incorporation into Islam probably followed a similar path of maintaining the traditional tribal framework of the pre-Islamic customary justice mechanisms while replacing its pre-Islamic pagan 'toolbox' with those of Islam (specifically Shari'a) as the Sulha's foundations.

The Islamic roots of Sulha are substantial. The practice is mentioned several times in the Qur'an and the Hadith. This is of significance to this work because it demonstrates the solid position of the practice within Islam – solidity that emanates from the apparent direct revelatory affiliation, as well as from the 'veteran status' of the practice within pre-Muslim customs and the preferential reference towards it by Muhammad.

One of the most prominent Qur'anic references to Sulha, one that also alludes to the practice's place as Islam's preferred method of dispute settlement, appears in Sura 42, Verse 40: 'The recompense of an injury is an injury the like thereof; but whoever forgives and thereby brings about a reestablishment of harmony, his reward is with God; and God loves not the wrongdoers'.

Another Qur'anic reference to Sulha says 'The believers are but a single Brotherhood: So make peace and reconciliation between your two (contending) brothers: And fear Allah that ye may receive Mercy'.[92] Here, too, the emphasis is on the reconciliation, rather than adjudication, aspect of the process.

Yet another Qur'anic reference reads:

> If two parties among the Believers fall into a quarrel make ye peace between them: but if one of them transgresses beyond bounds against the other then fight ye (all) against the one that transgresses until it complies with the command of Allah; but if it complies then make peace between them with justice and be fair: for Allah loves those who are fair (and just).[93]

Here, again, there is a stated preference for reconciliation, alongside the injunction to bring all available communal weight to ensure compliance with the supreme goal of conflict resolution.

And yet another Qur'anic verse lends explicit support to the concept of amicable settlement of disputes. It reads:

> In most of their secret talks there is no good: but if one exhorts to a deed of charity or justice or conciliation between men (secrecy is permissible): to him who does this seeking the good pleasure of Allah We shall soon give a reward of the highest (value).[94]

In addition to endorsing conciliation, the verse provides specific guidance regarding the actual practice of Sulha by endorsing 'secrecy' (confidentiality).

As noted earlier, there is evidence that Muhammad expressed a clear preference of Sulha, wherever possible, to the application of an arbitrative or Qadi procedure. Invoking a great Muslim authority to underscore this point, Sayen notes that

> Bukhari's Sahih (an early collection of traditions) includes a report of a dispute between two landowners who used the same stream for irrigation. The plaintiff had the legal right to exclusive use of the stream. The Prophet nevertheless suggested a reconciliation whereby the defendant could have the use of any excess water not needed for irrigation of plaintiff's land. Only when the defendant refused this compromise solution did the prophet give (arbitrative) judgment in accordance with plaintiff's legal right.[95]

Another example brought by Bukhari to illustrate Muhammad's preference of Sulha is a reported hadith by the Prophet: 'He who makes Peace (Sulh) between the people by inventing good information or saying good things, is not a liar (sic)'.[96] In addition to the promotion of Sulh as a practice, this hadith sets the historical and practical precedence for the practice of 'creative reframing' – a practice used extensively by Sulha practitioners whereby the peacemakers take extensive liberty with impressions and information that they convey to the disputing sides in the service of helping them develop a more positive attitude towards each other, even if it includes substantially misquoting or even inventing texts and narratives. According to Sulha practitioner Abu M'bada, the *Jaha* often goes beyond reframing to 'manufacturing' positive messages and narratives designed to help reduce negative feelings and foster positive attitudes between disputants.[97]

Another hadith seems to establish a financial reward to encourage Sulha making:

> There is a *sadaqa* [voluntary charity] to be given for every joint of the human body and for every day on which the sun rises there is a reward for the sadaqa for the one who establishes sulh and justice among the people.[98]

The practice of financially compensating interveners still exists among the Bedouins of the Negev desert in southern Israel. However, in the north of Israel Sulha makers, in an attempt to project an appearance of strict neutrality and total lack of commercial interest, do not take either alms and/or direct or indirect pay for their services; in fact, they often spend considerable sums out of pocket to facilitate Sulha processes.[99]

The social zone of practice for the Sulha process is the communal domain. In Ramahi's words:

Dispute resolutions in the Middle East are guided with an overarching principle of collective interests of the family, the tribe, the community and the country. The Arab's Islamic and tribal history places collective interest as the highest principle in a hierarchy of values in both dispute resolution and everyday dealings.[100]

Ramahi further expands on the subject of the centrality of the communal format, noting that:

> An individual's life is considered to be an element of the collective life; thus, the individual and the collective are considered to be one and the same. Therefore, any attack on the individual is considered to be an attack on the group and vice versa . . . All are collectively responsible for the punishment, revenge or compensation of any member of the tribe. All are jointly and severally liable for the compensation, punishment or revenge.[101]

This is a social setup that is vastly different from the predominantly individualistic Western approach. In the context of the Sulha, this communal perspective is essential because it touches the essence of the interclan dispute, above and beyond the dispute between individuals, as well as the need to resolve the interclan dispute in addition to the interpersonal dispute(s).

Political scientist Adeed Dawisha puts this supercommunal aspect into a broader historical, sociopolitical and dispute resolution perspective by linking communal hierarchy to Islam: 'Before the birth of the modern Arab state, the core societal units in the Arab world were (and perhaps continue to be) the tribe, the village, and the extended family'; he writes:

> For centuries, the pattern of political loyalty in the tribal and village communities was hierarchical, with power vested in the Sheikh or the Rais. Although he was bound by tribal and village laws and customs, the Sheikh or the Rais, assisted by elders and religious leaders, acted as the central authority, the final arbiter of power, and the ultimate dispenser of justice. Similarly, the extended

family has traditionally been hierarchically structured, with authority resting securely in the hands of the oldest member.

Dawisha points out an aspect of Arab culture that may be central to understanding the power of communal-based dispute resolution structures when he identifies what he terms 'Arab respect for and acceptance of hierarchical social structures with a clearly identifiable authoritative personage at the top'.[102]

In Mejelle (the Ottoman Civil Code), Sulha is defined as a contract between the parties to settle their differences amicably. The Sulha becomes a concluded contract once an agreement is reached and the disputants put their signature to a final document of reconciliation.[103]

Islam's preference for Sulha to other arbitrative/mediating means is based on the assumption that it conveys 'religious blamelessness' on the intervener and the disputants alike; there is also a recognition of the benefit of reconciling a dispute rather than adjudicating it, a process that often results in continued resentment, anger and even hatred between the disputants (including, importantly, in the aftermath of a verdict).[104]

Having examined the place of Sulha within the evolution of Islam and Islamic jurisprudence and within Muslim customary justice, it is important to explore the boundaries of this ubiquitous practice within Islam as a religion and a sociopolitical entity.

The practice of Sulha is strictly limited to '*huquq al-abad*' (rights of human beings), governing relations between people, where compromise and conciliation is the preferred path, as long as it is equitable and just and does not violate any provision of Muslim law (Shari'a). On the other hand, all issues concerning '*huquq Allah*' (rights of God) are strictly out of bounds for Sulha; this aspect of Muslim jurisprudence governs the relations between God and people, including 'Claims of God' (*hudud*), such as fornication and adultery; consumption of alcohol or other intoxicants; and apostasy, charity (*zakat*), and acts of prescribed atonement or penitence (*kaffarah*).

In many Arab countries (e.g. Jordan, Lebanon) failure to resolve a Sulha-allowed dispute by compromise causes it to be transferred to the domain of the formal court, where it becomes the duty of the Qadi to resolve the dispute, first by attempting to convince the disputants to reach a compromise solution and, if that fails, through proper adjudication. This procedure emanates directly from the instructions of the Prophet Muhammad.[105]

In Israel, Sulha and formal justice are strictly segregated from each other, and failure to resolve a Sulha simply results in the interclan conflict dragging on for years, sometimes decades. Eventually, all Sulha-bound disputes get resolved, though this can at times take as long as 30 years.[106] The one place within Islam where the practice of Sulha was coded into formal law was the *Mejelle* (*Mecelle*) – the civil code of the Ottoman Empire in the late nineteenth and early twentieth centuries, the first attempt to codify Shari'a-based law into an Islamic state's formal legal system.

Different types of cases are brought in for Sulha mediation/arbitration, including theft, rape, property damage and physical assaults (including murder). The view of Sulha makers is that if you do not deal with small, relatively less severe conflicts, they will eventually expand to major conflicts. Small (e.g. property) disputes command the attention of a single Sulha maker, whereas the more complex matters (notably murder) are dealt with by a full complement of interveners, sometimes extending to include a dozen dignitaries and more.[107]

After the death of Muhammad, the group of leaders that sustained his Islamic mission, known as 'The Companions', continued to promote Sulha. An indication of the continued preference for this practice is contained in a letter by the second caliph, Umar ibn al-Khattab, appointing Abu Musa Asharion to the position of Qadi. The letter contains guidance relating to the place and relevance of Sulha, stating that '[a]ll types of compromise and conciliation are permissible except those which makes haram anything which is halal and a halal is haram'.[108]

Med-Arb and Sulha

As we shall see, one of the Sulha's most distinguishing features is its use of a mix of mediation and arbitration tools. A seemingly similar, though essentially different, practice called Med-Arb is described in the literature; its features are helpful in highlighting the uniqueness of the Sulha.

In the words of political scientist Christine Harrington, Med-Arb is a 'technique that fuses the "consensuality" of mediation with the "finality" of arbitration'.[109] Although Med-Arb exhibits multiple different manifestations of dispute resolution approaches, depending on location and context of application, its core structure – a two-step process that utilizes mediation as the primary approach (used by the third-party intervener), followed by arbitration – is a distinguishing mode of practice that appears in all its variations.[110]

Med-Arb's legal origins can be traced to the Qur'an:

> If ye fear a breach between them twain appoint (two) arbiters one from his family and the other from hers; if they wish for peace Allah will cause their reconciliation: for Allah hath full knowledge and is acquainted with all things.[111]

The concept emanating from this verse arranges the available intervener's tools in sequential form: first there is a need to use the mediation tools to achieve conciliation, and only if such tools fail to produce the desired result – reconciliation – the intervener is instructed to move to an arbitration mode and utilize arbitration tools to bring the conflict to a resolution.

Zahidul Islam provides further substantiation to the broader legitimacy and use of a mixed mediation-arbitration mode of dispute resolution (outside the domain of marital law). He points to Article 1851 of the Mejelle, which supports the idea of going for arbitration when mediation attempts fail. This, he argues, proves that

Med-Arb is recognized and used in Islam, bringing additional examples of the use of mixed mediation-arbitration in other Muslim and non-Muslim countries such as Vietnam, Japan and Malaysia.[112]

Although this utilization of mixed-mode practice appears in a part of the Qur'an that deals with marital problems, it is of significance to the exploration of Sulha because this is the first (and only) time the Qur'an explicitly calls for the use of both mediation and arbitration tools in the same application – albeit in a way different from that used in the type of Sulha explored in this work. In Sulha, the interveners use mediation and arbitration applications interchangeably, when and where they see a need, throughout the process. Indeed, Zahidul Islam makes a distinct differentiation between arbitration and Sulha when he asserts that '[a]rbitration is governed by different regulations; therefore arbitration does not come under sulh'.[113] This assertion ignores the realities of the practice of Sulha as described in this work.

Other Muslim conflict resolution scholars also allude to the mediation-arbitration duality within Sulha. Ramahi provides a telling insight into this mixed practice, which distinguishes the Sulha from other Muslim and Western practices, when she writes: 'However, the disputing parties in sulh, also have the option to use an arbitrator in order to work towards a settlement. Thus, arbitration can be one of the means of sulh'.[114] However, although shedding light on this important phenomenon, Ramahi displays confusion regarding the place of arbitration in Sulha by presenting the arbitration part in Sulha as optional.

In the specific Sulha process examined in this work – that practiced in northern Israel by the region's Arab population – mediation and arbitration applications essentially coexist and are used alternately. Whereas in Med-Arb sequence is the central predicator of the process – prescribing the use of mediation followed by the use of arbitration, in Sulha the use of these two conflict resolution approaches is stage-dependent as well as context-dependent. The Sulha process always starts with an arbitrative process – the signing of the *Tafweeth* (Writ of Authorization), followed by a mediation approach to recruiting the victim's clan to the process. Later on, as the process proceeds, the interveners use mediation and arbitration tools interchangeably as needed and where needed. Indeed, as we shall see, this mixed use of these tools is an organic, and essential, part of the Sulha process.[115]

Notes

1 William Montgomery Watt, *Islam and the Integration of Society* (London: Routledge, 2001), p. 5.
2 Bernard Lewis, 'Islam and Liberal Democracy: A Historical Overview', *Journal of Democracy*, Vol. 7, No. 2 (1996), p. 54; Syed Khalid Rashid, 'Alternative Dispute Resolution in the Context of Islamic Law', *The Vindobona Journal of International Commercial Law and Arbitration*, Vol. 8, No. 1(2004), p. 95.
3 Alfred Guillaume, *The Life of Muhammad – A Translation of Ishaq's Sirat Rasul Allah* (Oxford: Oxford University Press, 1955), pp. 231–33.
4 George Sayen, 'Arbitration, Conciliation, and the Islamic Legal Tradition in Saudi Arabia', *University of Pennsylvania Journal of International Business Law*, Vol. 9, No. 2 (1987), p. 227.

5 Wael B. Hallaq, *The Origins and Evolution of Islamic Law* (Cambridge: Cambridge University Press. 2005), p. 3.
6 Majid Khadduri, 'Nature and Sources of Islamic Law', *George Washington Law Review*, Vol. 22, No. 3 (1953), p. 3. See also Judith, R. Wegner, 'Islamic and Talmudic Jurisprudence: The Four Roots of Islamic Law and Their Talmudic Counterparts', *American Journal of Legal History*, Vol. 26, No. 1 (1982), p. 26.
7 Shari'a (Way, Path) – Islamic Shari'a constitutes what is considered the divine body of laws as revealed by Allah to the Prophet Muhammad, purporting to cover the entire spectrum of human conduct in this world. Shari'a is fixed and remains unchanged. The laws of Shari'a are mostly general and deal with basic principles.
8 Ramahi, 'Sulh', p. 6.
9 Gulam Hyder, 'Dispute Management: An Islamic Perspective', *Arbitrator and Mediator*, Vol. 22, No. 3 (2003), pp. 6–7.
10 Author interview with Dr. Musa Abu Ramadan, an expert on Islamic law from the Academic Center, Carmel, and Bar Ilan University, Israel, 11 February 2011.
11 Gamal Moursi Badr, 'Islamic Law: Its Relation to Other Legal Systems', *American Journal of Comparative Law*, Vol. 26, No. 2 (1978), p. 189. See also Hyder, 'Dispute Management', p. 5; David Bonderman, 'Modernization and Changing Perceptions of Islamic Law', *Harvard Law Review*, Vol. 81, No. 6 (1967), pp. 1169–93; Mohammad Abu Nimer, 'Conflict Resolution Approaches: Western and Middle Eastern Lessons and Possibilities', *American Journal of Economics and Sociology*, Vol. 55, No. 1 (1996), pp. 35–52.
12 It is important to note that this chapter does not deign nor does it need to present a comprehensive picture of the evolution of Muslim jurisprudence; it presents the subject only in the context of its relevance to Muslim ADR in general and Sulha in particular, so as to provide the basic historical, chronological and functional contexts required for the exploration of Sulha.
13 Hyder, 'Dispute Management', p. 5
14 Badr, 'Islamic Law', p. 189.
15 Fiqh is the term defining Muslim jurisprudence (systematic deduction of law) and includes the rules and injunctions deduced from the Shari'a in the form of legal decisions and opinions written by Muslim jurists.
16 Ze'ev Maghen, 'Dead Tradition: Joseph Schacht and the Origins of Popular Practice', *Islamic Law and Society*, Vol. 10, No. 3 (2003), p. 276; Harald Motzki, *The Origins of Islamic Jurisprudence: Meccan Fiqh Before the Classical Schools*, translated by Marion H. Katz (Leiden: Brill Academic Publisher, 2002).
17 Noel, J. Coulson, *A History of Islamic Law* (Edinburgh: Edinburgh University Press, 1978), pp. 1–2. See also Patricia Crone Roman, *Provincial and Islamic Law: The Origins of the Islamic Patronate* (Cambridge: Cambridge University Press, 1987), p. 2.
18 Harald Motzki, 'Review of *The Origins of Islamic Law: The Qur'an, the Muwatta' and Madinan Amal*, by Yasin Dutton', *Journal of Law and Religion*, Vol. 15, No. 1/2 (2000–01), pp. 369–73.
19 Wael Hallaq, *A History of Islamic Legal Theories: An Introduction to Sunni Usul al-Fiqh* (Cambridge: Cambridge University Press, 1997), p. 1.
20 Author interview with Sheikh Ihye Abdel Rani (Abu Muhammad), head of the Sulha Committee of northern Israel's Arab community, 16 October 2012.
21 Joseph Schacht, *An Introduction to Islamic Law* (Oxford: Oxford University Press, 1983), pp. 70–1.
22 William Montgomery Watt, 'The Dating of the Qur'an: A Review of Richard Bell's Theories', *Journal of the Royal Asiatic Society* (New Series), Vol. 89, Nos. 1/2 (1957), pp. 46–56. See also Geoffrey Parrinder, 'And is it True?' *Religious Studies*, Vol. 8, No. 1 (1972), pp. 15–27.
23 Khadduri, 'Nature and Sources of Islamic Law', p. 3.
24 Ramahi, 'Sulh', p. 6.

32 *Sulha in Muslim jurisprudence*

25 Crone, *Roman, Provincial and Islamic Law*, p. 1.
26 Joseph Schacht, 'Foreign Elements in Ancient Islamic Law', *Journal of Comparative Law and International Law*, Vol. 32, Nos. 3/4 (1950), pp. 9–17; idem, *'The Origins of Muhammadan Jurisprudence'*, *Journal of Comparative Law and International Law*, Third Series, Vol. 33, Nos. 3/4 (1951), pp. 113–14. See also Ignacz Goldziher, 'The Principles of Law in Islam', in H.S. Williams (ed.), *The Historians' History of the World* (New York: Hooper and Jackson, 1908), p. 298.
27 Seymour G. Vesey-Fitzgerald, 'The Alleged Debt of Islamic Law to Roman Law', *The Law Quarterly Review*, Vol. 67, No.265 (1951), p. 86.
28 Hallaq, *The Origins and Evolution*, p. 19. See also Qur'an 2:213; 3:23; 4:58, 105; 5:44–5, 47; 7:87; 10:109; 24:48. For example, the Qur'an states (5:44): 'He who does not judge by what God has revealed is a disbeliever'.
29 *Ibid.*, p. 21.
30 Shelomo D. Goitein, 'The Birth-Hour of Muslim Law', *Muslim World*, Vol. 50, No. 1 (1960), p. 24.
31 Crone, *Roman, Provincial and Islamic Law*, p. 3. See also Wegner, *Islamic and Talmudic Jurisprudence*, p. 26.
32 William Montgomery Watt, *Muhammad: Prophet and Statesman* (Oxford: Oxford University Press, 1961), pp. 39–40.
33 Maghen, 'Dead Tradition', p. 340.
34 This section draws, among other sources, on Hani, S. Mahmassani, *The Philosophy of Jurisprudence in Islam*, trans. by Farhat J. Ziadeh (Leiden: Brill, 1961).
35 Samir Saleh, *Commercial Arbitration in the Arab Middle East* (Portland: Hart Publishing, 2006), p. 9.
36 Brandon M. Wheeler, *Applying the Canon in Islam: The Authorization and Maintenance of Interpretive Reasoning in Hanafi Scholarship* (Albany: State University of New York Press, 1996).
37 David J. Karl, 'Islamic Law in Saudi Arabia: What Foreign Attorneys Should Know', *George Washington Journal of International Law and Economy*, Vol. 25 (1991), pp. 131–70.
38 Andrew Rippin, *Muslims: Their Religious Beliefs and Practices* (London: Routledge, 2005). pp. 90–3.
39 *Ibid.*, p. 231.
40 Essam Alsheikh, 'Distinction Between the Concepts Mediation, Conciliation, Sulh and Arbitration in Shari'a Law', *Arab Law Quarterly*, Vol. 25 (2011), p. 372.
41 Author interviews with Khneifes, 24 July, 2007.
42 Irshad Abdal-Haqq, 'Islamic Law – An Overview of Its Origin and Elements', *Journal of Islamic Law and Culture*, Vol. 7, No. 1 (2002), pp. 27–82.
43 Majid Khadduri and Herbert Liebesny, *Law in The Middle East* (Washington, DC: The Middle East Institute, 1955).
44 Sayen, 'Arbitration, Conciliation', p. 226.
45 'Oh believers! Obey God and obey the Prophet and those among you who are in authority, and if you have a dispute over anything refer it to God and the Prophet if you believe in God and the last day. That is the best and fairest determination' (Qur'an 4:59).
    'We have sent you down the Book with the truth that you [Muhammad] may judge between the people by what God has shown you' (Qur'an 4:105).
    'Judge between them by what God has revealed and follow not their vain desires' (5:49).
46 Sayen, 'Arbitration, Conciliation', p. 227.
47 Gulam, 'Dispute Management', p. 1.
48 Sayen, 'Arbitration, Conciliation', p. 227.
49 Qur'an, 4:228.
50 Bonderman, 'Modernization and Changing Perceptions of Islamic Law', p. 1172.
51 *Ibid.*

52 Rahma Hersi, 'A Value Oriented Legal Theory for Muslim Countries in the 21st Century: A Comparative Study of Both Islamic Law and Common Law Systems', *Cornell Law School Inter-University Graduate Student Conference Papers*, Paper 29 (2009), http://scholarship.law.cornell.edu/cgi/viewcontent.cgi?article=1057&context=lps_clacp (accessed 26 May 2011); Patrick J. Bannerman, Islam in Perspective, A Guide to Islamic Society, Politics and Law (New York: Routledge, 1988), p. 19.
53 Gulam, 'Dispute Management', p. 6.
54 Ramahi, 'Sulh', p. 6.
55 Noel Coulson, *Commercial Law in Gulf States: The Islamic Legal Tradition* (London: Graham and Trotman, 1984), p. 19.
56 Jany János, 'The Four Sources of Law in Zoroastrian and Islamic Jurisprudence', *Islamic Law and Society*, Vol. 12, No. 3 (2005), p. 292.
57 Bernard Lewis, *The Arabs in History* (Oxford: Oxford University Press, 2002), p. 40.
58 Zahidul Islam, 'Provision of Alternative Dispute Resolution Process in Islam', *Journal of Business and Management* (IOSR-JBM), Vol. 6, No. 3 (2012), p. 31.
59 Mahdi Zahraa and Nora Hak, 'Tahkim (Arbitration) in Islamic Law Within the Context of Family Disputes', *Arab Law Quarterly*, Vol. 20, No. 1 (2006), p. 2.
60 Ramahi, 'Sulh'.
61 Ahmed Moussalli, 'An Islamic Model for Political Conflict Resolution: Tahkim', in Said, Funk and Kadayifcis (eds.), *Peace and Conflict Resolution in Islam*, p. 143.
62 Hudud infractions include theft, fornication and adultery (zina), consumption of alcohol or other intoxicants and apostasy.
63 Islam, 'Provision of Alternative Dispute Resolution Process in Islam', p. 33.
64 Author interview with Lawyer and Imam, Abdul Wahab, Shafaamer, Israel, 27 July 2011.
65 Walid Abdulrahim, 'Arbitration Under the Lebanese Law', https://sites.google.com/site/walidabdulrahim/home/my-miscellaneous-studies-in-english/5-arbitration-under-the-l (accessed 6 January 2013). See also Faisal M.A. al-Fadhel, 'Party Autonomy and the Role of the Courts in Saudi Arbitration Law', Thesis submitted for the Degree of Doctor of Philosophy in Law at Queen Mary College, University of London, 2010.
66 Islam, 'Provision of Alternative Dispute Resolution Process in Islam', p. 33.
67 Moussalli, 'An Islamic Model for Political Conflict Resolution', pp. 146–47, 157; Qur'an, 4:35.
68 Sayen, 'Arbitration, Conciliation', p. 229.
69 Author interview with Imam Abdul Wahab, 27 July 2011.
70 Ramahi, 'Sulh', p. 12.
71 Moussalli, 'An Islamic Model for Political Conflict Resolution', p. 149.
72 Efraim Karsh, *Islamic Imperialism: A History* (London: Yale University Press, 2006), pp. 12–3.
73 Lewis, *The Arabs in History*, p. 42.
74 Ali Khan, 'Commentary on the Constitution of Medina', in Hisham M. Ramadan (ed.), Understanding Islamic Law (New York: AltaMira Press, 2006), p. 201.
75 Muhammad Tahir-ul-Qadri, *The Constitution of Medina: 63 Constitutional Articles* (London: Minhaj-ul-Quran Publications, 2012).
76 Lewis, *The Arabs in History*, p. 32.
77 Moussalli, 'An Islamic Model for Political Conflict Resolution', p. 152; Author interview with Imam Abdul Wahab.
78 Sayen, 'Arbitration, Conciliation', pp. 227–28.
79 Ramahi, 'Sulh', p. 12.
80 Sayen, 'Arbitration, Conciliation', p. 229.
81 Barry Rubin, 'Pan-Arab Nationalism: The Ideological Dream as Compelling Force', *Journal of Contemporary History*, Vol. 26, No. 3/4 (1991), p. 545.
82 Sayen, 'Arbitration, Conciliation', p. 212.
83 *Ibid*, p. 218.
84 *Ibid.*, p. 247.

34 *Sulha in Muslim jurisprudence*

85 *Ibid.*, pp. 237–38.
86 *Ibid.*, p. 229.
87 Islam, 'Provision of Alternative Dispute Resolution Process in Islam', p. 31.
88 Jabbour, *Sulha*, p. 26. See also George Irani, 'Islamic Mediation Techniques for Middle East Conflicts', *Middle East Review of International Affairs* (MERIA), Vol. 3, No. 2 (1999), p. 11; Said, Funk and Kadayifci, *Peace and Conflict Resolution in Islam*, p. 182; Iqbal, *Dialogue and the Practices*, p. 1035; Author interview with Khneifes, 21 July 2007.
89 Jabbour, *Sulha*, p. 13.
90 Jane Smith, 'Women, Religion and Social Change in Early Islam', in E. Banks Findly and Y. Yazbeck Haddad (eds.), *Women, Religion, and Social Change* (Albany: State University of New York Press, 1985), pp. 19–37. See also Moussalli, 'An Islamic Model for Political Conflict Resolution', p. 145.
91 Ramahi, 'Sulh', p. 6.
92 Qur'an, 49:10.
93 *Ibid.*, 49:9.
94 *Ibid.*, 4:114.
95 Sayen, 'Arbitration, Conciliation', p. 228.
96 *The Translation of the Meanings of Sahih Al-Bukhari*, Volume 3, translated by Dr. Muhammad Muhsin Khan, Darussalam Publishers and Distributors: Riyadh, Saudi Arabia, 1997, p. 533.
97 Author interview with Abu M'bada, 13 November 2011.
98 *Sahih al-Bukhari*, hadith 3.857, www.alim.org/library/hadith/SHB/857/3 (accessed 24 November 2013).
99 Author interview with Khneifes, 2007. Khneifes describes one instance where his father, the late head of northern Israel's Jaha, paid out of pocket to 'drive back and forth about 50 times over a two-year period to reconcile a dispute between two families in the village of Mrar, about 25 miles from his home in the town of Shafaamr'.
100 Ramahi, 'Sulh', p. 2.
101 *Ibid.*, p. 5.
102 Adeed Dawisha, 'Power, Participation, and Legitimacy in the Arab World', *World Policy Journal*, Vol. 3, No. 3 (1986), p. 525.
103 Mejelle, Article 1531, http://majalla.org/books/2003/mejelle.pdf (accessed 19 October 2014).
104 Walid Iqbal, 'Dialogue and the Practices of Law and Spiritual Values: Courts, Lawyering, and ADR Glimpses into the Islamic Tradition', *Fordham Urban Law Journal*, Vol. (2001), p. 1041.
105 Islam, 'Provision of Alternative Dispute Resolution Process in Islam', p. 33.
106 Author interview with Khneifes, 15 July 2011.
107 *Ibid.*
108 David Samuel Margoliouth, 'Omar's Instructions to the Kadi', *Journal of the Royal Asiatic Society of Great Britain and Ireland*, Vol. 42, No. 2 (1910), pp. 311–12 (there are doubts regarding the letter's authenticity stemming from variations in the text as it appears in several sources).
109 Christine Harrington, Shadow Justice: The Ideology and Institutionalization of Alternatives to Court (Westport, CT: Greenwood Press, 1985), p. 126.
110 Sherry Landry, 'Med-Arb: Mediation with a Bite and an Effective ADR Model', *Defense Counsel Journal*, Vol. 63, No. 2 (1996), p. 264.
111 Qur'an, 4:35.
112 Islam, 'Provision of Alternative Dispute Resolution Process in Islam', pp. 31–6.
113 *Ibid.*
114 Ramahi, 'Sulh', 12.
115 This unique practice is explored extensively in Chapter 4.

2 The theoretical foundations of Sulha

This chapter explores some of the difficulties associated with the application of available conflict resolution theories and concepts to Muslim/Arab dispute resolution in general, and to Sulha in particular. This is done through an examination of the relevance (or lack thereof) of current, Western-origin theories to Eastern conflict resolution perspectives and practices, with a view to establishing the theoretical and functional rationale for the introduction of a new analytical concept – re-integrative honouring.

What is conflict?

The origins and dynamics of conflicts and the paths to their resolution appear to be intuitive and self-evident. Yet a review of the relevant research, theories and literature demonstrates a complexity at both the definitional and the application levels.

There are multiple definitions of conflict, including perceived differences in interests, views and/or goals;[1] opposing preferences;[2] and a belief in the impossibility of simultaneously satisfying the disputing parties' needs,[3] to name but a few. According to anthropologist Laura Nader,

> conflict results from competition between at least two parties. A party may be a person, a family, a lineage, or a whole community; or it may be a class of ideas, a political organization, a tribe, or a religion. Conflict is occasioned by incompatible desires or aims and by its duration may be distinguished from strife or angry conflicts arising from momentary aggravations.[4]

Such a divergence of approaches – combined with the fact that scholars need to resort to broad, inclusive descriptions, which at times fail to accurately distinguish between conflict and competition – reflect the difficulties associated with providing a reasonably universally acceptable definition of a conflict.

In the absence of a clear definition, several foundational observations may help illuminate the nature of conflict and its management:[5]

- Conflict is natural and exists in all relationships and in all cultures.
- Conflict is a cultural event, reflecting the experience, meaning and derived behaviours of the disputants and their environment.

- Conflict is neither chaotic nor disorderly, following an ordered social pattern and is 'embedded' in a conflict-practicing culture.[6]
- Conflict is an interactive process; it progresses (either towards resolution or exacerbation) through a search and creation of shared or divergent meaning.
- The interaction between disputants is rooted in their perceptions, interpretation, expressions and intentions; different disputants tend to approach conflicts and their resolution differently.

Muslim/Arab vs. Western conflict resolution perspectives

Although there is some literature exploring and describing the differences between Muslim and Western conflict resolution approaches and practices, a detailed examination and comparison of these issues is largely absent.

George Irani, one of the few scholars to explore both Western and Muslim/Arab conflict resolution practices, established the rationale for seeking to detect and define differences and similarities between cultures' conflict resolution perspectives and practices; in his words: 'Although conflict is a human universal, the nature of conflicts and the methods of resolving conflict differ from one sociocultural context to another'. He adds:

> In assessing the applicability of Western-based conflict resolution models in non-Western societies, theoreticians and practitioners alike have begun to realize the importance of being sensitive to indigenous ways of thinking and feeling, as well as to local rituals for managing and reducing conflicts.[7]

Political scientist Paul Salem, in his essay 'Critique of Western Conflict Resolution from a Non-Western Perspective', provides a number of possible explanations for some of the differences between Muslim/Arab and Western conflict resolution perspectives. Departing from the sociopolitical assumption that '[t]he Western community of conflict resolution theorists and practitioners operate within a macro-political context that they may overlook, but which colors (sic) their attitudes and values', Salem claims that Western conflict resolution perspectives, practices and theories are designed to maintain and sustain an 'imperial' status quo (ostensibly over Muslim/Arab cultures, perspectives and practices). In his words: 'All successful "empires" develop an inherent interest in peace. The ideology of peace reinforces a status quo that is favorable (sic) to the dominant power'.[8]

Salem then adds a 'religiosity-based' perspective by claiming that the Christian ethos promotes 'peace' whereas the Jewish, Muslim and Eastern ethos promotes peace while at the same time aggressively advocating war as a positive choice under certain circumstances. 'The centrality of the idea that peace is, in any conditions, "good" and war is necessarily and in all circumstances "bad" is to some degree peculiar to the Christian worldview', he writes.

> This exaltation – or over-valuation – of peace and blanket denigration of war and the traditional military virtues, is to a considerable degree, characteristic

of the Christian worldview; but it is not a central part of the ancient Greek, Babylonian, Roman, Jewish or Islamic worldviews.

On the contrary, Islam, 'although it places peace as an exalted virtue, openly declared a sacred political program, and set out unapologetically from the beginning to back up its proselytism (sic) with force'. The proof, according to Salem, lies in the fact that '[t]he Prophet himself and all the Rightly Guided Caliphs were proud warriors. In this context, war in itself is not shameful, nor is peace necessarily and always good'. His conclusion: 'With regard to conflict resolution, the Western blanket assumption that working for peace is always, regardless of circumstance and conditions, a good thing might be questionable in other cultural contexts'.[9]

Not only does Salem seem to have overlooked Western conflict resolution theories that go beyond the cultural/religious paradigm (e.g. need-based approaches viewing conflict as a corollary of unfulfilled basic needs, notably identity needs),[10] but contrary to his assertion there is quite a substantial body of Western literature that doesn't uphold conflict as necessarily bad.[11] Indeed, Salem contradicts his own characterization of Christian ethos as overly peaceable, if not pacifist, by describing pre–World War II Western history as 'largely marked by intense and often violent struggles to establish national unity, national independence, socio-economic equality, and/or popular government. The more successful among western nations also prospered by conquering other nations and struggling for world supply and consumer markets'.[12]

George Irani and Nathan Funk – in one of the foremost concerted efforts to explain the gap between Western and Eastern conflict resolution perceptions and practices – focus on identifying the differing profiles of both cultures. As they put it:

> Despite the rapid social and cultural changes wrought by modernization, the emergence of nationalism and state structures in the Middle East, the cultural profiles of Arab-Islamic societies still differ profoundly from those of Western societies. Although pastoral nomadism has declined rapidly in relation to village- and city-based modes of social life, nomadic peoples and their traditions have nonetheless left a deep imprint on Middle Eastern culture, society, and politics. Urban professional classes have indeed emerged, yet the peoples of the Middle East have not yet disposed of their attachment to families and their distinctive rituals of hospitality and conflict mediation.[13]

According to Irani and Funk, the result of this cultural 'stuckness' is that

> [e]ven today, the institutions of the state do not always penetrate deeply into society, and 'private' justice is often administered through informal networks in which local political and/or religious leaders determine the outcome of feuds between clans or conflicts between individuals. Communal religious and ethnic identities all remain strong forces in social life, as do patron-client relationships and patterns of patriarchal authority. Group solidarity, traditional

religious precepts, and norms concerning honor (sic) and shame retain their place alongside exhortations of service to the nation and the newer values of intellectuals, intent on profound social change.[14]

They then proceed to argue that Western conflict resolution conceptualizations largely do not integrate (and consequently fail to export) major social perceptions that are key to understanding Eastern life and conflict. The absence of these insights results in a 'theorization gap', which, in turn, is reflected in a 'practice gap' within Muslim/Arab societies:

> In Arab-Islamic societies, Western techniques of conflict management and resolution are learned and adopted by urban professional groups such as businessmen or businesswomen, bankers, and engineers. For most people, however, conflict control and reduction are handled either by state-controlled courts or by traditional means. In this context, one of the basic criticisms launched against Western conflict resolution techniques is that they are either too mechanistic or based on therapy-oriented formulas that do not correspond with the idiom of daily life. Although some professionals find Western techniques and skills relevant and useful within the context of their own pursuits and activities, they also recognize a need to adapt these methods to indigenous cultural realities.[15]

Not surprisingly, severe difficulties often arise when Muslim/Arab conflict resolution practitioners, largely Western educated, explore indigenous and imported conflict resolution practices. Conflict resolution scholar Oussama Safa describes some of the difficulties associated with the conceptual and functional split (both real and perceived) between Western and Muslim conflict resolution theories and practices:

> Certain sectors in the Arab World and even some conflict resolution activists consider the field of conflict resolution to be a Western invention and thus alien to the local culture. This draping of the field of conflict resolution with foreign flags produces two practical challenges for conflict resolution organisations in the Arab World. First, externally these organisations face political, cultural and sometimes even philosophical challenges and obstacles from various authorities, who at best dismiss the efforts of these organisations as culturally irrelevant or inapplicable in the Arab World, and in the worst case accuse them of being cultural or even political lackeys of the West. The second challenge is related to the first one but more internal in nature: it is created by the buy-in of some local conflict resolution activists into the above arguments and thus the creation of internal conflicts among activists, who experience a strong tension between their desire to be true to their culture and environment and the urge to enhance their practices with conflict resolution skills and techniques that can be learned abroad.[16]

Sulha and conflict resolution theories

By way of surmounting these definitional and perceptual obstacles, this section explores Sulha within the context of several major conflict resolution theories (or theories that bear major relevance to the understanding of conflict resolution), including social identity theory (SIT), interdependence theory (IT), realistic conflict theory (RCT), Maslow's needs theory and restorative justice theory.

The assumed relevance of these theories rests primarily in the fact that they examine inter-relations from a group perspective (as opposed to exploring them exclusively from an individual perspective), including the fulfilment of human needs and the collaboration between disputants to resolve conflicts, within a communal context and in cooperation with the community. Because Sulha is a practice focused on resolving inter- (and intra-) group conflicts, it is reasonable to assume that such theories may present an acceptable medium of examination.

Sulha and social identity theory

Social identity theory (SIT) – sometimes bundled together with self-categorization theory (SCT) to form social identity approach[17] – postulates that mere membership in a group leads to the creation of an 'in-group' that favours the parent group at the expense of all others (defined as the out-group).[18]

According to sociologists Jan Stets and Peter Burke, 'a social group is a set of individuals who hold a common social identification or view themselves as members of the same social category'.[19] This definition dovetails with the description of the *hamula* (clan), the social group that is at the core of each Sulha-related conflict, defined by anthropologist Scott Atran Man as 'the village patronymic group'.[20]

Groups in general, and blood-related groups in particular, occupy a central place in the context of Muslim/Arab conflict resolution practices. In the words of Irani: 'Far more is at stake than the interests of individuals; disputing families and lineage groups solicit the intervention of prominent individuals to prevent the escalation of the conflict and the disruption of communal symbiosis'.[21]

Indeed, based on SIT, it may be possible to argue that the clan-based communal format prevalent in Arab communities, together with the realities of close-proximity living conditions, create a social topography that is conducive to producing out-group bias and resultant conflicts. As social psychologists Henry Taifel and John Turner write: 'The mere awareness of the presence of an out-group is sufficient to provoke intergroup competitive or discriminatory responses on the part of the in-group'.[22]

But a closer examination shows that SIT provides only a partial description and explanation of Sulha-related conflicts where in-group/out-group bias by itself, though clearly present, does not always provide a sufficient explanation as to the cause for the eruption of a conflict. A simple example will help illustrate the need to also explore the random nature (outside the domain of the out-group bias) at the root of many conflicts: two drivers find themselves squabbling over a parking space (this type of conflict actually happens quite often in Israel); in the heat of the argument, one driver stabs or shoots the other, creating an instantaneous interclan conflict between the victim's and the perpetrator's clans – groups that may have been cohabiting peacefully for decades, possibly even bonded by intermarriage, commercial and other links. Although the posteruption characteristics of the conflict are undoubtedly bound to group identities and demonstrate all the hallmarks of an in-group–out-group clash, it is quite clear that the eruption of the described feud (along with many similar conflicts) has nothing to do with the group affiliation, but is more associated with personal, individual, behavioural issues.

It is obvious that an exploration of the causes of the eruption of conflict is lacking without the insight gained from looking into the contribution of individual, identity-based elements. Stets and Burke provide a unique insight and offer an approach to exploring such composite conflict situations by proposing to merge group-related SIT with individual-focused identity theory (IT), possibly providing a way to reconcile the tension between the group-related perspectives and the manifestations of individual aspects of conflict situations. In their words: 'In this regard we discuss the cognitive processes of depersonalization (in social identity theory) and self-verification (in identity theory) as well as the motivational processes of self-esteem (in social identity theory) and self-efficacy (in identity theory)'.[23]

Another aspect worth exploring in this context is the behavioural impact of the transition from 'just' groups into specific conflict-defined groups. For example, once conflict erupts, the groups – now disputants – add to their characterization a specific, hitherto nonexistent, identity element: that of either a victim or a perpetrator group. Each such designation predicates certain designation-specific behaviours. For example, if a person belongs to the victim's group, that person is supposed to seek revenge on the perpetrator's group and is supposed to feel that his or her collective and individual sense of honour was damaged and hurt significantly (at least at the start of the conflict). By entering the conflict zone, hitherto amorphous concepts such as honour, revenge and forgiveness become concrete, essential and central.[24]

Yet another aspect worth noting when using SIT to explore Sulha-related conflicts is that the definition of an in-group within SIT is totally context free; that is the affiliation between group members can be completely nonsensical (e.g. selected by a flip of a coin).[25] This is, of course, not the case with Sulha-related conflicts, where the affiliation between group members is substantial, spanning blood relations, familial, cultural and sometimes economic and even political bonds. So, whereas it is possible to argue with confidence that the mere existence of more than one clan predisposes out-group bias, the eruption of conflicts may be seen as essentially external to the described SIT-related bias, requiring additional theoretical support outside of SIT.

Sulha and realistic conflict theory

Realistic conflict theory (RCT), also known as realistic group conflict theory (RGCT), represents another attempt to expand the examination of interpersonal relationships (conflicts in particular) from the individual to the group. The basic premise of RCT is that competition over limited resources leads to negative relations (i.e. intergroup conflict), whereas cooperation and collaboration lead to positive relations.[26] In the words of psychologist Donald Campbell, 'Real conflict of group interests causes intergroup conflict'.[27]

An important characteristic of resources is that they are finite, particularly in the context of competition and/or conflict (e.g. water, land, money). If a resource is finite, a success by one individual/group to maximize its possession necessarily leads to a reduction or depletion of that same resource's availability from the perspective of those not included in the group associated with the maximized possession. Therefore, it is reasonable to assume that any social interaction involving utilization of finite resources poses a risk of evolving into a conflict, reflecting the competition over specific finite resources.

As for conflicts that are managed through Sulha, these are mainly (though not exclusively) perceived by the disputants, the interveners and the community at large as linked directly to a perception of loss of honour and the restoration of honour and trust between the disputants' clans. Therefore, in order to establish the relevance (or lack thereof) of RCT to Sulha, it is necessary first to decide whether honour is a resource.

In honour-based cultures, such as that of northern Israel's Muslim/Arab community, honour is central to the relations between groups involved in Sulha-related conflicts, and without it, no dispute will be resolved.[28] Sheikh Ihye Abdel Rani, head of northern Israel's Arab community's *Jaha* over the past eleven years and a member of the *Jaha* since 1974, argues that 'honour is the heart of Sulha. Conflicts start because of damaged honour and are solved through restoration of honour'.[29] Elias Jabbour, a long-time conflict resolution practitioner in the Arab community of northern Israel, writes: 'Honor (sic) is, by far, the most important aspect of Sulha'.[30]

It seems that it is possible (and reasonable) to view honour as one of the core values that are utilized as resources (both individual and public/communal) within the Sulha process.[31] In that context, honour is used to (re)build trust – a major lubricant of social interaction both at the individual and communal levels. Honour is also directly connected to self-image (as well as one's perception of one's image in the eyes of others – the community and individuals). It appears that improving self-image is a clear motivator.[32] This can explain both the motivation to avenge and the transformed motivation to forgive, predicated on one's perception of self-image (in one's own and outsiders' eyes).

Yet, even as we identify honour as a resource, it appears that its place in Sulha is more complex and nuanced than that of a 'regular' resource because even though it is a resource, it is not the finite, mutually exclusive resource that is usually thought about in conflict observance and/or analysis.[33] As shall be shown later, honour (or rather its perception in the eyes of the disputants and the relevant community) is a resource that can increase or decrease simultaneously, on both sides of the dispute, in response to different behaviours and social cues. One side's perception of increased honour is not necessarily predicated on the other side's perception of decreased honour. Furthermore, it can be divided and shared between the disputants without creating an unsatisfied need, and its resultant conflict, on the part of any side.

Because of this unique feature of honour, it is difficult to demonstrate that in Sulha-related conflicts the disputing groups (clans) are actually in conflict *over the resource* of honour. A more reasonable view is that the core of the intergroup conflict in such situations is *not* a conflict *over* a limited resource (i.e. honour), but over the honour-related self-perceptions of the clans, as well as the perceptions of the clans regarding their honour in the eyes of the community at large. Viewed in such light, it is argued that the interests of both groups rest in simultaneously sustaining and restoring their honour in their own eyes and in the eyes of their community of reference.[34]

Such interests are, then, not mutually exclusive; actually, both the disputants and the relevant communities know that exclusiveness in such circumstances will most likely result in extending the conflict ad infinitum by possibly reversing the polarity of the victim–perpetrator axis as the conflict spirals in an infinite revenge–counter-revenge cycle.

Obviously, this subject requires much additional examination, but this is outside the scope of this work. Suffice it to say that RCT does not cover some of the complexities apparent in honour-based, Sulha-related conflicts.

Sulha and interdependence theory

Interdependence theory (IT) stipulates that the relationship between groups may be characterized by a constant effort to maximize rewards (e.g. exchanged resources that provide gratification) while concurrently striving to minimize costs (e.g. exchanged resources that are seen as promoting loss, insult and/or punishment).[35] Furthermore, IT stipulates that a characteristic feature of an ideal (and for that matter, stable) relationship – either between individuals, or intercommunal – is the presence of high levels of rewards compared with low levels of costs. Deviation from that proportional (im)balance is likely to lead to conflict, hence the relevance of IT to conflict.

Here, too, it appears that the 'infinite' characteristic of honour as a resource makes Sulha a private case of IT. Indeed, the main task of the Sulha practitioners is to ensure maximization of the honour resource by both disputing clans. It is necessary and possible for all disputants to maximize their honour perception, availability and utility without contributing to the competition over it along with its attendant possible conflict. Only when such a condition is fulfilled can the process move toward resolution.

Sulha and Maslow's hierarchy of needs

Psychologist Abraham Maslow's hierarchy of needs theory postulates that as people attend to their needs, they aspire to first meet the more basic ones, such as survival, health (food, water, shelter) and safety. Other, less urgent, needs, according to Maslow (e.g. belonging, esteem, self-actualization), will not be attended to until the basic needs are satisfied.[36] Applying this theory to conflict situations, Paul Sites argued that it is possible to hypothesize that in such situations disputants will first address their more basic needs because until and unless these needs are fulfilled, there will be no progress towards satisfying the less basic needs.[37]

Following these two basic premises, it is reasonable to assume that the first needs disputants will attend to as they attempt to resolve a conflict would be related to their basic survival and security. Irani sheds light on this assumed direction, writing:

> From a Western psychological perspective, conflict usually erupts because some basic needs have not been fulfilled, such as needs for shelter, food, self-esteem, love, knowledge, and self-actualization. The non-fulfilment of these needs, exacerbated by acute feelings of victimization, inevitably leads to conflict and may eventually lead to war.[38]

But in the course of researching the ways disputants in Israel's Arab community respond to specific types of conflicts, particularly those involving perceived offenses against family honour by female family members or violence against a clan member, it appears that disputants position honour and identity as basic needs of a higher priority than health and safety. Put simply, it appears that in the immediate aftermath of the eruption of those particular kinds of conflict, disputants tend to focus more on satisfying family honour and belonging (identity) needs as they perceive them while ignoring or allocating secondary or tertiary places to what Maslow and Sites mark as the most basic needs (survival and safety), including derivatives of these needs, such as health, freedom from incarceration and economic security.[39]

One such relevant conflict context, called 'honour killing', involves a situation in which a male relative whose relationship can be traced exclusively through males (known as an agnate relative)[40] murders a female family member (mother, daughter, sister) in order to restore what he perceives as the family's lost honour because of perceived improper behaviour on the part of the female family member – usually of a sexual nature. Here, in what may appear as a somewhat bizarre role reversal, the perpetrator, as perceived by many family and community members, is the murdered female family member, and the perceived victim is the agnate family member(s) – along with the woman's entire clan – who then acts to restore their lost honour by killing the allegedly errant female family member.[41]

The act of restoring the family's honour by murdering the perceived female offender demonstrates the primacy of honour needs because it often takes place with total disregard of the severe ramifications of such an act, including almost certain destruction of the immediate family unit, extended incarceration of one or more male family members, significant financial hardship for the entire family due to incurred legal costs and loss of income from one or more male family members.[42]

If the murdered woman is not a direct relative of her husband (first cousin), as is sometimes the case, the husband's clan may see the killing as an offence to the husband's honour (and that of his entire clan, of course) and declare a conflict, despite the fact that the killing allegedly took place to restore male honour. Such a conflict will require a Sulha to resolve.

Because the primary need in a Sulha-related conflict is restoration of honour, such a conflict seems to challenge Maslow's basic needs hierarchy.

Blood feuds, the second type of conflict where it is possible to witness behaviour that challenges Maslow's basic needs priority assumptions, involves a situation in which a member of an extended family kills a member of another clan. In the immediate aftermath of such a killing, the honour-restoring instinct of a victim's *hamula* is to seek revenge for the damage done to his or her clan's honour, regardless of the ramifications associated with such an act. In such situations, male members of the victim's clan view every male member of the killer's clan as a legitimate target for revenge by virtue of clan 'circles of responsibility'.[43] It is worth noting that those attempting or carrying out an act of revenge put *all* their male clan members in mortal danger because *all* male members of the disputing clan are obliged to defend each other with their lives and to avenge any attack with equal ferocity to restore *their* damaged honour.

Both blood feuds and honour killings conflicts are handled in many cases by the Sulha process, which seems particularly suitable for dealing with such issues because the Sulha itself is based, first and foremost, on restoration of honour needs and therefore seems to be conversant with the central needs of disputants in such conflicts. Another aspect of the Sulha that makes it particularly suitable for handling such conflicts is the fact that it provides a clan-level solution – a significant advantage when dealing with conflicts that are mainly clan based.

In order to accommodate the different hierarchy of needs as presented by disputants in Sulha-related conflicts, one should define a different hierarchy of needs within the Sulha's conflict resolution practice. Such a hierarchy does indeed exist, and Figures 2.1 and 2.2 depict the difference between Maslow's approach and the

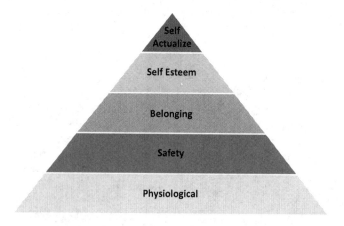

Figure 2.1 Maslow's hierarchy of needs

The theoretical foundations of Sulha 45

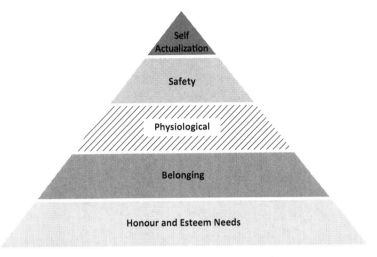

Figure 2.2 Sulha's hierarchy of needs

hierarchy of needs in honour-related conflicts in northern Israel's Arab community (and, probably, with varying degrees of accuracy, within much of the Arab/Muslim world), whereby the base of the needs pyramid is honour.[44]

Here, again, is an illustration of a Western theory that does not quite successfully explain or predict honour-based conflicts in a non-Western cultural context in general, and that of the Sulha in particular.

Sulha and fundamental attribution error

In the context of conflict resolution, fundamental attribution error, also known as the overattribution effect, describes the existence of a pervasive tendency on the part of disputants to overestimate the primacy of personality and underestimate the influence of situational constraints on the observed behaviour of their counterparts in a conflict situation.[45] This is part of a broader attribution theory whose central effort is to explain how people understand, explain and respond to their observations and consequent interpretation of the behaviour of others.[46]

As will be demonstrated later, the gradual process of the Sulha is designed to introduce the disputing clans to the situational reality of their counterparts. This is achieved through presentations made by the interveners when they meet with each disputing clan. As Sulha maker Faraj Khneifes explains:

> When we sit with each clan, we try to make them understand that this unfortunate event is not because the other clan is fundamentally evil, but because someone 'lost it' in the heat of the argument and made a terrible mistake that everyone now regrets.[47]

It appears that this approach, repeated multiple times during discussions between the *Jaha* and each of the disputing clans (particularly, but not exclusively, the victim's clan),[48] aims at creating a sense of accountability, or what psychologist Philip Tetlock describes as 'pressures to justify one's causal interpretations of behaviour to others'. It also appears that creating such accountability may help mitigate the overattribution effect by introducing the disputing clans to the perspective that their reality is, in fact, similar to that of the other side, making reconciliation – between equals of sorts in this case – a more acceptable option.[49]

In contrast to the previous examples, this is one of the instances where Western concepts and theories find accurate expression and practice within Sulha without requiring the introduction of exceptions or alternative 'indigenous' options.

Sulha and the illusion of transparency

The illusion of transparency concept describes a phenomenon in negotiations that psychologists Leaf Van Boven, Thomas Gilovich and Victoria Husted Medvec define as 'the belief that their [negotiating side] private thoughts and feelings are more discernible to their negotiation partners than they actually are'.[50] This is a particularly relevant issue in the context of Western dispute resolution practices, where, according to social psychologist Dean Pruitt, negotiating with all disputants at the same time and location is a practice used extensively.

That is a valid proposition if we assume that disputants have reasonable control and understanding of how well (or not well) they manage to convey or conceal their intentions and/or preferences during the negotiation process. Yet research shows that 'people overestimate their ability to conceal private information. But there is also evidence that people experience the illusion when trying to convey private information'.[51]

In the context of Sulha, where a significant effort is dedicated to preventing the victim's clan from avenging its loss (of life and honour), as well as preventing the perpetrator's clan from retaliating, the illusion of transparency can become a major problem, and its resultant perspectives may lead to potentially dangerous situations, including the threat of loss of life – if one side misinterprets the other side's cues, or even interprets them accurately as attempts to exacerbate the conflict.

This is why in all Sulha situations in northern Israel interveners create a complete separation between the disputing parties, eliminating the danger of misunderstanding, and instead making exclusive use of the vehicle of private caucus.[52] In the course of the Sulha process, the *Jaha* meets each disputing clan multiple times, mostly in the privacy of the clan's own compound, completely avoiding the option of bringing the disputing parties together (even on neutral ground).

This practice gives the members of the *Jaha* the necessary time and opportunity to identify a change in posture by either disputant group and to introduce it properly for the other group, giving them ample time to internalize and to respond in kind. Conversely, this 'separation of disputants' approach gives the *Jaha* the space required to creatively reframe disputants' statements and use them to promote reconciliation.[53]

Sulha and restorative justice theory

Restorative Justice Theory (RJT) argues that repairing the harm caused by criminal behaviour is preferred to simply punishing the perpetrator. In addition, RJT proposes that the best way to accomplish this goal is through a collaborative process between the parties (victims, perpetrators and communities). This collaborative process should ideally transform the attitudes of the disputants, their relationship and their relations with the relevant community.[54]

Australian criminologist John Braithwaite defined restorative justice as

> a process where all stakeholders affected by an injustice have an opportunity to discuss how they have been affected by the injustice and to decide what should be done to repair the harm. With crime, restorative justice is about the idea that because crime hurts, justice should heal. It follows that conversations with those who have been hurt and with those who have afflicted the harm must be central to the process.

Elsewhere Braithwaite sheds light on the broader communal aspects of restorative justice, writing that one of the core tasks of this concept is 'expanding the issues beyond those that are legally relevant, especially into underlying relationships'.[55]

It is worth noting that although many researchers refer to restorative justice as a relatively new Western concept, a review of its principles and practice reveals significant similarities with indigenous customary justice practices in general, and Sulha in particular. George Irani and Nathan Funk define Sulha explicitly as a restorative justice process when they argue that the term 'has been used to refer both to a ritualized process of *restorative justice* (sic) and peacemaking and to the actual outcome or condition sealed by that process.'[56] Gellman and Vuinovich also refer to Sulha as a specific restoration practice, writing that 'Sulha furnishes a culturally appropriate means for restoring values'. Further, they note that '[w]hat Sulha is able to offer more broadly is a systematic process for recognizing a basic human right to dignity through restoration of honor'(sic).[57]

In Africa, for example, restorative justice practices found practical expression within South Africa's "Truth and Reconciliation" commission, as well as within Rwanda's Gacaca courts.[58] Similar practices took place in Chile as that country tried to deal with the legacy of Augusto Pinochet's dictatorship.[59]

In addition to locating Sulha firmly as a restorative practice, these descriptions position it as a process based on re-integrative honour, a concept that will be introduced, defined, described and discussed extensively throughout this work.

Restorative justice and re-integrative shaming theory

Re-integrative shaming theory (RST) was developed by Australian criminologist John Braithwaite in conjunction with the Restorative Justice Theory. RST aims at providing practical tools to be applied within the restorative justice concept. RST highlights the centrality of shame in the creation of a bond between the offender and the community. Re-integrative shaming, Braithwaite argued, assists in re-integrating the offender back into the community by affecting the offender's conscience and by facilitating the construction of a relationship of respect and approval between the offender and the community (as well as the victim's kin group).[60]

Braithwaite further argued that there are two types of shaming: disintegrative and re-integrative; the former, in his words, 'creates a class of outcasts and thus prevents offenders from re-joining the society', whereas the latter 'maintains bonds of respect or love, and sharply terminates disapproval with forgiveness'.[61]

This is the theoretical foundation for the exploration of shame as a constructive restorative component within conflict resolution.[62] According to criminologists Hee Joo Kim and Jurg Gerber, 'Braithwaite's Re-integrative Shaming Theory (1989) underpins the conferencing alternative, and Re-integrative shaming is an essential part of the RJ (Restorative Justice) conference'.[63] Lode Walgrave and Ivo Aertsen similarly locate shaming within the core of restorative justice practices, arguing that it 'can be a powerful aspect in the informal process that brings the victim and the offender together in their search for a just restorative solution to their conflict'. They further put re-integrative shaming within the context of community conflicts, writing '[r]e-integrative shaming is about the positive power of human relationships to deal with offenses and other types of behaviour that jeopardize harmonious community living.'[64]

To further clarify the place of shame in restorative justice, it is worth noting the distinction between guilt and shame. Theologian John Elliott describes two essential culture types: shame and guilt. In his view, shame cultures

> differ from industrialized "guilt cultures" in that their members are group-oriented and governed in their attitudes and actions primarily by the opinion and appraisals of significant others. In contrast to "guilt cultures" with their developed sense of individualism, and internalized conscience and an interest in introspection, in "shame cultures" what "other people will say" serves as the chief sanction of conduct.[65]

Despite attempts by Braithwaite and others to frame shame as a constructive element, it is evident that shame is essentially based on lack of worthiness. Educational psychologist Jessica Van Vliet links the worthiness and social connection elements that appear to be essential in the Sulha context when she writes: 'Shame is conceptualized as an assault on the self, where the individual's self-concept, social connection, and sense of power and control come under attack'.[66]

The culture of Sulha is clearly that of shame. Yet when the Sulha process is examined, it is evident that the use of shaming, under any pretext, does not, and cannot possibly, assist in any way in the resolution of conflicts, whereas the use of honouring, the very opposite of shaming, provides the re-integrative element that is so essential for reconciliation in this cultural context.

The theoretical foundations of Sulha 49

Where do we go from here?

This rather exhaustive examination of the Sulha within the context of multiple theories and concepts makes it clear that locating and describing a theoretical foundation that adequately describes and explains this practise is hardly a trivial task; it also appears that existing theories, for the most part, fail to explain Sulha wholly and properly. This may be because virtually all existing and relevant conflict resolution theories are both young (post–World War II), Western in origin and orientation and rely on Western-based assumptions, creating a gap (sometimes even a conflict) between Western-generated perspectives and 'indigenous' practices.

That is a less-than-ideal situation, as this lack of sufficient universal or, alternatively, 'indigenous' theoretical foundation affects the ability to adequately learn and analyze Muslim/Arab conflict resolution practices by Western scholars, mostly because scholars usually end up exploring such practices using, by and large, their own cultural, theoretical and analytical values and tools.[67]

This apparent lack of solid theoretical foundation for the study of the Sulha raises the need to seek and, if possible, introduce a more coherent perspective that will describe and explain some of the unique features of Muslim/Arab customary justice in general, and Sulha in the north of Israel in particular. Therefore, following the exploration of existing conflict resolution theories and their relevance (or lack thereof) to Sulha, this chapter introduces a new concept of Re-integrative Honouring that may be used to locate, describe and predict the transformation of the disputants' honour, revenge and forgiveness attitudes as they go through the Sulha process.

Re-integrative honouring concept

Re-integrative honouring concept (RHC) is a new perspective that seeks to explain how the Sulha works by suggesting that during the Sulha process the interveners manipulate the disputants' perception of their honour – restoring the hurt sense of honour of the victim's clan while ensuring that the perpetrator's clan's sense of honour is not degraded – thus facilitating a gradual transformation of the disputants' attitudes, from a desire to avenge to a willingness to forgive, to eventual reconciliation.

The re-integrative honouring concept appears to be similar to re-integrative shaming theory (RST), its Western restorative justice theory 'twin', but with the major difference that RST uses shaming as *the* main transformation-affecting mechanism, whereas RHC views honouring, rather than shaming, as the conflict's central transformative vehicle.

Furthermore, it is argued that within the cultural context of Sulha, the process of re-integrative honouring requires the alternate use of both mediation and arbitration tools. Whereas shaming-based RST describes a chronological sequence of shame-acknowledgement-transformation,[68] the honouring-based RHC proposes a sequence of honour-acknowledgement-transformation. Whereas RST puts the individual offender and victim at the heart of the transformative effort, RHC proposes that the transformation take place at the level of the disputants' expanded kin groups (clans) and that the centre of attention within this process is the victim's clan, since it is the one group that requires major honour restoration and re-integration assistance.

Anthropologist Jane Schneider asserts that 'shame [is] the reciprocal of honor'.[69] This is helpful when exploring the use of these tools in the context of conflict resolution in general, and Sulha in particular, and it may be valuable to expand on this pairing to clarify some of their relevant reciprocal aspects. For example, sociologist Brene Brown defines shame as the 'fear of disconnection'.[70] If this is indeed the case, and if honour is the reciprocal of shame, then it may be defined as '*hope for connection*'.

Thus it is argued that the key difference between re-integrative shaming and re-integrative honouring lies in the distinction between the two concepts' prime motivation: fear of disconnection vs. hope for connection, respectively. This work argues that, whereas shame works on the reaction to fear of disconnection (a negative sanction), re-integrative honouring, the concept proposed as the foundation of Sulha, is predicated on hope for connection (or reconnection, in many cases).

Notes

1 Morton Deutsch, *The Resolution of Conflict* (New Haven: Yale University Press, 1973).
2 Peter Carnevale and Dean Pruitt, *Negotiating in Social Conflict* (Philadelphia: Open University Press, 1993).
3 Jeffrey Rubin, Dean Pruitt and Sung Hee Kim, *Social Conflict: Escalation, Stalemate and Settlement*, 2nd ed. (New York: McGraw-Hill, 1994).
4 Quoted in *International Encyclopaedia of the Social Sciences*, Vols. 3/4 (New York: Macmillan & Free Press, 1968), p. 236. See also Jeffrey Rubin, Dean Pruitt, Sung Hee Kim, *Social Conflict: Escalation, Stalemate and Settlement*, 2nd ed. (New York: McGraw-Hill, 1994).
5 These observations are loosely based on John Paul Lederach, *Preparing for Peace: Conflict Transformation Across Cultures* (Syracuse: Syracuse University Press, 1995).
6 Georg Elwert, Stephan Feuchtwang and Dieter Neubert (eds.), *Dynamics of Violence: Processes of Escalation and De-Escalation in Violent Group Conflicts* (Berlin: Duncker & Humblot, 1999).
7 Irani, 'Islamic Mediation Techniques for Middle East Conflicts', pp. 1–2.
8 Paul Salem, 'A Critique of Western Conflict Resolution From a Non-Western Perspective', in Salem (ed.), *Conflict Resolution in the Arab World*, p. 1.
9 *Ibid.*, p. 2.
10 See, for example: Joseph V. Montville, 'Psychoanalytic Enlightenment and the Greening of Diplomacy', in Vamik D. Volkan, Joseph V. Montville and Demetrius A. Julius (eds.), *The Psychodynamics of International Relations* (Lexington: Lexington Books, 1991), Col. 2.
11 See, for example: Dennis J.D. Sandole, 'Traditional Approaches to Conflict Management: Short-Term Gains vs. Long-Term Costs', *Current Research on Peace and Violence*, Vol. 9, No. 3 (1986), pp. 119–24; Leonard Greenhalgh, 'SMR Forum: Managing Conflict', *Sloan Management Review*, Vol. 27 (1986), pp. 45–51.

12 Salem, 'A Critique of Western Conflict Resolution From a Non-Western Perspective', p. 2.
13 George Irani and Nathan Funk, 'Rituals of Reconciliation – Arab-Islamic Perspectives', *Arab Studies Quarterly*, Vol. 20, No. 4 (1998), p. 59.
14 Ibid.
15 Ibid., p. 60.
16 Oussama Safa, 'Conflict Resolution and Reconciliation in the Arab World: The Work of Civil Society Organisations in Lebanon and Morocco', *Berghof Research Center for Constructive Conflict Management* (2007), p. 14, www.berghof-handbook.net/documents/publications/safa_handbook.pdf (accessed 27 January 2013). See also Abu-Nimer, 'Conflict Resolution Approaches'.
17 Matthew J. Hornsey, 'Social Identity Theory and Self-categorization Theory: A Historical Review', *Social and Personality Psychology Compass*, Vol. 2, No. 1 (2008), p. 204.
18 Henri Tajfel and John C. Turner, 'An Integrative Theory of Intergroup Conflict', in Stephen Worchel and William G. Austin (eds.), *The Social Psychology of Intergroup Relations* (Monterey, CA: Brooks-Cole, 1979), pp. 33–47.
19 Jan E. Stets and Peter J. Burke, 'Identity Theory and Social Identity Theory', *Social Psychology Quarterly*, Vol. 63, No. 3 (2000), p. 225.
20 Scott Atran Man, 'Hamula Organisation and Masha'a Tenure in Palestine', *New Series*, Vol. 21, No. 2 (1986), p. 271.
21 Irani and Funk, 'Rituals of Reconciliation', p. 64.
22 Taifel and Turner, 'An Integrative Theory of Intergroup Conflict', p. 38.
23 Stets and Burke, 'Identity Theory and Social Identity Theory', p. 224.
24 Halim Barakat, *The Arab World: Society, Culture and State* (Berkeley: University of California Press, 1993). See also Abu-Nimer, 'Conflict Resolution Approaches, p. 44.
25 Hornsey, 'Social Identity Theory', p. 205.
26 Jay W. Jackson, 'Realistic Group Conflict Theory: A Review and Evaluation of the Theoretical and Empirical Literature', *Psychological Record*, Vol. 43, No. 3 (1993), pp. 395–415.
27 Donald T. Campbell, 'Ethnocentric and Other Altruistic Motives', in David Levine (ed.), *Nebraska Symposium on Motivation* (Lincoln: University of Nebraska Press, 1965), p. 287.
28 Abu-Nimer, 'Conflict Resolution Approaches', p. 46; Irani, 'Islamic Mediation Techniques for Middle East Conflicts', pp. 6, 9.
29 Author interview with Sheikh Rani, 16 October 2012.
30 Jabbour, *Sulha*, p. 41.
31 Irani, 'Islamic Mediation Techniques for Middle East Conflicts', p. 6.
32 Dan Ariely, *The Upside of Irrationality* (New York: Harper Collins, 2010), p. 64.
33 See, for example, Victoria Esses, Lynne Jackson, John Dovido and Gordon Hodson, 'Instrumental Relations Among Groups: Group Competition, Conflict and Prejudice', in John Dovido, Peter Glick and Laurie Budman (eds.), *On the Nature of Prejudice, Fifty Years After Allport* (Malden, MA: Blackwell Publishing, 2005), p. 229.
34 Gellman and Vuinovich, 'From Sulha to Salaam', p. 140. See also Abu-Nimer, *Nonviolence and Peace Building in Islam*, p. 96.
35 Harold, H. Kelley and John W. Thibaut, *Interpersonal Relations: A Theory of Interdependence* (New York: Wiley-Interscience, 1978); Susan Sprecher, 'Social Exchange Theories and Sexuality', *Journal of Sex Research*, Vol. 35, No. 1 (1998), pp. 32–43.
36 Abraham H. Maslow, 'A Theory of Human Motivation', *Psychological Review*, Vol. 50, No. 4 (1943), pp. 370–96.
37 Paul Sites, *Control: The Basis of Social Order* (New York: Dunellen Publishing Company, 1972).
38 Irani, 'Islamic Mediation Techniques for Middle East Conflicts', p. 3.

52   The theoretical foundations of Sulha

39 Peter Dodd, 'Family Honor and the Forces of Change in Arab Society', *International Journal of Middle East Studies*, Vol. 4, No. 1 (1973), pp. 40–54. See also John Elster, 'Norms of Revenge', *Ethics*, Vol. 100 (1990), pp. 862–85; Barakat *The Arab World*; Doron Pely, 'When Honor Trumps Basic Needs: The Role of Honor in Deadly Disputes within Israel's Arab Community', *Negotiation Journal*, Vol. 27, No. 2 (2011a), pp. 205–25.
40 The murdered woman's father, brother and/or son.
41 For an extended discussion of 'honour killings' see Chapter 3.
42 Author interview with Khneifes, 2007.
43 Jabbour, *Sulha*, p. 73.
44 Pely, 'When Honor Trumps'.
45 Edward Jones, 'The Rocky Road from Acts to Dispositions', *American Psychology*, Vol. 34 (1979), pp. 107–17. See also Lee Ross, 'The Intuitive Psychologist and His Shortcomings: Distortion in the Attribution Process', in Leonard Berkowitz (ed.), *Advances in Experimental Psychology* (New York: Academic Press, 1977).
46 Harold H. Kelley, 'Attribution Theory in Social Psychology', in David Levine (ed.), *Nebraska Symposium on Motivation*, Vol. 15, 1967.
47 Author interview with Khneifes, 14 June 2009.
48 Author observations made during Jaha meetings with disputing clans.
49 Philip Tetlock, 'Accountability: A Social Check on the Fundamental Attribution Error', *Social Psychology Quarterly*, Vol. 48, No. 3 (1985), p. 227.
50 Leaf Van Boven, Thomas Gilovich and Victoria Husted Medvec, 'The Illusion of Transparency in Negotiations', *Negotiation Journal*, Vol. 19, No. 2 (2003), p. 117.
51 Dean G. Pruitt, 'Process and Outcome in Community Mediation', *Negotiation Journal*, Vol. 11, No. 4 (1995), p. 369.
52 Author interview with Sheikh Abdel Rani (16 October 2012).
53 See discussion of reframing in Chapter 5.
54 John Braithwaite, 'Restorative Justice and De-Professionalization', *The Good Society*, Vol. 13, No. 1 (2004), pp. 28–31.
55 Ibid., p. 28; idem, *Restorative Justice and Responsive Regulation* (Oxford: Oxford University Press, 2002), p. 249.
56 Irani and Funk, 'Rituals of Reconciliation', p. 52.
57 Gellman and Vuinovich, 'From Sulha to Salaam', p. 140.
58 Claire Moon, *Narrating Political Reconciliation: South Africa's Truth and Reconciliation Commission* (Lanham: Lexington Books, 2009); See also Rutagengwa Claude Shema, Regional Coordinator, Great Lakes Peace Initiative (GLPI), Gacaca Jurisdictions In Rwanda: Hope And Hopeless, www.author-me.com/nonfiction/gacacaqjurisdictions.htm (accessed 19 October 2014).
59 *Report of the Chilean National Commission on Truth and Reconciliation* (Notre Dame, Indiana: University of Notre Dame Press, 1993), www.usip.org/sites/default/files/resources/collections/truth_commissions/Chile90-Report/Chile90-Report.pdf (accessed 19 October 2014).
60 John Braithwaite, *Crime, Shame and Reintegration* (Cambridge: Cambridge University Press, 1999), p. 12.
61 Ibid., p. 12.
62 This discussion accepts Braithwaite's assertion and when referring to RST assumes the latter case.
63 Hee Joo Kim and Jurg Gerber, 'Evaluating the Process of a Restorative Justice Conference: An Examination of Factors That Lead to Re-Integrative Shaming', *Asia Pacific Journal of Police and Criminal Justice*, Vol. 8, No. 2 (2010), p. 1.
64 Lode Walgrave and Ivo Aertsen, 'Reintegrative Shaming and Restorative Justice', *European Journal on Criminal Policy and Research*, Vol. 4, No. 4 (1996), p. 85.

65 John H. Elliott, 'Disgraced Yet Graced. The Gospel According to 1 Peter in the Key of Honor and Shame', *Biblical Theology Bulletin*, Vol. 24 (1994), p. 168.
66 Jessica Van Vliet, 'Shame and Resilience in Adulthood: A Grounded Theory Study', *Journal of Counselling Psychology*, Vol. 55, No. 2 (2008), p. 233.
67 Abu-Nimer, 'Conflict Resolution Approaches', p. 36.
68 Eliza Ahmed, Nathan Harris, John Braithwaite and Valerie Braithwaite, *Shame Management Through Reintegration* (Melbourne: Cambridge University Press, 2001), p. 60.
69 Jane Schneider, 'Of Vigilance and Virgins: Honor, Shame and Access to Resources in Mediterranean Societies', *Ethnology*, Vol. 10, No. 1 (1971), p. 1.
70 Brene Brown, *I Thought It Was Just Me (But It Isn't), Telling the Truth About Perfectionism, Inadequacy and Power* (New York: Gotham Books, 2007), pp. 89–90.

3 Honour, revenge and forgiveness in Sulha

The concepts of honour, revenge and forgiveness were, for the most part, 'imported' into Islam from existing pre-Islamic social tribal norms; they are, nonetheless, deeply embedded in Islam and play a central role in the Muslim perception of morality and ethics, as well as in the ethos and practice of Muslim dispute resolution in general and Sulha in particular.

Historian Reuven Levy traces the concepts of honour and revenge in Islam directly to the Prophet Muhammad and his practice of enabling the continuation of pre-Islamic concepts so long as they did not collide with the central themes of Islam. As he put it:

> As was his general policy, whether deliberately or not, Muhammad in his demands made comparatively few changes in the ordinary mode of life of his converts, and although he introduced certain important reforms, particularly in the matter of sexual relationships, he was content to accept the common moral ideas of his tribe. What they were is comprised in the term *muruwwa* (literally 'virtue'), to which 'chivalry' in many respects corresponds, but which is more fully represented by 'honour and revenge'.[1]

Co-opted to Islam, pre-Islamic tribal, honour and revenge concepts find substantial expression in Muslim law, both formal and customary. In the words of Farrukh Hakeem, Maria Haberfeld, and Arvind Verma:

> The law of *Qisas* [retaliation] can be understood after looking at the ancient customs of the Arabs prior to the advent of Islam. Hostility was a characteristic feature of the tribesmen of pre-Islamic Arabia. Friendly co-operation was a way of life only among the members of the same tribe. The main feature for this state of hostility was personal revenge for homicide. One of the most compelling reasons for the motive of revenge among Arab tribesmen was their belief that after the death of a murdered person a night-bird known as *Ham*, would stand on the grave and cry, 'I am thirsty, give me a drink'. This implied that revenge should be taken in order to quench its thirst. As a consequence, revenge was taken not only against the culprit, but also against the culprit's tribesmen.[2]

The concept of forgiveness also occupies a prominent place in Islamic religious dogma and Muslim legal practice. The Qur'an speaks directly to forgiveness ('Keep to forgiveness . . .')[3] and places it on a higher moral plateau than revenge and punishment. It states that '[t]he recompense of an injury is an injury the like thereof; but whoever forgives and thereby brings about a reestablishment of harmony, his reward is with God; and God loves not the wrongdoers'.[4] This phrase is considered the main theological underpinning of the Sulha. In the words of Islamic scholar Muhammad Kamali, the Qur'an

> distinguishes a superior course of conduct from that which may be considered as ordinary. Punishing the wrong-doer, for example, is the normal course enjoined by the *Sharia*, but forgiveness may at times be preferable (*ahsan*) and would thus represent the higher course of conduct.[5]

Within Sulha, honour, revenge and forgiveness are central functional as well as perceptual concepts around which evolve both the conflict and its resolution. The concatenation of honour, revenge and forgiveness concepts establishes the ultimate purpose and practice of the Sulha – transforming the disputing clans from a desire to avenge to a willingness to forgive, through the restoration of honour.

Sharon Lang highlights the link between honour and revenge – the central motivator of the Sulha – when she writes: 'To avenge the murder of a close kinsman is honourable; to fail to do so is dishonourable'.[6] Elias Jabbour elaborates on the link between Sulha and forgiveness, and on the absolute need for forgiveness to establish reconciliation, writing that 'Sulha is first and foremost based on forgiveness. If the offended side does not forgive, there will be no Sulha and there will be no peace'.[7]

This chapter locates and defines these core elements and their theoretical and functional foundations in preparation for a detailed analysis of their functional, emotive and ritualistic place within each specific stage of the Sulha. Furthermore, the insights derived from this exploration will be used later on to demonstrate the validity of the Re-integrative Honouring Concept (RHC).

About honour

The centrality of honour in cultures has been extensively researched,[8] with the issue traced to the early monotheistic period. In the words of theologian David de Silva: 'The culture of the first-century world was built on the foundational social values of honor and dishonor'.[9]

Several researchers have located honour (*Karame*, *Sharaf*) as *the* core value and motivator in Muslim/Arab cultures in general and in customary Muslim dispute resolution in particular.[10] Abu-Nimer links the utilitarian use of honour to the prevailing cultural norms, including those of dispute resolution in the Muslim/Arab Middle East, when he writes:

> [T]he initiation and implementation of intervention are based on the social norms and customs of the society . . . These values are maintained and

preserved by the disputants in their social context. Even if a dispute is over scarce resources (such as money or debts, or land) values such as 'honour,' 'shame,' 'dignity,' 'social status,' and religious beliefs are at stake.

He also points to the competition between values such as honour and disputes over scarce resources (health and safety-associated needs), and the importance that 'preserving the social values' has in framing the prioritization of needs in the cultural context of such conflicts.[11]

Irani explores another facet of honour in the Muslim/Arab context by examining the sociopolitical constructs in Middle Eastern cultures and their impact on disputes and dispute resolution modes and on the centrality of honour in this context. In his view,

> [c]lientelism and the absence of citizenship in the Western sense of the word have profound implications for reconciliation and processes of conflict reduction in the Middle East. Private justice is meted out through a network in which political and/or religious leaders determine the outcome of feuds between clans or conflicts between individuals. Ideologies of honour and shame also play a key role in this context.[12]

Western cultures generally embrace the perception of individualism – where people can mostly dishonour themselves, and possibly their immediate family, but not their entire clan, and where a loss of personal honour is seen as a significant but not necessarily disastrous drawback.[13]

Psychological economist Dan Ariely adds another dimension to the discussion of honour by linking it to trust and defining trust, 'the opposite of revenge', as a resource used to support rational thinking (to the extent it exists).[14] Because in Sulha, the opposite of revenge is forgiveness, trust and forgiveness find themselves on the same side of the equation.

Within the clan-based social structure of northern Israeli Arabs (and that of many other Arab and Muslim communities throughout the world), the state of the honour of the individual reflects immediately and crucially on the perception of honour of the entire clan (both as seen by the clan's members and by the community at large), and committing what is perceived as a dishonourable act or, conversely, being the target of a dishonouring act, reflects negatively on the entire clan.[15]

Yet despite the extensive attention to honour in the literature, there appears to be a lack of a clear definition of this concept in a social context. Furthermore, there is little exploration of the ramifications of honour's centrality on the perceptions and/or actions of disputants, or on the priorities they assign to their needs as a result of these perceptions.

Even more interesting is the fact that, despite its centrality, the term honour is often used in an evocative 'folkloristic' form of maintenance and/or restoration of social esteem – both self and externally perceived. In the words of social anthropologist Unni Wikan:

> Honour is a word with a very special quality. Unlike most of the words used in anthropology, it holds an alluring, even seductive appeal. I think that its

spell derives from its archaic and poetic overtones: it harks back to more glorious times when men were brave, honest and principled. (What women were is beside the point since they, in both anthropological and popular conceptions, have no honour of their own to defend.) This unacknowledged evocative quality has diverted the anthropological treatment of honour away from a concern with meaning in everyday life towards normative moral discourse, among men.[16]

Such a 'folkloristic' perspective tends to obscure the utilitarian role of honour in dispute resolution in general, and in Sulha in particular. This role is essential to understanding the process and stages of Sulha, and will be explored in detail in this work.

In order to facilitate a discussion of the place of honour in Muslim dispute resolution and Sulha, the following definition of honour in its social context will be used: *a nonmaterialistic, meritorious, emotive as well as functional value, denoting the perception (self and societal) of an individual and/or group's social status and prestige.*

'Honour killing'

A stark demonstration of the centrality of the perception of honour (and the practical ramifications of its perceived loss) in Arab culture – indeed, at the core of the Arab family, which is the centre of Arab society – is offered by the phenomenon of 'honour killing'. In what is termed honour killings, fathers, brothers and other agnatic male kin murder their female flesh and blood (daughter, sister, mother) to restore the honourable status of the family whenever they perceive a female relative to have violated it.[17] In the words of conflict resolution scholar and practitioner Oussama Safa:

> Honour killing and revenge is commonly accepted as a way to restore family honour and often tolerated by the legal system. In most instances, women are the victims in the retributive killings and perpetrators usually receive light sentences, if any.[18]

Honour (or in this case, the maintenance of honour) appears to be so important and central to life in the Arab world that some Arab legal systems and penal codes recognize it as a formal extenuating circumstance in murder cases justifying reduction or elimination of penalty (e.g. Article 340 of the Jordanian Penal Code).[19]

The phenomenon of honour killings has been explored from different angles by several scholars. Sociologist Manar Hasan looked at the sociopolitical aspects of these murders,[20] political scientist Catherine Warrick explored the sociolegal aspects,[21] and Middle East scholar Yotam Feldner and journalist Suzanne Ruggi looked at the ethnographic, economic and legal aspects.[22] Interestingly, no scholar has yet examined honour killings from the perspective of the perpetrator's prioritization (i.e. why the perpetrator apparently positions 'honour' ahead of all other needs).

Sociologist Peter Dodd sheds light on the interfamilial links and the normative framework that may help explain the cultural background leading to 'honour' killings. He writes:

> The family forms the core productive unit in Arabian society, and it represents the foundation for unity in the community. Members of a family share responsibilities and duties, and enjoy its successes and failures. They feel proud when a member of the family achieves success, and feel ashamed when a member of the family fails in a job or a task. If some member of the family makes a mistake, or does something shameful, this is considered a disgrace to the whole family. Therefore, the relationships between members of the family are simply relations between interconnected members of a cohesive unit. Each member plays his/her role, but remains closely linked to roles of the other members; like the father, the wife, the husband and the children. Each one of them 'lives' his character, but feels responsible for the others. His/her behaviour affects all other members of the family. For example, when a girl misbehaves, she is not only violating traditions, but also bringing shame to the whole family. This is where the roots of the crimes of killing on the basis of honour lie. The family undertakes such a crime to attempt to re-establish the honour of the family.[23]

Other scholars of Middle Eastern cultures and Middle Eastern dispute resolution traditions highlight the predominance of the family, with its strong patriarchal orientation, as a central social structure in many Arab cultures, including among Israel's Arab community.[24] Indeed, general ethnographic Muslim, as well as Muslim dispute resolution literature contains significant discussion of the inter-relations within the traditional Arab family. Cultural anthropologists Amalia Sa'ar and Taghreed Yahia-Younis describe the competition and conflicts that dissect multiple patriarchal power regimes, simultaneously oppressing Arab Israeli women and creating fleeting opportunities of escape from oppression.[25] Sa'ar presents several additional explorations of gender relations within Israel's Arab community.[26] Historian Samira Haj describes the violent treatment of women at the hands of their husbands and the rationalizations used by the husbands to justify such violence.[27]

But, here again, it seems that the literature, though rich, includes no examination of the impact of interclan conflict on women and/or (and even more importantly from the perspective of this work) on the impact of women on the process of dispute resolution (Sulha).

The United Nations estimates that about 5,000 women and girls are murdered worldwide every year by members of their own families.[28] Psychologist and psychotherapist Phyllis Chesler disputes these figures as woefully low and provides a competing picture of the scope of the phenomenon and the social attitudes that accompany and foster it. She writes:

> In 2000, the United Nations estimated that there are 5,000 honour killings every year. That number might be reasonable for Pakistan alone, but

worldwide the numbers are much greater. In 2002 and again in 2004, the U.N. brought a resolution to end honour killings and other honour-related crimes. In 2004, at a meeting in The Hague about the rising tide of honour killings in Europe, law enforcement officers from the U.K. announced plans to begin reopening old cases to see if certain murders were, indeed, honour murders. The number of honour killings is routinely underestimated, and most estimates are little more than guesses that vary widely. Definitive or reliable worldwide estimates of honour killing incidence do not exist.[29]

The place of honour in Sulha

Sulha-related literature identifies the central role of honour within the practice. As Gellman and Vuinovich argue, 'the values most applicable to Sulha are honour, saving face, wisdom, generosity, respect, dignity and forgiveness'.[30] It is interesting to note in this context that within this extended list of seven values, most are directly related to honour (saving face, wisdom, respect and dignity); only two (generosity and forgiveness) are not directly related to this factor. This apparent redundancy further highlights the centrality of honour in Sulha.

Political scientist Raymond Cohen also places honour at the core of the *hamula*-based society, where Sulha is just about the only inter-*hamula* dispute resolution tool. In his words:

> In this segmented, honor-based society, clan rivalry is endemic. Conflicts may ignite over matters of honor, which can be anything concerning women, land, property, and one's good name or that of one's family. Equally, a dispute may start out as an argument over something trivial and quickly escalate into an affair of honor.[31]

Aseel Ramahi connects the context of honour within Sulha to pre-Islamic practices, claiming that 'many of the rules of conduct practiced before Islam continued to be honoured after the rise of Islam especially customs relating to personal honour, hospitality and courage'.[32]

Disputants participating in Sulha also indicated the centrality of honour in the context of the disputes they were involved in and the high priority they assigned to honour and its maintenance and recovery. A member of a victim's clan in a yet-unresolved dispute in the town of Nazareth told the author of this book: 'They [the perpetrator's clan] sullied our honour, and there will be no peace until we regain it'.[33] A member of the victim's clan in yet another killing-related dispute in the village of Dir al-Assad similarly said: 'They [the perpetrator's clan] behaved like animals; they have no honour and they hurt our honour. We are the largest clan in this village. We must regain our honour'.[34]

Yet despite the obvious attention and recognition given to the centrality of the perception of honour within the Sulha practice, there has been no attempt to measure the possible impact and/or influence of this perception by the disputants within the Sulha. One of the central arguments advanced by this work is that the Sulha process is predicated on the ability of the interveners to facilitate the restoration of the perception of the sense of honour of the victim's side in a dispute (a clan in this case), while maintaining (as opposed to degrading) the perception of the sense of honour of the perpetrator's clan – the other side to a Sulha-managed dispute. An examination of the validity of this assertion is performed through interviews with Sulha makers and disputants and through the analysis of a questionnaire administered to members of victim clans. Extensive examination of this process is described in the analysis section of this work (Chapter 4).

It is important to stress in this context and in light of sensitivities regarding such cultural constructs that the positioning of honour within Arab culture in general and Arab dispute resolution in particular is not an 'Orientalist'[35] social artefact manufactured by Western 'outsiders' viewing Eastern cultures as naïve, irrational and emotive. As the scholarship cited in this chapter indicates, plenty of 'native' Muslim/Arab scholars, as well as 'non-native' scholars, have identified the same constructs. Furthermore, the perspective of their analysis positions these constructs as functional, rational and considered elements of the examined phenomenon.

Revenge and forgiveness

Revenge and forgiveness are two central and recurring themes in conflict management and resolution in general, and in Muslim/Arab dispute resolution in particular. Evidence, historical and current, of the desire by disputants to avenge real and perceived wrongs is present in abundance; forgiveness is an equally prominent feature of dispute resolution practices. Practitioners use a variety of tools to try to transform the disputants and the disputes and bring the disputants to embrace forgiveness in place of revenge.[36]

Islam is quite explicit about the duality of revenge and forgiveness within its conflict resolution perspective. As noted earlier in this chapter, the Qur'an prescribes revenge as the appropriate religious/cultural response to an injury, but in the same breath extols the virtue of forgiveness and proposes that God prefers forgiveness to the proscribed revenge.[37]

This complex Qur'anic construct, confusing as it is, encapsulates the major theological underpinnings of the Sulha process. The confusion emanating from the inherent conflict between revenge and forgiveness invites a transformative process and actually creates the functional foundation of the Sulha, in addition to its philosophical underpinning.

It is obvious that in order to facilitate progress towards resolution of disputes, a necessary condition is to transform the disputants' attitudes from a desire to avenge to a willingness to forgive. This is precisely what the Sulha is supposed to do. In fact, the Sulha process includes a number of task-specific, restorative justice steps designed to do just that: facilitate a transformation of the disputants' perspectives (particularly, but not exclusively, those of the victim's side) from a desire for revenge to a willingness to forgive.[38]

This section explores the theoretical foundation for understanding revenge and forgiveness and their contextual posture within dispute resolution in general and Muslim/Arab dispute resolution in particular.

About revenge

Revenge predates monotheism, and is probably rooted in the very existence of human beings within social structures.

Homer's *Odyssey* offers a vivid illustration of the deeply embedded place of revenge and forgiveness – in this context, at the ancient relational interface between gods and mortals. In Homer's words:

> And Jove said, 'My child, what are you talking about? How can I forget Ulysses than whom there is no more capable man on earth, nor more liberal in his offerings to the immortal gods that live in heaven? Bear in mind, however, that Neptune is still furious with Ulysses for having blinded an eye of Polyphemus king of the Cyclopes. Polyphemus is son to Neptune by the nymph Thoosa, daughter to the sea-king Phorcys; therefore though he will not kill Ulysses outright, he torments him by preventing him from getting home. Still, let us lay our heads together and see how we can help him to return; Neptune will then be pacified, for if we are all of a mind he can hardly stand out against us'.[39]

The passage describes the reason for revenge ('Neptune is still furious with Ulysses'), its purpose ('torment' Ulysses), and one possible path to resolution (creating a coalition to pacify Neptune).

Despite (or maybe because of) its ancient roots, revenge has been a hotly debated feature of human existence for as long as humanity remembers and records itself. Opinions about the rationality (or lack thereof) and about the functionality of revenge vary widely, and it is unlikely that the argument about it will be resolved anytime soon.

Western scholars tend to view revenge as an act of individuals. In the words of psychologists Noreen Stuckles and Richard Goranson: 'The vengeful act is essentially personal'.[40] This is a view that does not take into account the communal nature of revenge, a practice that is deeply rooted in tribal communities'. Stuckles and Goranson also view revenge as an act that takes time to carry out: 'it is usually committed after a period of reflecting on harm done to oneself'.[41] This is also a view that fails to consider the prevailing practice in some cultures, where revenge, as we shall see, is not the product of extended reflection, but a product of almost instinctive (and many times, rapid) response.

Economist Richard Posner explores the economic (cost–benefit) dilemma encapsulated within revenge, writing:

> The passion for revenge may seem the antithesis of rational, instrumental thinking. In particular it flouts the economist's commandment to ignore

sunk costs, to let bygones be bygones. When there is no possibility of legal redress to deter [the] aggressor, potential victims will be assiduous in self-protection. But that can be extremely costly and often is futile. The alternative is retaliation against the aggressor after he has victimized you. Yet if you are [a] "rational man" you will realize that the harm is a sunk cost. No matter how much harm you do to the aggressor in return, the harm you have suffered will not be annulled. Whatever dangers or other burdens you take on in order to retaliate will merely increase the cost to you of the initial aggression. To deter aggression in a revenge culture, the potential victim must convince potential aggressors that he will retaliate even if the expected benefits of retaliation, calculated *after* the aggression has occurred, are smaller than the expected costs at that time. He must in other words make a credible commitment to act in a way that may be irrational when the time to act comes. But the making of such a commitment may be rational (as conventional economic analysis might overlook): it may deter enough aggression to generate benefits greater than the costs of having sometimes to honor the commitment by retaliating, instead of cutting one's losses.[42]

Posner's perspective, quite popular among economists, is that what may seem irrational on an individual level relevant to the particular loss from the offense (sunk cost) is actually very rational in the context of deterring future offensive acts against an individual or a group. It is a known strategy for monopoly behaviour (called retaliatory pricing).[43]

Regardless of one's perspective about revenge, one thing is clear: it is a universally central element of human culture. In the words of Dan Ariely: 'Revenge is one of the deepest-seated instincts we have'. Ariely reviews the motivations, drivers and inhibitors for revenge and concludes that 'it seems that the threat of revenge – even at great personal expense – can serve as an effective enforcement mechanism that supports social cooperation and order'.[44]

Indeed, Keith and Charlotte Otterbein used the ethnographic material contained in the Human Relations Area Files (HARF) Probability Sample to examine blood revenge following homicide in fifty distinct cultures around the world and concluded that blood revenge was 'infrequent'.[45] But a consequent examination of their work by psychologists Martin Daly and Margo Wilson discovered that they did not count in their analysis cases where 'blood money' was accepted by the victim's family in lieu of revenge.

Because it is reasonable to assume that in the absence of a revenge norm there would have been no need for a revenge-substitute mechanism such as blood money, Daly and Wilson concluded that fifty-seven of the sixty cultures they examined had 'some reference to blood feud or capital punishment as an institutionalized practice or specific accounts of particular cases, or at least, some articulated expression of the *desire* for blood revenge'.[46] In short, revenge, in their opinion, is an integral part of most (if not all) human cultures.

Revenge and forgiveness literature divides roughly between those who see revenge as a disease and forgiveness as its cure and those who see revenge and forgiveness as part of a human arsenal of evolutionary adaptations. The current Western view of revenge holds that it is basically an irrational social ill, afflicting the weak of character and countered only by the 'medicine' of forgiveness.[47] Michael McCullough describes this view in a rather dramatic fashion when he explores the reigning Western perspective on revenge:

> [R]evenge is an infection that invades a vulnerable host (perhaps one whose resistance to the infection has been weakened by a poor constitution or a bad childhood), releases a toxin that poisons the host morally, physically, and psychologically, and then wreaks destructive effects on the avenger and the objects of his or her vengeance – sometimes spreading from one host to another until the outbreak reaches epidemic proportions.

McCullough calls this view 'the disease model of revenge'.[48]

John Elster proposes the 'irrational' perspective of revenge, defining it as 'the attempt, at some cost or risk to oneself to impose suffering upon those who have made one suffer, because they have made one suffer'.[49] An article by psychiatrist Colin Parkes in the *British Journal of Psychiatry* lists 'obsessive revenge seeking' as a 'diagnostic category' alongside post-traumatic stress disorder, panic syndromes, major depression and anxiety disorders.[50]

Philosopher Trudy Govier presents a similar view of revenge. 'When we seek revenge, *we seek satisfaction by attempting to harm the other (or associated persons) as a retaliatory measure*', she writes. 'We expect to feel better if we can somehow express our negative feelings in actions intended to "get back" at those who have harmed us'.[51] Govier actually ignores a possible starting point for a more challenging analysis of revenge when she writes: 'Seeking revenge is one way to reassert ourselves'.[52] And neither Govier nor other researchers use this challenging insight as a trigger for extended analysis that may examine their 'satisfaction' thesis (because reassertion is completely different from satisfaction).

Such perspectives do not create space for a possible exploration of a potential rational foundation of revenge other than the retaliatory one, focusing on 'satisfaction' and 'getting even' as the main motive.

There is, however, a competing view of revenge, upholding that both revenge and forgiveness are selected evolutionary adaptations or, simply put, that they are part of human nature. In McCullough's words:

> The desire for revenge isn't a disease to which certain unfortunate people fall prey. Instead, it's a universal trait of human nature, crafted by natural selection, that exists today because it was adaptive in the ancestral environment in which the human species evolved.[53]

This view provides additional insight to help decipher the expression of revenge as part of the process of conflict management within Muslim/Arab cultures.

The most prominent proponent of the 'evolutionary' argument for vengefulness is Charles Darwin. He writes in *The Descent of Man*:

> It has, I think, now been shewn (sic) that man and the higher animals, especially the Primates, have some few instincts in common. All have the same senses, intuitions, and sensations – similar passions, affections, and emotions, even the more complex ones, such as Jealousy, suspicion, emulation, gratitude, and magnanimity; they practice deceit and are revengeful.[54]

Economist Alan Hamlin uses Elster's 'irrational revenge' argument as the foundation of a counterargument that demonstrates the potential rationality of revenge: 'The definition of revenge is taken immediately to indicate a prima facie difficulty for any attempt at a rational choice explanation of revenge'. He writes:

> Revenge is backward looking, whereas rationality is forward looking – so the two fail to engage . . . The fact that someone has inflicted suffering (of a particular type) on you may be a necessary condition for your taking vengeance on that person, but some further forward-looking condition may need to be satisfied before vengeance will actually be taken. This possibility is sufficient to open the door to possible rational choice explanations of revenge.

Hamlin strengthens the case for a possible rational explanation of revenge (away from the disease model) by linking revenge and honour. As he puts it:

> If honor is the key to understanding revenge, that is, the key to understanding the pattern of approval and disapproval associated with a norm-based practice of revenge – and I agree that it is – the behavior of revenge must be recovered from an analysis of honor.[55]

Likewise, having discussed a host of experiments in both humans and apes, Ariely concludes that 'punishing betrayal, even when it costs us something, has biological underpinnings'.[56]

And McCullough summed up the current evolutionary perspective on revenge: 'Today, we may view revenge as a problem . . . but through the lens of evolution, it's also a solution'.[57]

There still remains the question of why, beyond its religious foundations, revenge has been and still is a pervasive sentiment and practice in the Middle East, as opposed to, for example, Western Europe.

One possible explanation is that it has been shown that retaliatory action by perceived victims is more likely to happen, and will be stronger when it does, when a familiar audience has witnessed the provocation or the attack.[58] Because much of the Arab community in northern Israel resides in rural settings, where, literally, everybody knows everybody (and in many cases are related to them), the impact of witnessing an honour-damaging provocation or an injurious infraction is very significant on both the victim and the witnesses: the victim knows that kin and neighbours are direct or indirect witnesses to his or her loss and its attendant hurt and loss of honour; the witnesses are intimately familiar with the victim and the offender and are quite likely to disseminate the details of the dispute, along with their own interpretation, throughout the immediate and not-so-immediate areas.

Another possible explanation comes from the examination of the conflict behaviour of nomadic herders, as opposed to that of sedentary farmers, when it comes to revenge. It has been shown that herder communities were very vulnerable to existential threats resulting from theft of their livestock, making it beneficial for them to cultivate a reputation for being the kind of people who respond fiercely to any slight. The situation is apparently different with sedentary farmers, whose existence is much less threatened in the long run by belligerent acts (take away a cow, and the herder is permanently without livelihood; take away a crop, and the farmer can grow another crop on the same soil).[59]

McCullough lends support to this argument when he writes: 'Europeans who settled the American Northeast came predominantly from places such as England, Germany and Holland, where intensive farming was the traditional way of life – a way of life that didn't require people to be so obsessed with honour'.[60] The implication is that if one is not 'so obsessed with honour', one may be less inclined to revert to vengeance as a mode of preserving or restoring perceived loss of honour.

The place of revenge in Sulha

The place of revenge in Sulha is associated directly with the fact that in the Muslim/Arab clan-based cultural context, revenge is pretty much the only culturally and functionally sanctioned path available to disputing parties (particularly to the victim's side) to restore lost honour. Sheikh Ihye Abdel Rani, acting head of northern Israel's Sulha Committee, a practitioner with decades of experience advocating and conducting Sulha processes and agreements, shrugs his shoulders when asked about the 'need' to avenge and says: 'If we don't have our honour, we have nothing . . . and without Sulha, revenge is the only way we know to redeem lost honour'.[61]

Irani and Funk identify the prevention of revenge attacks as the main purpose of the Sulha process. In their words:

> The purpose of private sulh is to achieve restorative justice and to make sure that revenge will not take place against the family of the perpetrator, leading to an escalation of conflict . . . The actual ritual of settlement and reconciliation follows a similar format in most of its usages. For example, in a case of murder, the family of the murderer will act quickly in order to thwart any attempt at blood revenge.[62]

A unique feature of the 'administration' of revenge within Israel's Arab community (and within many other communities in the Muslim and Arab world) emanates from the structuring of these communities along super-extended family clan lines, the *hamula* (plural *hamail*). Demographically, each Arab village, and many towns, can be viewed as a mosaic of large and small Hamail. Individuals in these contexts are intimately affiliated with their *hamula*.[63]

Clinical psychologist Susan Nathan writes: 'The importance of the Hamula cannot be overstated: it is the ultimate body to which members of traditional Arab society owe their loyalty'.[64] Raymond Cohen links 'clan rivalry' to revenge, noting that in this social context '[c]onflict risks igniting blood revenge or retribution (*tha'r*), a cycle of murderous feuding between clans that might smolder (sic) for years'.[65]

When an individual in an Arab community commits an infraction, his entire *hamula* with its 'circles of loyalty/responsibility' is held responsible for the act and for its consequences – including, most importantly, by becoming targets for revenge attacks by the victim's clan.[66]

It is also the *hamula*, not the individual – in the form of its leadership (elders) – that is responsible for handling the resultant conflict, initially pursuing revenge as a way to restore the clan's lost honour, and ultimately making the effort, again on behalf of the entire clan, to manage/resolve the conflict, using the traditional tool of Sulha.

It is important to recognize that in the same way that the *hamula* may be the key to resolving conflicts, it might actually be seen as the cause of the creation and festering of some conflicts. The 'group' social format of *hamail* in Arab communities, together with the realities of close-proximity living conditions, may create a social topography that, according to social identity theory (SIT), is conducive to producing out-group bias and resultant conflicts. As Taifel and Turner put it: 'The mere awareness of the presence of an out-group is sufficient to provoke intergroup competitive or discriminatory responses on the part of the in-group'.[67]

So it is seemingly possible to see a logic behind the propensity for revenge, particularly in the Middle East. As McCullough concludes: 'It protected our ancestors from aggressors . . . it protected their efforts to benefit from large-scale cooperative behaviour'.[68]

About forgiveness

A useful definition of forgiveness is a response involving letting go of negative feelings and designs (e.g. hate, revenge) directed towards a perceived offender. In some cases, forgiveness may also involve positive feelings such as compassion toward the perceived perpetrator.[69]

It appears that forgiveness is a universal trait (as opposed to a cultural artefact). An examination of sixty different cultures documented the presence of this sentiment, as well as of conciliation concepts (or both) in fifty-three of the sampled cases (93 per cent): a 95 per cent threshold defines a phenomenon as a 'statistical human universal'.[70]

Hannah Arendt traces the 'discovery' of the role of forgiveness as far back as Jesus. 'The discoverer of the role of forgiveness in the realm of human affairs was Jesus of Nazareth', she writes. 'The fact that he made his discovery in a religious context and articulated it in a religious language is no reason to take it less seriously in a strictly secular sense'.[71] This perspective ties in with the 'disease' concept of revenge by providing the 'cure' part of the dichotomy illness (revenge)–cure (forgiveness).

From an evolutionary perspective, the picture is different. Using the same conceptual tools of evolutionary science used to analyze revenge, it is possible to conclude that forgiveness is neither the 'civilized' side of 'primitive' revenge nor a shoddy attempt at masking our failings with, in the words of Michael McCullough, 'a thin veneer of civility'.[72]

McCullough explored forgiveness in a number of works, including its theoretical foundations and instruments of measurement. Placing forgiveness as an essential basic feature of human adaptation, McCullough does not mince words:

> [O]ur capacity for forgiveness is every bit as authentic as our capacity for revenge ... The human capacity for forgiveness, like the human capacity for revenge, solved critical evolutionary problems for our ancestors, and it's still solving those problems today.

He pointed out that forgiveness reduced the motivation to seek revenge against a perceived aggressor and that this sentiment is based on two concepts: forgiving as a motivational construct, and forgiving as a pro-social construct.[73]

McCullough adds additional insight into the behavioural context of forgiveness when he writes: 'Even though our basic behavioural inclinations are shaped by natural selection, we humans aren't slaves to our instincts'. He then adds:

> Because our large brains enable us to reflect on our own condition, to view things from the perspective of other people, to reason about the causes of our behaviour and the behaviour of others, to exert control over our appetites and emotions in the service of higher ideals, and to inspire and persuade others to do the same, there is every reason to believe that we can construct social institutions that will encourage forgiveness rather than revenge.[74]

McCullough continues to broaden the examination of the place of forgiveness, both within a conflict between individuals and in a communal context:

> To forgive a stranger or a sworn enemy, we have to activate the same mental mechanisms that natural selection developed within the human mind to help us forgive our loved ones, friends, and close associates. To encourage more forgiveness in our communities and on the world stage, we must create the social conditions that will activate those mechanisms.[75]

The psychological and behavioural components of forgiveness mean that the disputants no longer view each other's kin group as enemies and instead revert to seeing them as equal members in the community with all privileges and duties, transcending the dispute and its memory of continuous conflict.[76]

The place of forgiveness in Sulha

In Arab culture, and within the context of Muslim/Arab dispute resolution, forgiveness is a central value. Abu-Nimer points out the centrality of the value of forgiveness within the context of dispute resolution in the Arab/Muslim culture, describing it as a tool used to mitigate disputes; in his words: 'The Arab tradition of forgiveness and dignity, an important value which elders have traditionally utilized to encourage certain behaviors (sic) of tolerance and respect'.[77]

The Qur'an indirectly bonds forgiveness with honour by positioning forgiveness as the only path, short of revenge, to redemption of lost or damaged honour by disputing or victimized parties.[78]

Jabbour elaborates on the direct and essential link between Sulha and forgiveness, writing: 'Sulha is first and foremost based on forgiveness. If the offended side does not forgive, there will be no Sulha and there will be no peace'.[79]

And, indeed, forgiveness and reconciliation in Sulha are expressed in several ways, the most common of which are a willingness to give and receive public apologies, a willingness to give and receive compensation, a willingness to participate in religious and quasi-religious rituals (relevant to the conflict) and a willingness to engage the services of third-party interveners to help resolve the conflict. This sentiment is expressed most vividly during the Sulha ceremony, embedded in its three central pillars: *Musafacha* (hand shaking), *Musamacha* (a declaration of forgiveness by the victim's clan) and *Mumalacha* (a sharing by the disputants of a meal prepared by the perpetrator's side).[80]

McCullough adds a life sciences perspective to forgiveness when he asserts that '[e]very neurologically intact person comes into this world outfitted with the capacity to forgive under certain circumstances'.[81] This is the foundation on which the Sulha process rests. The role of the Sulha is to create exactly these 'certain circumstances'.

Forgiveness, within the context of Sulha, is not limited to present disputants, but covers past, present and future generations. The public, written nature of the forgiveness takes it out of the private, personal domain and makes it a formal declaration of peace between the two clans in their entirety, for all generations past, present and future, with the community as witness. The text is very specific: 'This peace is valid for all those who are present here, and all those who are absent. For every embryo in the womb of its mother or for every sperm from the back of the father'.[82] This means that the community (and in particular the victim's family) has a ritualistic and a practical obligation to forgive (though, of course, not the duty to forget) and that the act of reconciliation is binding for the victim's 'circles of responsibility' structure.

Forgiveness and reconciliation

Sulha uses forgiveness to achieve interclan (as well as individual) reconciliation. Forgiveness is not the *only* tool used to facilitate reconciliation, but it is one of the platforms – albeit a major one – used to reach that goal.

Forgiveness and reconciliation appear to be two related concepts, both epistemologically and functionally. According to McCoulough, '[r]econciliation and forgiveness aren't conceptually identical, but they probably have the same evolutionary roots'. He further elaborates on the internal mechanism that links forgiveness and reconciliation, using forgiveness as an enabler of reconciliation carried forward on a foundation of a newly (re)generated sense of goodwill: 'So forgiveness is an internal process of getting over your ill will for an offender, experiencing a return of good will, and opening yourself to the possibility of a renewed positive relationship with the offender'. Renewed positive relationship with the offender is the reconciliation part of the process. In McCoulough's opinion, forgiveness and reconciliation are so tightly bonded, that, in his words 'reconciliation, at least in humans, seems to be the point of forgiveness'.[83]

The link between forgiveness and reconciliation may be used to measure the former by way of the latter. One of the main methods to measure reconciliation used by psychologists, sociologists and primatologists calculates the conciliatory tendency (CT) – examining the tendency of people and/or primates to exhibit conciliatory behaviour before and/or after conflict.[84] CT values range between 0 (subjects are not any friendlier towards each other after conflicts than they were before) and 1 (subjects are friendlier after conflict than they were before the conflict).

An illuminating observation regarding CT tests to children is that, in the words of McCoulough,

> [t]he strategies that preschool children use for reconciling conflicts are a lot like the ones that we adults use when we've offended someone at work, angered a neighbour, or hurt our spouse's feelings. They [the children] explicitly apologize, invite each other to resume playing, offer to share the objects or goodies that they were fighting over, hug each other and hold hands.[85]

Comparing these strategies to those used to seal the Sulha process during the closing ceremony shows striking similarities, including apologies (by the offending side), shaking hands (the equivalent to holding hands), sharing food (the equivalent of sharing objects or goodies) and invitation to reconcile (equivalent to invitation to resume playing). In fact, the Sulha ceremony exhibits all the signs of a functioning, high-level conciliatory tendency.

It thus seems that the main distinction between forgiveness and reconciliation is that it takes one to forgive, but it takes two (at least) to reconcile.[86] This is a major distinction that the Sulha process recognizes; hence, although much of the process is dedicated to restoring the honour of the victim's clan, significant resources are also dedicated to maintaining the sense of honour of the perpetrator's clan, possibly with a view to reconciliation – beyond the forgiveness by the victim's side. In other words, the process aims at 'returning the rights and dignity to the families of both the offender and the offended'.[87]

The place of ritual in forgiveness and reconciliation

The challenge of the Sulha – a multistage, tightly choreographed, reconciliation ritual – is to essentially provide an alternative to revenge that is perceived by the disputants and the community as even more honourable than this option.

Sociologist Anthony Giddens points out the general importance of rituals both to the individual's emotional well-being and to communal harmony and social integration. He writes:

> Without ordered ritual and collective involvement, individuals are left without structured ways of coping with tensions and anxieties . . . Communal rites provide a focus for group solidarity at major transitions . . . [while] allocating definite tasks for those involved.[88]

Indeed, the importance of ritual in Sulha is evident when watching the solemnity and exactitude with which both disputants and interveners approach each of the process's stages. In Jabbour's words:

> We learn to be careful not to forget one word or item because one forgotten word, one simple mistake, one forgotten step in the process of the Sulha and the Sulha will break down. We must lay it on a very solid foundation step by step, with no misunderstanding.[89]

Gellman and Vuinovich also focus on the primacy of the ritual for resolving inter-/intracommunal disputes. They write: 'Ritual is a technical, aesthetic, and communicative process that plays an important role in conflict resolution and reconciliation'. They further expand on the specific restoration-of-honour role of the ritual, arguing that 'Sulha, as ritualized behaviour, creates a space for regaining dignity and honour where it has been lost'.[90]

The interplay of honour, revenge and forgiveness in Sulha

Because Sulha is the *only* communal (as opposed to the individual-oriented state legal system) dispute resolution tool available to the *hamail*-based communities of the Arabs in north Israel, it is reasonable to assume that in its absence and in the absence of its attendant promotion of a cultural option of forgiveness, the only path to restoration of honour left to clan members who perceive their honour to have been damaged is revenge. Without the Sulha, the offended party *must* avenge an offence or stand to suffer severe societal sanctions.

John Elster highlights an essential link between honour and revenge when he writes: 'In societies with a strict code of honour, the ostracism suffered by a person who fails to avenge an offence can be crippling'.[91] This formulation encapsulates the main difficulty facing interveners in Arab communities – an offended party *must* avenge an offence or stand to suffer severe societal sanctions (e.g. loss of honour, ostracism).

That puts a heavy burden on the Sulha process: it has to provide an alternative to revenge that is even more honourable, for otherwise, why would disputants choose that option? It is important to bear in mind that the basic cultural instinct still tilts heavily in the direction of preservation of honour through revenge, so it is arguable that by offering the honourable forgiveness option, Sulha works at the same time *with* ingrained cultural norms *against* other equally ingrained cultural norms.

So the Sulha provides the vehicle that helps concretize the concept of advantageous forgiveness within a conflict context beyond its Qur'anic foundations. The practical meaning of forgiveness is a cessation of conflict between disputing clans in the sense that the victim's side forgives the perpetrator's party and stops seeking revenge. Effectively, this means that the families of the disputants may return to live in the same neighbourhood, trade with each other and move about without fear of belligerent acts by any side. Even more so, it means that life in the entire relevant community can resume gradual normalcy.

Examining the Sulha process in detail shows that the basic premise of the entire enterprise is to transform disputants (and the community along with them) from the personal, clan-based and communal need for revenge to an understanding that reconciliation and forgiveness are even more honourable than revenge. This is no small task in a patriarchal, tribal community where honour is a man's – and, more importantly, a clan's – most prized possession, valued much more than money or material possessions and, in many cases, much more than life itself. But when the entire community – dignitaries, officials and lay members – put themselves in the forgiveness corner and convey to the disputants a uniform message that positions forgiveness above revenge as the real honourable thing to do, in many instances, the message sinks in and the disputants subscribe to the same view despite their desire for revenge.

Sulha is by no means a cast-iron guarantee of forgiveness as a replacement of the revenge option; but as the authors of a detailed report on Arab traditional justice note:

> Despite the fact that informal justice sometimes failed to maintain social harmony in the long term, with the re-emergence of the dispute by way of revenge, even if this comes after many years as noted above, it did however in many cases prevent reactions leading to escalation of the dispute through prompt initiation of the proceedings of Atwa and *sulh*.[92]

Although there is evidence of revenge taking before, during and even after Sulha, these episodes are few and are considered an aberration by the community.[93] This is, apparently, why Sulha has endured for over 1,500 years.

Notes

1 Reuven Levy, *The Social Structure of Islam* (Cambridge: Cambridge University Press, 1969), p. 191.
2 Farrukh B. Hakeem, Maria R Haberfeld and Arvind Verma, *Policing Muslim Communities: Comparative and International Context* (New York: Springer, 2012), p. 15.
3 Qur'an, 7:199.
4 *Ibid.*, 42:40.

5 Muhammad Hashim Kamali, *Principles of Islamic Jurisprudence* (Britain: Islamic Texts Society, 2006), p. 221.
6 Lang, *Sulha Peacemaking*, p. 54. See also Gellman and Vuinovich, 'From *Sulha* to Salaam', p. 133.
7 Jabbour, *Sulha*, p. 31.
8 See, for example: Elvin Hatch, 'Theories of Social Honour', *American Anthropologist*, Vol. 91, No. 2 (1989), pp. 341–53; Ahmed S. Akbar, *Islam under Siege: Living Dangerously in a Post-Honour World* (Cambridge: Polity Press, 2003).
9 David A. de Silva, *Honor, Patronage, Kinship and Purity: Unlocking New Testament Culture* (Downers Grove, IL: Inter Varsity Press, 2000), p. 23.
10 Dodd, 'Family Honor and the Forces of Change in Arab Society', pp. 40–54; Barakat, *The Arab World*; Gideon Kressel, 'Shame and Gender', *Anthropological Quarterly*, Vol. 65, No. 1 (1992), pp. 34–46.
11 Abu-Nimer, 'Conflict Resolution Approaches', p. 46.
12 Irani, 'Islamic Mediation Techniques for Middle East Conflicts', p. 9.
13 Richard L. Abel, 'The Rise of Capitalism and Transformation of Disputing: From Confrontation Over Honor to Competition for Property', *UCLA Law Review*, Vol. 27 (1979), pp. 223–55.
14 Ariely, *The Upside of Irrationality*, p. 127.
15 Jabbour, *Sulha*, p. 69.
16 Unni Wikan, 'Shame and Honour: A Contestable Pair', *Man, New Series*, Vol. 19, No. 4 (1984), p. 635.
17 Joseph Ginat, *Blood Disputes Among Bedouin and Rural Arabs in Israel: Revenge, Mediation, Outcasting and Family Honour* (Pittsburgh: University of Pittsburgh Press, 1987); Pely, 'When Honour Needs Trump Health'.
18 Safa, 'Conflict Resolution and Reconciliation', p. 5.
19 Raymond Cohen, 'Language and Conflict Resolution: The Limits of English', *International Studies Review*, Vol.3, No.1 (2001), pp. 25–51; Catherine Warrick, 'The Vanishing Victim: Criminal Law and Gender in Jordan', *Law and Society Review*, Vol. 39, No. 2 (2005), pp. 315–48.
20 Manar Hasan, 'The Politics of Honour: Patriarchy, the State and the Murder of Women in the Name of Family Honour', *Journal of Israeli History: Politics, Society, Culture*, Vol. 21 (2002), pp. 1–37.
21 Warrick, 'The Vanishing Victim: Criminal Law'.
22 Yotam Feldner, '"Honor" Murders – Why the Perps Get Off Easy', *Middle East Quarterly*. Vol. 7, No. 4 (2000), pp. 41–50. See also Suzanne Ruggi, 'Commodifying Honor in Female Sexuality: Honor Killings in Palestine', in *Power and Sexuality in the Middle East*, Middle East Report, Vol. 28, No. 206 (1998), pp. 12–5.
23 Dodd, 'Family Honor and the Forces of Change in Arab Society', p. 43.
24 Abu Nimer, 'Conflict Resolution Approaches'; Nathan, *The Other Side of Israel: My Journey Across the Jewish/Arab Divide* (New York: Random House, 2005); Jabbour, *Sulha*; Joseph Suad, 'Gender and Family in the Arab World', in S. Sabbagh (ed.), *Arab Women Between Defiance and Restraint* (New York: Olive-Branch Press, 1996), pp. 194–202; Rita Giacaman, Islah Jad and Penny Johnson, 'For the Common Good? Gender and Social Citizenship in Palestine', in S. Joseph and S. Slyomovics (eds.), *Women and Power in the Middle East* (Philadelphia: University of Pennsylvania Press, 2001).
25 Amalia Sa'ar and Taghreed Yahia-Younis, 'Masculinity in Crisis: The Case of Palestinians in Israel', *British Journal of Middle Eastern Studies*, Vol. 35, No. 3 (2008), pp. 305–23.
26 Amalia Sa'ar, 'Feminine Strength: Reflections and Gender in Israeli-Palestinian Culture', *Anthropological Quarterly*, Vol. 79, No. 3 (2006), pp. 397–430.
27 Samira Haj, 'Palestinian Women and Patriarchal Relations', *Signs: Journal of Women in Culture and Society*, Vol. 17, No. 4 (1992), pp. 761–78.

28 'Impunity for Domestic Violence: 'Honour Killings' Cannot Continue – UN Official', www.un.org/apps/news/story.asp?NewsID=33971#.UQ50JaXoRNk (accessed 3 February 2013).
29 Phyllis Chesler, 'Worldwide Trends in Honour Killings', *Middle East Quarterly*, Vol. 7, No. 2 (2010), p. 3.
30 Gellman and Vuinovich, 'From Sulha to Salaam', p. 140. See also Lang, *Sulha Peacemaking*, p. 53; Kressel, 'Shame and Gender', 34.
31 Cohen, 'Language and Conflict Resolution', p. 37.
32 Ramahi, 'Sulh', p. 6.
33 Author interview (on 6 November 2011) with one of the leaders of a clan whose member was killed in a clash with one of Nazareth's main clans (interviewed on condition of anonymity).
34 Author interview (on 12 July 2011) with a member of a clan in Dir al-Assad, whose nephew was murdered in 2007 (interviewed on condition of anonymity).
35 Edward Said, *Orientalism* (New York: Vintage, 1979).
36 Trudy Govier, *Revenge and Forgiveness* (London: Routledge, 2002). See also Kenneth Cloke, 'Revenge, Forgiveness, and the Magic of Mediation', *Conflict Resolution Quarterly*, Vol. 11, No. 1 (1993), pp. 67–78.
37 Qur'an, 42:40.
38 Jabbour, *Sulha*, p. 31.
39 *Homer's Odyssey*, Book I, p. 1, www.sacred-texts.com/cla/homer/ody/ody01.htm (accessed 28 November 2013).
40 Noreen Stuckless and Richard Goranson, 'The Vengeance Scale: Development of a Measure of Attitudes Toward Revenge', *Journal of Social Behavior and Personality*, Vol. 7, No. 1 (1992), p. 26.
41 *Ibid.*
42 Richard Posner, *Law and Literature* (Cambridge: Harvard University Press, 1988), p. 76.
43 Darren Bush and Salvatore Massa, 'Rethinking the Potential Competition Doctrine', *Wisconsin Law Review*, Vol. 1035, No. 4 (2004), pp. 1036–124.
44 Ariely, *The Upside of Irrationality*, pp. 123–24.
45 Keith Otterbein and Charlotte Otterbein, 'An Eye for an Eye, a Tooth for a Tooth: A Cross Cultural Study of Feuding', *American Anthropologist*, Vol. 67, No. 6 (1965), pp. 1470–82. See also David Levinson, 'The Human Relations Area Files', *Reference Services Review*, Vol. 17, No. 3 (1989), pp. 83–90.
46 Martin Daly and Margo Wilson, *Homicide* (New York: Aldine de Gruyter, 1988), p. 226.
47 Michael E. McCullough, *Beyond Revenge: The Evolution of the Forgiveness Instinct* (San Francisco: Jossey-Bass, A Wiley Imprint, 2007).p. 5.
48 *Ibid.*
49 Elster, 'Norms of Revenge', p. 862.
50 Colin M. Parkes, 'Psychiatric Problems Following Bereavement by Murder or Manslaughter', *British Journal of Psychiatry*, Vol. 162 (1993), p. 49.
51 Govier, *Revenge and Forgiveness*, p. 2 (emphasis in the original).
52 *Ibid.*
53 McCullough, *Beyond Revenge*, p. 10.
54 Charles Darwin, *The Descent of Man, and Selection in Relation to Sex* (Chicago: University of Chicago Press, 1952; originally published in 1871), p. 294.
55 Alan P. Hamlin, 'Rational Revenge', *Ethics*, Vol. 101, No. 2 (1991), p. 377.
56 Ariely, *The Upside of Irrationality*, p. 126.
57 McCullough, *Beyond Revenge*, p. 11.
58 Bert R. Brown, 'The Effects of Need to Maintain Face on Interpersonal Bargaining', *Journal of Experimental Social Psychology*, Vol. 4 (1968), pp. 107–22. See also Sung Hee Kim, Richard, H, Smith and Nancy L. Brigham, 'Effects of Power Imbalance

and the Presence of Third Parties on Reactions to Harm: Upward and Downward Revenge', *Personality and Social Psychology Bulletin*, Vol. 24 (1998), pp. 353–61; Robert Kurzban, Peter DeScioli and Erin O'Brien, 'Audience Effects on Moralistic Punishment', *Evolution and Human Behavior*, Vol. 28 (2007), pp. 75–84.
59 Richard E. Nisbett and Dov Cohen, *Culture of Honour: The Psychology of Violence in the South* (Boulder: Westview 1996). See also Jacob Black-Michaud, *Cohesive Force: Feud in the Mediterranean and the Middle East* (Oxford: Basil Blackwell, 1975).
60 McCullough, *Beyond Revenge*, p. 53.
61 Author interview with Rani.
62 Irani and Funk, 'Rituals of Reconciliation', p. 62.
63 Izhak Schnell, 'Urban restructuring in Israeli Arabs settlements', *Middle Eastern Studies*, Vol. 30, No. 2 (1994), pp. 330–50. See also Izhak Schnell and Michael Sofer, 'Embedding Entrepreneurship in Social Structure: Israeli-Arab Entrepreneurship', *International Journal of Urban and Regional Research*, Vol. 27, No. 2 (2003), pp. 300–18.
64 Nathan, *The Other Side of Israel*, p. 118.
65 Cohen, 'Language and Conflict Resolution', p. 37.
66 Jabbour, *Sulha*, p. 73.
67 Taifel and Turner, 'An Integrative Theory', p. 38.
68 McCullough, *Beyond Revenge*, p. 61.
69 Forgiveness, *A Sampling of Research Results: American Psychological Association* (Washington, DC: Office of International Affairs, 2006), p. 5. See also Michael J. Subkoviak, Robert D. Enright, Ching-Ru Wu, Elisabeth A. Gassin, Suzanne Freedman, Leanne M. Olson and Issidoros Sarinopoulos, 'Measuring Interpersonal Forgiveness in Late Adolescence and Middle Adulthood', *Journal of Adolescence*, Vol. 18 (1995), pp. 641–55.
70 McCullough, *Beyond Revenge*, pp. 121–22. See also Donald Brown, *Human Universals* (Boston: McGraw-Hill, 1991).
71 Hannah Arendt, *The Human Condition* (Chicago: University of Chicago press, 1975), p. 214.
72 McCullough, *Beyond Revenge*, p 13.
73 Ibid. pp. 43, 44. See also idem 'Forgiveness as Human Strength: Theory, Measurement, and Links to Well-Being', *Journal of Social and Clinical Psychology*, Vol. 19, No. 1 (2000), p. 43.
74 Idem, *Beyond Revenge*, p. 19.
75 *Ibid.*, p. 16.
76 Jabbour, *Sulha*, pp. 56–7.
77 Abu-Nimer, 'Conflict Resolution Approaches, p. 44.
78 Qur'an, 42:40.
79 Jabbour, *Sulha*, p. 31.
80 The Sulha's three pillars are discussed in Chapter 4.
81 McCullough, *Beyond Revenge*, pp. 88–9.
82 Jabbour, *Sulha*, p. 53.
83 McCullough, *Beyond Revenge*, pp. 114–16.
84 *Ibid.*, p. 119.
85 *Ibid.*, p. 121.
86 Ervin Staub, 'Constructive Rather Than Harmful Forgiveness, Reconciliation, Ways to Promote Them After Genocide and Mass Killing', in Everett Worthington (ed.). *Handbook of Forgiveness* (New York: Routledge, 2005), pp. 443–60.
87 Jabbour, *Sulha*, p. 95.
88 Anthony Giddens, *Modernity and Self-Identity: Self and Society in the Modern Age* (Palo Alto: Stanford University Press, 1991), p. 204.
89 Jabbour, *Sulha*, p. 33.

90 Gellman and Vuinovich, 'From Sulha to Sallam', p. 133.
91 Elster, 'Norms of Revenge', p. 864; Lang, Sulha Peacemaking, p. 54.
92 Institute of Law, Birzeit University, 'Al-Kada' Gayrel Nethamee: Seyadat al-Kanun wa-Hal al-Niza'at Fee Falasteen' (Informal Justice: Rule of Law and Dispute Resolution in Palestine. National Report on Field Research Results), 2006, pp. 192–209.
93 Author interview with Faraj Khneifes, 14 June 2009.

4 Sulha
Structure and characteristics

The Sulha is the most ubiquitous customary justice mechanism in the Muslim/Arab world in general and within Muslim/Arab communities in northern Israel in particular. It is designed to facilitate reconciliation across many types of disputes, from simple honour-affecting insults like the pushing of another man's wife, through property disputes, to assaults and murders. The severity of the offence is measured by its potential honour-losing impact and/or by its consequent potential to evolve into a much more serious dispute.

By way of shifting a group of grieving, angry and provoked disputants from a desire to avenge and restore lost honour through the infliction of pain on the perceived offender's clan to a willingness to forgive and reconcile, Sulha makers must take the disputants, separately, yet together, through an elaborate, seven-step transformative and restorative journey; the stages are designed to gradually restore the honour of the victim's clan without damaging the honour of the perpetrator's clan and to simultaneously introduce the concept of forgiveness as an individually and communally preferred option to the conflict *and* to revenge – leading ultimately to reconciliation.

As such, the Sulha's purpose is not to re-engineer human behaviour but to provide disputants with an honour-restoring alternative to revenge (forgiveness in the Sulha framework), as well as to provide the disputants with a formalized conduit that will maximize the likelihood of their choosing forgiveness over revenge as they respond to a conflict and to their perceptions of their status within the community resulting from a conflict.

If, for example, as Michael McCullough claims, 'the desire for revenge is a conduit for pain',[1] then reconciliation in general and the Sulha process in particular should equip the disputants with another, possibly more successful, pain-relieving conduit that at worst will help the disputants keep the desire as just that – a desire – and at best provide them with a culturally preferred substitute in the form of an honour-enhancing forgiveness. In Lang's words, 'Sulha alleviates emotional and social pressures and serves as a legitimate alternative to retaliation'.[2]

This chapter uses existing literature, survey questionnaires, interviews, statistical analysis and qualitative analysis to demonstrate how Sulha uses a gradual re-integrative honouring process, utilizing task-specific mediation, arbitration and improvisation tools to facilitate the restoration of the victim clan's sense of honour while maintaining that of the perpetrator's clan, so as to effect a transformation from a desire to avenge to a willingness to forgive.

Re-integrative honouring concept (RHC)

The central theoretical foundation of this discussion is the re-integrative honouring concept (RHC), postulating a transformative process that uses a gradual application of honour-restoring acts and rituals to enable the victim's clan to restore its lost and/or hurt sense of honour, thereby creating the social space needed to allow it to replace its almost instinctive revenge 'reflex' with an increasing willingness to forgive the perpetrator and his clan.

As shown in Chapter 2, RHC differs from the existing re-integrative shaming theory (RST) mainly in that in re-integrative shaming the primary object of transformation is the perpetrator and the primary vehicle of transformation is shaming, whereas in re-integrative honouring the primary object of transformation is the victim's clan and the primary vehicle of transformation is honouring.

RHC seeks to provide a way to observe, describe, explain and predict disputants' perception and attitude changes throughout the Sulha process, leading ultimately to a willingness by the victim's clan to publically announce their communal forgiveness, an act that creates the required social infrastructure for the enacting of the Sulha ceremony, through which the disputing clans, the region's dignitaries and the local (and sometimes regional) community put their seal of approval on a reconciliation agreement while at the same time creating the ritualistic and social framework required to hold the disputing parties responsible for upholding the agreement and maintaining the reconciliation process on course, past the rituals and ceremonies, into the future.

Although RHC seems like a promising research direction, it is important to acknowledge that because of variations in Sulha processes throughout the Middle East region and elsewhere in the world, in order to gain broader validation, the claims made by the RHC will require additional examinations against different conflict backgrounds, tracking changes in honour perception by the victim's clan in other environments (outside the north of Israel) and their relation to relevant revenge and forgiveness tendencies.

RHC survey

A survey was used to monitor the perceptions of several members of each examined victim's clan with respect to their state of honour, revenge and forgiveness, both at each stage of the process and as they go through the various stages of the Sulha process. The survey's eleven interviewees were volunteers from eight different clans representing eight different disputes that took place between 2003 and 2011 in northern Israel.[3] All interviewees were men and all insisted on total anonymity, including details of their clan, names, domiciles and any other identifying detail regarding themselves or the specific disputes they were associated with.[4]

All interviewees were given a Likert scale–like questionnaire using a modified model of a Forgiveness Likelihood Scale to measure possible attitude modifications along three areas of examination: perception of damage to their sense of honour, desire for revenge and willingness to forgive. Each of the three areas of examination was measured for every stage of the Sulha process, and the responses were grouped to produce median, range and average calculations. The data were then analyzed as ordinal data (each individual question separately), using the dot plot method of presentation because data are not continuous). The central tendency was summarized by average and median, and the variability was summarized by range.[5]

The range of possible answers to each question in the questionnaire was Strongly Disagree, Disagree, Neutral, Agree, Strongly Agree. (See Appendix B for a copy of the questionnaire.)

The survey questionnaires covered seven stages of the Sulha (S1–S7), exploring the memories of the interviewees regarding their emotions with respect to honour, revenge and forgiveness perspectives, at specific times within the Sulha process and their recollection of their resultant attitudes at each stage. It posed the victims' clan representatives essentially the same set of questions at each stage, with minor variations designed to reflect the distinct stages of the Sulha.

The rationale underlying this method rests on the assumption that people remember events through recollection of their emotional state during the specific event. In the words of psychologist Lawrence Sanna: 'When remembering life experiences, individuals often relate not just to what happened but also how they remembered feeling at the time. Indeed, the most meaningful and memorable experiences of our lives are typically those that evoked strong emotions'.[6]

The subject of recollection of emotion is a controversial one. According to Sanna, 'investigators have taken radically different positions on whether and how people remember past emotions. Some argue that emotions are stored in memory directly, whereas others argue that emotions must first be transformed into cognitive representations'.[7]

Furthermore, it has been suggested that current events reshape recollections of memory in general and emotions in particular. Psychologist Linda Levine, for example, argues that 'memories for emotional responses are partially reconstructed or inferred on the basis of current appraisals of events'. Yet she also upholds that 'in contrast to some current models, memories for past emotions were not indelible, and a general tendency to overestimate the intensity of past emotions was not observed'.[8]

Regarding the question of people's recollection of past emotions, as it relates to this specific survey, the assumption when planning the survey was that people remember very well their emotions during various traumatic and post-traumatic events and rituals. Indeed, the rituals are designed to leave a memorable impression on disputants and their relevant communities. The survey aimed at exactly that: eliciting in Sulha participants on the victim's side a recall of their impressions at key junctions in the process (mostly, as we shall see, marked by strong ritualistic activity). To that end, indeed, interviewees almost always remarked that

'I remember it like it was yesterday'. Not one interviewee claimed to have forgotten how he felt in the aftermath of these stages and rituals.

The statements in the questionnaire's form were mixed (i.e. they were not presented sequentially) so interviewees would not be able to use their relative location as a place marker to associate a specific statement with a specific Sulha stage or relative to other statements in the questionnaire. Each statement was given a coded number that was later used to associate it with a specific stage and examined sentiment (i.e. honour, revenge or forgiveness).[9]

Data collection took place during a series of eight interviews, each lasting three to five hours, between 13 May 2013 and 21 July 2013. Mr. Faraj Khneifes, a senior member of the region's Sulha Committee, assisted in scheduling and facilitating the meetings with the clans' representatives and participated in the interviews to the extent that he performed the introductions, explained the purpose of the interview and survey and helped clarify questions and contexts when necessary.

Assumptions

The assumption underlying this line of inquiry is that every stage of the Sulha can be observed and analyzed along the time axis of the process so as to provide a time-stamp view of the 'state of dispute' as well as a concurrent picture of the 'state of honour'. If honour is indeed an element in the reintegration, we should see a change in the honour perception of the victim's clan as it moves through the Sulha process – from a perception of denigration and lost honour to a perception of a restored honour. In the specific case of this survey, the purpose was to measure the decline in the perception of the victim's clan interviewees that their clan's honour was damaged considerably.

Conversely, if the assumed change in damaged honour perception does indeed occur, it is reasonable to assume that there should be concurrent evidence of a change in the desire to avenge by the victim's clan – namely, it should decrease as the Sulha process progresses. Simultaneously, if such a transformation does take place and the sense of damaged honour decreases, along with a concurrent decline in the desire to avenge, the victimized clan's willingness to forgive should increase, reflecting their restored sense of honour, which in turn enables them to contemplate (and practice) a readiness to forgive as an emotional and functional 'replacement' of the desire for revenge. The culmination of the process comes when the victim's clan feels that their honour was restored, enabling them to forgive and consequently reconcile.

Another assumption is that in order for the process to move forward towards an eventual agreement (forgiveness, reconciliation), the preceding stage must conclude successfully, in the 'accounting' sense that the damaged honour perception of the victim's clan has declined (or remained consistent), while at the same time the drive to avenge has gradually been replaced by the option to forgive. If, at the end of the process these conditions are fulfilled (decline in the perception of damaged honour, decreased need for revenge and increased willingness to forgive), there will be an agreement and the Sulha process will have achieved its functional and cultural goals. As Elias Jabbour put it: 'We learn to be careful not to forget one word or item because one forgotten word, one simple mistake, one forgotten step in the process of the Sulha, and the Sulha will break down'.[10]

Sulha stages

The transformation from a desire to avenge to a willingness to forgive through a restoration of the victimized clan's damaged sense of honour consists of seven stages:

- Conflict eruption and the recruitment of the offender's clan.
- Recruiting of the victim's clan.[11]
- Signing of the *Tafweeth* by the victim's clan.
- Payment of Atwa and initiating a Hudna (temporary truce).
- Negotiations with the disputants.
- Deciding on a verdict.
- Conducting the Sulha ceremony.

The analysis of each stage evaluates the transformation of the perception of members of the victim's clan as they go through the Sulha process, locates changes in perceptions at key points and investigates the possibility of a correlation between the three 'states' (honour, revenge and forgiveness) as they change through the process.

Stage 1: conflict eruption and recruiting the offender's clan[12]

Unlike the response expected from the state's formal legal authorities in the aftermath of an apparent infraction (e.g. the discovery of a dead body) – namely the launch of a formal investigation – the 'authorities' responsible for the implementation of the customary, restorative justice process – in this case the Sulha Committee – do not automatically initiate the Sulha process. In the words of Elias Jabbour:

> Several formal steps should usually take place before the Sulha process can officially start, and it is important that these steps take place in the right format and sequence, for the process to start as soon as possible, so as to forestall situations such as revenge killings and other forms of retaliation.[13]

Traditionally, the first step in initiating a Sulha process is for representative(s) of the offender's clan to contact at least one known member of the area's Sulha Committee (*Jaha*), assume initial responsibility for the infraction of their clan member, express regret on behalf of the offender and the clan and sue for reconciliation with the victim's family.

Petitioning the Sulha practitioners (at this point they are not yet a formal *Jaha*) to launch the reconciliation process on their behalf is the offending clan's only practical as well as honour-preserving and enhancing venue available. Without the

Sulha process, suing for reconciliation would have been looked at by the perpetrator's clan as a dishonouring act of cowardice (in the face of a potential retaliatory vengeance attack); but the status of the Sulha's institution as a platform that can increase honour through substituting forgiveness (magnanimity) for the urge for revenge, together with the personal clout of the interveners and the opportunity to behave in a way that will be appreciated by the interveners because it shows a willingness to take concrete steps towards a formal initiation of the reconciliation process, provides the perpetrator's clan with a necessary honour-enhancing platform. In the words of Faraj Khneifes: 'If they [the perpetrator's clan] honour us [the Sulha practitioners], this shows a respect for the Sulha and we return the respect when we agree to take on the case'. Furthermore, in the eyes of the community, suing for reconciliation signifies a willingness of the offender's family to honour the community's desire for harmony.[14] Accommodating the general will wins the perpetrator's clan respect within their community.

According to Jabbour, the exact words the representatives of the perpetrator's clan should say to the Sulha practitioner(s) are: 'We are in your house and you must help us. We are in serious trouble: one of our sons committed a crime and we are in your hands'.[15] The reason for what seems like a rush to assume responsibility by the perpetrator's clan is that the period of time immediately attending the eruption of a dispute is rife with potential for attempted retaliatory revenge by the victim's family members. As Khneifes put it:

> The blood of the members of the victim's clan is said to be 'boiling with anger' because of the pain of their loss and the insult to their honour; someone [from the victim's clan] may rush to avenge before the Sulha process even starts.[16]

So from the offender's family's perspective, the sooner the 'official' Sulha process kicks off, the sooner they will be able to avail themselves of some protection from vengeance.

According to Jabbour, in the context of this first meeting with the offender's clan, the dignitaries also have a specific text that must be delivered. They say: 'You requested that we intervene. We, as a *Jaha*, want to hear your authorization and receive it in writing'.[17]

The *Jaha*-to-be uses at this stage a strict arbitrative approach. They *demand* from the representatives of the offending clan (not beseech or even ask them) to sign on to the Sulha process through their endorsement of a *Tafweeth* – an irrevocable writ of authorization to act on the family's behalf comprising two parts: a request by the perpetrator's clan from the *Jaha* to intercede on their behalf with the victim's family and to conduct the Sulha – as well as an authorization to do so – and, no less significantly, an obligation by the perpetrator's clan to abide by whatever verdict the *Jaha* reaches.

The *Tafweeth* is effectively an arbitration contract. It gives the interveners the same powers that a Western-style arbitrator or a Muslim Hakam (a *Tahkim* practitioner) has. This is a powerful tool that puts the *Jaha* in a dominant position with respect to its ability, when necessary, to coerce the perpetrator's clan into an agreement. In reality, this tool is rarely used in such a forceful way; for the most part, its importance rests in the symbolic and potential powers of coercion it gives the *Jaha* – implied power acknowledged by all involved parties, whose 'spirit' hovers over the proceedings throughout the process.[18]

In some instances, the offender's family does not step forward promptly and it is up to the Sulha dignitaries or to local elders to assess the gravity of the situation and to decide whether to act immediately (to 'force-start' the process) or to wait. If the dignitaries deem the situation dangerous (e.g. that there is an imminent danger of revenge killing), it is acceptable for the Sulha Committee or one of its members to contact the offender's family and to cajole them to start a Sulha process.[19]

At this stage of the process no formal temporary truce has yet been agreed upon by the disputants, and the potential for revenge attack is high. Hence the Sulha makers evaluate the situation and try to decide whether the tension between the disputants is volatile enough to merit the application of a *Tarhil* (exile in Arabic)[20] – a compulsory relocation order that Sulha makers can impose on the offender's clan. This is an ancient practice, originating in nomadic times, where in the event of a dispute the family of the offender would pack its tents and move far away from the tent of the victim's family to reduce irritation and the subsequent potential for additional acts of belligerency.[21]

Today, for social and practical reasons (it is difficult to uproot and move large families), *Tarhil* is practiced only under extreme circumstances of anticipated, imminent violence. But it is still practiced where the *Jaha* decides that it is absolutely essential.

Stage 1: data analysis

To measure the perspectives of the victim's clan interviewees immediately after the eruption of the conflict, they were asked to respond to the following three statements:

- Immediately after the start of the conflict you were very angry and wanted to take revenge.
- Immediately after the start of the conflict you were willing to forgive the killer's clan.
- Immediately after the start of the conflict you felt your clan's honour was hurt badly.

Table 4.1 and Figure 4.1 present the basic descriptive statistics derived from the aforementioned data.

Stage 1: discussion

The time immediately attending the eruption of a conflict is fraught with emotions and tension for the disputing clans and the community. Often the village is inundated with uniformed and armed police, on foot and in vehicles, patrolling the areas where the two disputing clans reside in an attempt to forestall any rush to

Table 4.1 Stage 1: descriptive statistics – victim's clan

Median			Range			Average		
Revenge	Forgiveness	Honour	Revenge	Forgiveness	Honour	Revenge	Forgiveness	Honour
4.0	2.0	4.0	3.0	2.0	3.0	4.0	1.7	4.0

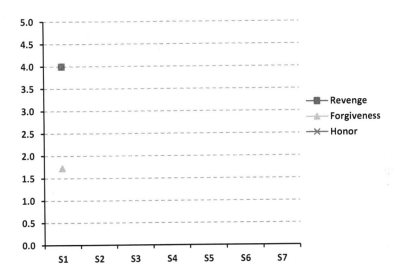

Figure 4.1 Stage 1: depicted averages – victim's clan

Note: The depicted states of Honour and Revenge are identical at this stage (see Table 4.1), and therefore they overlay each other. This is why it looks like there are only two depicted states on this graph.

avenge or any other activity that might exacerbate the conflict. Businesses in the immediate area usually close down, especially those belonging to the disputing clans.[22] Members of the perpetrator's clan living in close proximity to those of the victim's clan usually pick up basic belongings and depart rapidly to more distant locations, mostly camping temporarily with relatives, either in the village or in neighbouring villages.[23]

The assumption is that at this stage the desire to avenge will be high, as will be the sense of hurt honour, whereas the willingness to forgive will be low.

The survey findings support this assumption. As shown in Table 4.1, the average measured value of the willingness to forgive was low, whereas the average measured values of the desire to avenge and the sense of hurt honour were high.

PERCEPTION OF HURT SENSE OF HONOUR

Asked about their perception of their state of honour, informants were quite adamant. In the words of one: 'Honour? What honour? They not only killed our son;

they dishonoured us in front of the entire village!' Another informant stressed the magnified sense of hurt resulting from the actual loss of a clan member, combined with the strong sense of loss of honour, saying: 'The pain from what they did, was doubled by the pain from their huge disrespect towards us'.

Eighty-one per cent of the interviewees agreed with the statement that at the start of the conflict they felt their honour was badly hurt, whereas 18 per cent disagreed with this statement.

The observed and measured states of the victim clan's perceptions confirm the RHC hypothesis; at this early stage of the conflict, no real action has taken place yet to modify or mitigate any of the perceptions and feelings, so there is no reason to expect that they would change on their own. The only possible significant modifier other than concrete action by some actor within the process (i.e. interveners, community or disputants) is the passage of time, which may be reasonably assumed to have an impact on the disputants.

DESIRE TO AVENGE

Many of the interviewees expressed recollection of their clan's collective and individual anger, which in their words fuelled an almost uniform desire to get back at the perpetrator's clan, inflict suffering and disrespect on them, and in the process redeem their own clan's sense of respect and honour. In the words of one informant: 'My brother was incredibly angry and humiliated. He wanted to go out with a machinegun and kill every xxxx Hamula man he could find'. Another informant said: 'We were neighbours, friends, and their son did this to us [murdered our son]; the only thing we could think about was revenge'. [24] About 72 per cent of the interviewees indicated that at the start of the conflict they were very angry and wanted to take revenge. About 9 per cent indicated disagreement with this sentiment.

It is worth noting that the surveyed population includes a segment that completely opposes the Sulha process, as well as the process's driving cultural sentiments, such as revenge. However, during times of conflict, dissenting voices tend to quiet down, although they do not disappear.

WILLINGNESS TO FORGIVE

Informants responded emotionally to the proposition that they consider forgiveness at this early stage of the conflict. One informant said: 'Forgiveness? God should forgive them, not us!' Another added that 'I was sure [immediately after the eruption of conflict] that there was no way in the world I would ever forgive the killer's clan'. Yet another member of a victim's clan, the brother of a murdered young man, said in a filmed interview soon after the murder: 'Nothing in this world will cause me to shake the hand of the murderer's clan'.[25]

About 81 per cent of the interviewees disagreed with the statement that at the start of the conflict they were willing to forgive the victim's clan. None of the interviewees indicated agreement with this statement.

Stage 2: recruiting the victim's family

Recruiting the victim's clan to the Sulha process turns out to be completely different from the ritual performed to incorporate the perpetrator's clan. For one thing, the victim's family rarely takes the first step in the Sulha process; it is considered a huge loss of honour for the aggrieved side to seek a Sulha, mainly because in the traditional sequence of expected cause-and-effect events in such a conflict context, once a clan perceives that an offence was committed against one of its members, it is expected to take rapid honour-restoring action in the form of revenge – an equal or more severe measure of retaliatory punishment against the members of the perceived offender's clan.[26]

Save for revenge, the only honour-restoring option available to the victim's clan is its prerogative to accommodate (or sometimes reject) an appeal from the Sulha dignitaries to join the Sulha process and postpone the act of attempted vengeance. Sharon Lang quotes an anonymous Sulha practitioner who describes the cultural rationale underlying the honour-for-revenge interchange concept in the following words: 'If it is an act of *sharaf* [honour] to avenge, it is more honor not to revenge; that is why we call him (who forgives) a great person. If he takes revenge, then he is like any other normal person, but when he says, "I could have killed the killer, but I chose not to," that is a great man.'[27]

By way of activating this honour-restoring option to revenge, the Sulha dignitaries, now armed with the authorization to initiate contact as signed by the offender's clan, come to the compound of the victim's clan. Here, the *Jaha*-to-be uses self-humbling, honouring postures to start restoring the honour perception of the victim's clan. The dignitaries stand at the doorway of the victim's clan compound, and their leader declares 'We were sent and are authorized as *Jaha* by the killer's family, and we invite you to consider us'.[28] Both the narrative and the posture are explicitly designed to avoid any appearance that the Sulha makers are coercing, commanding or even instructing the victim's family to join the process. On the contrary, they put themselves deliberately in a passive, responsive role and *invite* the victim's clan to take the active, honour-enhancing role of 'considering' the option to communicate with the dignitaries about their misfortune.

This role-reversing ritual is designed to enhance the victim's family's sense of control and reduce their sense of helplessness (which is likely to be very high at this point), but at the same time divert them, with ample communal support, from the urgent desire to avenge and into the culturally preferred option of conciliation that may ultimately lead to forgiveness – something that is unthinkable at this stage, but still figures prominently in the grand scheme of things.

Furthermore, at this preliminary stage in the process, and as a deliberate act designed to facilitate the recruitment of the victim's clan to the Sulha, the dignitaries may also resort to the extraordinary measure of acting as venting buffers for the victimized family's sense of rage, helplessness and frustration. When this happens, the dignitaries may be abused verbally, sometimes in quite an aggressive manner, by the victim's family members – particularly women and youngsters.[29] This is a turn of events that goes against all accepted norms in the strict patriarchal environment where it takes place, and is designed to provide the victim's family with another significant outlet for their rage, together with an acknowledgment of their suffering and their need to recover their lost honour. This venting process is considered essential by the dignitaries, for in its absence it is unlikely that the victim's family would be able to bring itself to accept the initial request to join the Sulha process.

Lang provides a detailed description of the venting process and its underlying social rationale, which she calls 'reverse musayara' (reverse social etiquette/ingratiation) whereby

> [n]otables constituting the *Jaha*, while negotiating with the injured family, treat the victim's family, from the beginning to the end of the process, with the elaborate respect and consideration normally reserved for persons of high status. This process may usefully be regarded as a performative reversal of the standard patron-client relationship prevalent in Arab society. In relationships of patronage (*wasta*), the client's request for a favor is flattering for the patron, and each wasta favor can be seen as a transaction wherein *sharaf* [honour] flows from the client to the patron. The *Jaha* – the most reputable men in the community – symbolically turn this relationship on its head (reverse musayara) by beseeching an ordinary family (currently reeling under the humiliation of a killing) to be so kind as to grant them a favor (sic) – to make peace rather than to avenge themselves. This reverse positioning is extraordinarily flattering for the injured family; the weakened party is placed in a (temporary) position of 'patronage' over society's most esteemed men. Such treatment helps to assuage feelings of humiliation further and to effect a partial restoration of lost *sharaf*.[30]

The use of this powerful subritual at this preliminary stage of the reconciliation process is a prominent demonstration of the importance of honour as a currency in the gradual transaction of the social contract designed to facilitate the recruitment of the victim's family to participate in the Sulha. If the family agrees and cooperates, it is rewarded with a massive increase of their perceived honour status by the community and the dignitaries alike; if, however, it declines to cooperate, it causes the dignitaries a loss of face (through loss of authority) and is itself affected similarly as their refusal is marked (again by the community at large) as the main reason for this loss of face and for the continuing paralysis in the reconciliation process.

Stage 2: data analysis

To measure the perspectives of victim's clan interviewees when the *Jaha* (at this point dignitaries) met with them soon after the eruption of the conflict, they were asked to respond to the following three statements:

- When the *Jaha* came to talk with you for the first time after the conflict started, you felt you still wanted to take revenge.

- When the *Jaha* came to talk with you for the first time after the conflict started, you were willing to forgive the perpetrator's clan.
- When the *Jaha* came to talk with you for the first time after the conflict started, you felt your clan's honour was hurt badly.

Table 4.2 and Figure 4.2 present the basic descriptive statistics derived from the aforementioned data.

Discussion

Traditionally, soon after the eruption of a conflict the members of the victimized clan gather at the victim's home or, absent that, at the home of one of the *hamula*'s leaders, where they establish a 'mourning tent'. This is an area covered by some temporary shade-producing material, such as a tarpaulin, under which rows of plastic chairs are arranged to accommodate the visitors who start streaming in soon afterwards to express their condolences. Members of the victim's clan (gender-segregated) lounge about, talking and smoking; young members of the clan distribute light snacks, water, tea, coffee and fruits. Whenever a visitor comes into the area (men only; women visitors go to the women's section), the leaders of the

Table 4.2 Stage 2: descriptive statistics – victim's clan

Median			Range			Average		
Revenge	Forgiveness	Honour	Revenge	Forgiveness	Honour	Revenge	Forgiveness	Honour
4.0	2.0	4.0	3.0	2.0	3.0	3.6	1.8	4.0

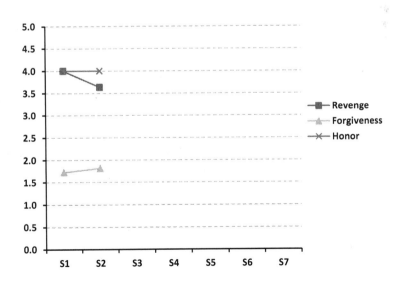

Figure 4.2 Stage 2: depicted averages – victim's clan

victim's clan stand up, form a reception line and shake the hands of the visitors, listening to words of consolation and usually saying little. Sounds of heavy crying are often heard from the women's section and many of the men also shed tears in public, though they usually do not cry audibly.

The RHC assumption is that at this early stage of the conflict the victimized clan's desire to avenge will remain high, their sense of hurt honour will be high and their willingness to forgive will be low. The survey data support this assumption. As seen, the averaged measured value of the willingness to forgive is low, whereas the averaged measured values of the desire to avenge and the sense of hurt honour are high.

PERCEPTION OF HURT SENSE OF HONOUR

At this point, despite the visit by the dignitaries, it appears that the victimized clan's hurt sense of honour as they first meet the *Jaha* remains the same as it was immediately after the eruption of the conflict. The wound, physical and emotional, is apparently still fresh, and members of the victim's clan are immersed in their agony and humiliation. In the words of one interviewee: 'We didn't want to talk to the *Jaha* at all; we listened to them only out of respect for them'.

No change is seen in the perceptions of the interviewees regarding their clan's hurt honour. About 81 per cent of the interviewees agreed with the statement that when they met the *Jaha* for the first time they felt their honour was badly hurt; about 18 per cent disagreed with this statement. It is interesting to note that there are no expressions of neutrality with respect to this sentiment. People either feel that their honour was hurt or they do not.

The observed and measured states of the victimized clan's perceptions at this stage fit the basic RHC assumptions. At this stage, no real work by the *Jaha* towards changing the perceptions of the victim's clan has taken place. What little change that was observed in the desire to avenge and the willingness to forgive may be attributed to the passage of time and the attendant start of contemplation by the members of the victim's clan regarding the complexity of the conflict at hand.

DESIRE TO AVENGE

At this early point in the conflict (usually, about twenty-four hours after its eruption), many interviewees recollected feeling a strong sense of frustration and rage and a strong need to vent those sensations. The targets for such venting were the consoling friends, family members and members of the community, as well as the visiting dignitaries (not a formal *Jaha* at that point), who were just beginning their efforts to gain some control over the fresh conflict and put it on a formal track. In the words of one interviewee: 'They [*Jaha*] visited us in the mourning shed; they wanted to talk about Sulha, but all we could talk about was our anger, and how they [the killer's clan] should stay away from here if they don't want to die a terrible death'.

About 54 per cent of the interviewees indicated that when the dignitaries came to visit them for the first time they were very angry and wanted to take revenge. Eighteen per cent indicated disagreement with this sentiment, and about 27 per cent expressed a neutral stance. These findings show a slight reduction in the desire for revenge, possibly as a result of the ability to vent extensively. This may also be a time when members of the victim's clan begin expressing more individual stances as the reality of the situation sinks in and discussions take place regarding what can and needs to be done to redress the insult and the injury. Some family members are completely opposed to the concept of revenge, some are ambivalent and many talk about revenge as a way of venting anger, dealing with their sense of helplessness and attempting to assuage their hurt sense of honour.

Women also talk about anger, frustration and desire to see their men-folk exact revenge. Often, they express themselves in quite blunt and audible terms, particularly as they gather to make arrangements for the funeral and carry out the purification rights (washing and dressing up the deceased and preparing him or her for burial).

WILLINGNESS TO FORGIVE

The victim's clan's recollections of their willingness to forgive at this early stage of the conflict show just a slight change in the direction of accepting the concept of forgiveness. There is little or no real discussion about reconciliation at this point. In the words of one interviewee describing the first visit of the dignitaries to their mourning shed: 'The *Jaha* didn't say anything about forgiveness; that would not be proper at this stage'.

Seventy-two per cent of the interviewees disagreed with the statement that when they met the *Jaha* soon after the eruption of the conflict they were willing to forgive the victim's clan. Twenty-seven per cent expressed neutrality regarding this statement, indicating a budding start of willingness to contemplate such a possibility, possibly as a result of the presence of the reconciliation-talking dignitaries.

Stage 3: signing the Tafweeth *and forming the Jaha*

The signing of the *Tafweeth* is a two-step process, taking place separately first between the *Jaha* and the perpetrator's clan and then between the *Jaha* and the victim's clan. As described in stage 1, the perpetrator's clan ought to sign the authorization document to effectively invite the dignitaries of the would-be *Jaha* to start putting together the foundations for the Sulha process. The *Jaha* then moves to the victim's clan (usually at their mourning tent location) to attempt to get them to sign off on the *Tafweeth*, effectively recruiting the victim's clan to the Sulha process and enabling it to formally begin.

Following the venting and reverse musayara sessions described in stage 2, the would-be-*Jaha* sits down with the representatives of the victim's clan to discuss their terms for signing off on the *Tafweeth*. The dignitaries are not supposed to take too long to initiate discussions with the victim's family, as this, too, may appear to be a sign of disrespect, which will further increase the latter's sense of hurt honour.[31]

During the discussions/negotiations, the representatives of the victim's clan often make demands that the would-be-*Jaha* cannot accommodate, such as a prima facie agreement that the perpetrator's immediate family leave the village in perpetuity. When that happens, the dignitaries patiently explain that they are not authorized to discuss such issues until the Sulha process has started formally; they may, however, advise the family of the perpetrator to leave the village for the time being so as to give the victim's clan the sense that the *Jaha* is attuned to their agony and to forestall possible revenge attacks by grieving clan members.

The negotiations may take several hours, days or, at times, even weeks. If the process takes longer than a day or two the dignitaries may try to convince the representatives of the victim's clan to agree to the implementation of a temporary, informal truce to create the space required for the preliminary negotiations to conclude without further complications. To that end, the dignitaries invite the representatives of the victim's clan to honour them (the dignitaries) and grant them a temporary truce. If the victim's clan agrees, it wins praise and honour from the dignitaries for its noble consideration of the good of the community at large.

When the interveners succeed in recruiting the victim's clan to the Sulha, the clan's representatives must formally enlist in the process and – much like the perpetrator's clan – authorize the dignitaries to intervene on their behalf by countersigning the *Tafweeth* writ of authorization. At this point, the group of dignitaries formally becomes a Sulha Committee, or *Jaha* (referred to henceforth by the participants as '*al-Jaha al-Karim*' – The Respectable *Jaha*).[32]

The Sulha Committee

The task of transforming disputants' attitudes from a pure desire for revenge to readiness to adopt a nonbelligerent stance, to an eventual willingness to forgive, rests exclusively with the men of the Sulha Committee – the body of mediators/arbitrators entrusted by the disputants and the community to navigate this demanding transformative path.

Depending on the particulars of the case, the *Jaha* members use their experience; status; precedence; Islamic law; Islamic lore; current and former relations with and between the disputants; the economic, financial and political circumstances over which the dispute plays itself out; and the collective will of the community to mediate, arbitrate, discuss, coax, convince, cajole and sometimes coerce the disputing clans away from desire to avenge towards forgiveness – all through a constant effort to restore the victim's clan's sense of hurt honour.[33]

At the head of the Sulha Committee presides its most senior member – a man of reputation, experience and authority[34] – charged with managing its activities and steering both *Jaha* and disputant's clan members through the often-rocky road to an agreement. Much depends on the clout of the *Jaha* leader, and it is important that his credibility and credentials be impeccable and unassailable in the community.[35]

The *Jaha* draws its power and authority primarily from the status of the practice, as well as the status of its head and individual members within the community at large and the disputing clans in particular. In the words of Sheikh Ihye Abul Rani, head of the Sulha Committee of northern Israel's Arab community: 'If the disputants do not have total confidence in our honour and honesty, there cannot be a Sulha'.[36]

The makeup of the *Jaha* changes from case to case with the number of its members ranging from one to twenty, reflecting the complexity and probably also the importance of the dispute within the community. According to Khneifes, the goal of the interveners is to avoid creating a top-heavy committee that will be difficult to administer and steer, yet to include in it a number of members with the relevant experience, the connections with the disputing clans and the reputation within the community of reference.[37]

Assembling the *Jaha* for the nascent process may take several days, at times even a week or two; while the offender's and victim's clans are not allowed to dictate conditions for the operation of the *Jaha*, they have significant input regarding its makeup. For example, the disputants can veto the participation of individual *Jaha* members. The head of the Sulha Committee and the dignitaries make an effort to construct a *Jaha* that will be the most effective, in the sense that it will acceptable by all sides, as well as have the most potential influence on the disputants so as to increase the chances of bringing them to accept the (eventually) proposed agreement.

Determining the makeup of the Sulha Committee requires the interveners to present the disputants with the names of the proposed members. The committee head is always the titular (and sometimes functional) leader of the *Jaha*. The disputants are not allowed to contest his leadership because he represents the authority of the process, and without him the process loses its position in the eyes of the community.[38]

Regarding the rest of the committee members, the disputing clans can veto those of them whom they have a reason to suspect of being prejudicial to their case. For example, if a *Jaha* member had a commercial or personal conflict with a member of the disputants' clans (one or both), this is considered an acceptable reason for his exclusion from the committee. When that happens, the head of the *Jaha* assigns a new member, and the disputing clans have a chance to consider his credentials. In general, the committee head tries to assign to each dispute a mixed group of interveners from different towns and villages and different religions to ensure the engagement and commitment of the broadest community subset to both the process and its outcome.

Occasional complications can, and do, arise; for example, if a clan objects to too many proposed committee members, the process can drag on for a long time – something the *Jaha* members are loath to accept. This puts the dignitaries in a position where they are at the same time willing to accommodate the disputants but also unwilling to give them 'free rein' over the process. In the words of Sheikh Abu Riad Ali Shtewe: 'We are willing to accommodate [the disputants], but if things become complicated we tell them to stop the haggling and get the process moving before another murder takes place'.[39]

92 Sulha: structure and characteristics

To resolve such impasses, the dignitaries sometimes resort to aggressive, even coercive, arguments to persuade the disputants to accept the proposed line-up. Arguments in favour of accepting a dignitary's place in the *Jaha* range from descriptions of the man's dispute resolution exploits in the past and in similar cases, but can also extend to explaining to the objecting disputants that a rejected dignitary may resent their veto and hold a grudge against the clan.[40]

Allowing the disputing sides to participate in the determination of the *Jaha*'s makeup, and even giving them a limited veto power, has a functional as well as a psychological reason. It is yet another step in the habituation of the disputants into a reconciliation process and away from the revenge option. Regardless of their perceptions and sentiments at this stage of the process, by virtue of their involvement, the leaders of the disputing clans are actively engaged in taking action towards reconciliation and moving away from the tendency to 'stew in their own juices' of frustration, a place where contemplation of vengeful modes of honour restoration is more likely.

Conversely, the community at large, monitoring the process from the sidelines with great interest, receives another calming demonstration that the disputants are working towards forming the *Jaha*, increasing the stature of the disputants as they match wits with the dignitaries in order to accommodate the communal desire for progress toward reconciliation.

Stage 3: data analysis

To measure the perspectives of victim's clan interviewees after signing the *Tafweeth* and effectively starting the Sulha process, they were asked to respond to the following three statements:

- Immediately after signing the *Tafweeth*, you were very angry and wanted to take revenge.
- Immediately after signing the *Tafweeth*, you were willing to forgive the killer's clan.
- Immediately after signing the *Tafweeth*, you felt your clan's honour was hurt badly.

Table 4.3 and Figure 4.3 present the basic descriptive statistics derived from the aforementioned data.

Table 4.3 Stage 3: descriptive statistics – victim's clan

Median			Range			Average		
Revenge	Forgiveness	Honour	Revenge	Forgiveness	Honour	Revenge	Forgiveness	Honour
3.0	2.0	4.0	3.0	3.0	4.0	3.2	2.5	3.5

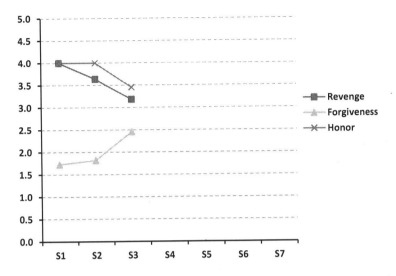

Figure 4.3 Stage 3: depicted averages – victim's clan

Discussion

The signing of the *Tafweeth* by the victim's clan is a watershed event in the life of the Sulha process. It signifies the full and formal incorporation of the disputants into the reconciliation process. In the words of one of the *Jaha* members:

> They don't know it, but once they sign the *Tafweeth*, they are committed to reconciliation; it may take a short time, or it may take a long time; it may be an easy one, or it may be a difficult and painful one – but a reconciliation it is.

The observed and measured changes in the perceptions of the victimized clan's representatives with respect to all three measured states may reflect the first transformative instance in the process. It may be that the clan's representatives, though still in the thick of the conflict, are starting to internalize the 'inevitable' direction of the process – forgiveness in lieu of revenge. This shift may be enabled by the measured reduction in the perception of hurt honour, the start of a restorative process, creating the foundations of self-confidence and trust (both in themselves and their community) that enable the gradual surrender of the need to use revenge as an honour-restoration measure, making place for forgiveness to become a player in the process.

Reconciliation is not yet achieved; it may still be a long, at times convoluted, road to a final agreement, but the disputants are visibly and formally on track, ready to take conciliation-making steps towards each other and towards the attending community – with the *Jaha*'s help and guidance.

PERCEPTION OF HURT SENSE OF HONOUR

The extensive honour-restoration effort exerted by the dignitaries in their attempt to bring the victim's clan to the Sulha process finally starts to show results, with about 54 per cent of interviewees indicating a sense of hurt honour, compared with 81 per cent at the earlier stage. In the words of an informant: 'The *Jaha* members really know how to make you feel better. They understand what we've gone through and do everything they can to help us get back on our feet'.[41]

Yet the shift in a direction of honour restoration is tentative at this stage, with a significant 27 per cent now expressing a neutral stance regarding the perception of hurt honour, demonstrating the start of a change; the same 18 per cent of the interviewees still hold to the more conciliatory posture, refusing to acknowledge their hurt honour. This is an interesting phenomenon that requires further studying. It may be that this group (those who from the start do not perceive their clan's honour to have been hurt) belong to the more 'liberal' or 'modern' part of the clan which would like to see a radical change in clan politics and a move away from a collective honour perception – with all that is entailed.

DESIRE FOR REVENGE

The signing of the *Tafweeth* by the victim's clan has an immediate impact on their perceived desire to avenge, which begins to weaken visibly. This is not surprising because the victim's clan, by signing the *Tafweeth*, has effectively embraced the Sulha-based solution of replacing revenge with forgiveness. Yet such a transformation is difficult to internalize and carry out to completion without the proper ritual so soon after the eruption of the conflict. In the words of one informant: 'It's a strange feeling; you're still burning to avenge the insult and pain, but you go along with the process, because you're not alone, and you have to think of your family, the village, the future generations'.[42]

The data show that 45 per cent of interviewees indicated that after signing the *Tafweeth* they were very angry and wanted to take revenge. This is a marked decline compared with 54 per cent who indicated a similar sentiment earlier in the process.

About 36 per cent of interviewees indicated disagreement with this sentiment, and 18 per cent expressed a neutral stance. These findings show the first significant change in attitudes on the part of the victim's clan, where for the first time more people are against revenge than for it.

WILLINGNESS TO FORGIVE

At this stage of the process, willingness to forgive is still a concept that is not expressed out in the open by the victim's clan, though in private many admit that they are fully cognizant of the direction the process they just signed on will take them. In the words of one informant:

> I'll tell you, if you sign the *Tafweeth*, you already know that you're going to forgive them someday, but you don't think or talk about it a lot, because the pain and humiliation are still too strong to even allow you to think about that.[43]

The collected data reflect this ambivalent attitude. About 54 per cent of interviewees disagreed with the statement that after they signed the *Tafweeth* they were willing to forgive the victim's clan. That is a marked decline from 72 per cent. About 27 per cent expressed neutrality regarding this statement, the same proportion measured in the earlier stage; but for the first time, 18 per cent of interviewees indicated agreement to forgive – the first appearance of such a sentiment.

Stage 4: atwa and hudna: *formalizing a truce*

With the *Tafweeth* signed by both disputing clans and the committee makeup agreed upon, the Sulha makers – now a formal *Jaha* – try to capitalize on the momentum and start a process that they hope will eventually lead to forgiveness and reconciliation.

However, in order to do this, the *Jaha* still has to complete another significant ritual – the payment of the Atwa (token of goodwill in Arabic), followed rapidly by the declaration of a formal truce (*hudna*) – often viewed as one ritual because, in the words of Faraj Khneifes, 'There is no Atwa without Hudna, and no Hudna without Atwa'.[44]

In the Atwa ritual, the interveners ask the offender's clan to deposit with them a monetary token of goodwill payment. This sum, usually amounting to about $2,000 (c. £1200) in cash, is supposed to serve a twin purpose: demonstrating in a symbolic and practical way the agreement of the perpetrator's clan to participate in earnest in the Sulha and its adherence to the rules of the process (including the binding arbitration clause) and indicating the offending clan's willingness to assume responsibility for its role in the dispute, thus getting it further habituated to its 'role' as the perpetrator side in the process.[45]

The *Jaha* then takes the Atwa money and brings it to the victimized clan's compound, where they offer it to the clan representatives. Sometimes, when the *Jaha* attempts to hand over the Atwa, the victim's clan declines the payment but accepts a Hudna without Atwa. This is called '*Honour Hudna*' or '*Honour Atwa*' (*Atwa Tsharaf*) – another honour-boosting act aimed at enhancing the victimized clan's sense of honour by giving it a chance to demonstrate magnanimity and disregard for material forms of intervention.

Although the *Jaha* considers such an arrangement less effective than a fully paid Atwa, it will allow it, should the victim's clan insist so as to help boost its dignity. In some cases, the committee declares an Honour Hudna for a week, after which the victim's clan accepts the cash Atwa.[46]

As soon as the victim's family takes the Atwa or declares an Atwa Tsharaf, a Hudna goes into effect.[47] As noted above, despite the two distinct terms and rituals, many Sulha makers see the Atwa and Hudna as one concatenated continuum demarcated only by a formalized sequence that predicates an Atwa before a Hudna.

In cases of murder, it is important for the *Jaha* to move fast and try to establish a Hudna before the victim's family has an opportunity to carry out or to attempt a blood revenge act of retaliation against a male member of the offender's family. Sulha practitioner Abu M'bada said that there are three days after a murder when it is impossible to set a Hudna because of what he termed 'boiling blood' – a period when anger and frustration preclude any possibility of a rational discussion or action.[48] But this was disputed partially by other Sulha Committee members, who explained that the three days were the traditional Muslim mourning period, during which discussing a Hudna is more difficult, and that in reality the *Jaha* often insists on achieving even a short-term Hudna before the *Hitme* (end of mourning period).[49]

With the Hudna in place, the disputants are on their way to a gradual journey of habituation towards the nonviolent option, a sort of a prelude to forgiveness (it is too early to talk about real forgiveness at this stage). Under the umbrella of the Hudna, the disputants' families can resume something close to normal lives, relieved from the pressure to consider defensive or offensive measures as a matter of daily concern. This reduces the tension, enhances the quality of life throughout the community and thus creates additional positive incentives to avoid revenge and a resumption of hostilities. Without the Hudna, the disputants remain steeped in the 'routine' of talking about revenge, sometimes actively planning a retaliatory attack, and their ability to experience firsthand the positive effects of nonbelligerence would be hindered.

Usually, the initial Hudna is set for a short period of three to six months, and when/if this Hudna expires before the completion of the Sulha process (which is quite likely), the *Jaha* requests extensions from both sides until a final Sulha agreement is reached.[50] The cumulative length of the Hudna(s) depends on the judgment of the *Jaha* and the sentiments of the disputants, and may last from several days to several years.

Thus, the Atwa and Hudna agreements mark another gradual shift in the course of the conflict as it moves from revenge to forgiveness, giving the victim's clan another opportunity to restore their damaged sense of honour. Hudna, for the purpose of the Sulha, may be looked at as a 'forgiveness training wheel'.

Stage 4: data analysis

To measure the perspectives of victim's clan interviewees after receipt of the Atwa and acceptance of a Hudna, they were asked to respond to the following three statements:

- After you agreed to the Atwa and Hudna, you felt you still wanted to take revenge.
- After you agreed to the Atwa and Hudna, you were willing to forgive the perpetrator's clan.
- After you agreed to the Atwa and Hudna, you still felt your clan's honour was hurt badly.

Table 4.4 and Figure 4.4 present the basic descriptive statistics derived from the aforementioned data.

Table 4.4 Stage 4: descriptive statistics – victim's clan

Median			Range			Average		
Revenge	Forgiveness	Honour	Revenge	Forgiveness	Honour	Revenge	Forgiveness	Honour
3.0	3.0	3.0	2.0	2.0	2.0	3.1	2.7	3.2

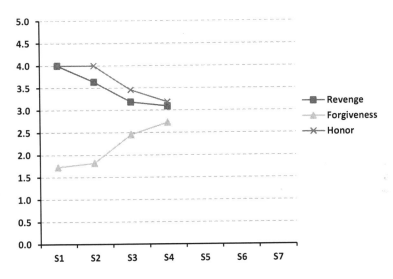

Figure 4.4 Stage 4: depicted averages – victim's clan

Discussion

The Atwa's acceptance by the victim's clan followed by the Hudna mark a major change in the attitude of the victim's clan both towards itself and towards the perpetrator's clan and the conflict. This is the first deliberately collaborative act for the two clans in the context of a reconciliation process (the perpetrators offer the Atwa, and the victims accept), and neither clan is blind to its significance. The stage is used to give the victim's clan another opportunity to buttress its recovering sense of honour by choosing the 'Honour Atwa' path. For the perpetrator's clan this stage symbolizes another step towards an assumption of responsibility as the culpable party in the process.

These rituals take place in private caucus, with only the *Jaha* and either victim or perpetrator clan's representatives present, yet they often involve substantial shows of emotion, with declaratory statements by the leaders of both clans echoed by repeating cries of acquiescence by the participants (*Jaha* and clan leaders).[51]

PERCEPTION OF HURT SENSE OF HONOUR

The effort to begin constructing an acceptable rationalization for the shift from the culturally sanctioned path of revenge towards the now almost inevitable forgiveness needs to be based on solid foundation of a restored sense of honour, and the words of one informant reflect this sentiment. He said (about his clan's agreement to accept the Atwa and Hudna): 'People kept telling us that we were doing the right, honourable thing, to agree to a Hudna'.[52]

The portion of interviewees indicating a persistent sense of hurt honour at this stage continues to decline and now stands at about 36 per cent. The majority of interviewees (about 45 per cent) are now 'parked' in the neutral zone reflecting a gradually restored sense of honour, but still lacking confidence in the reality or permanence of this restoration – a sort of cultural 'sulking'. The portion of interviewees that indicate no hurt honour remains constant at about 18 per cent.

DESIRE TO AVENGE

The acceptance of the Atwa, followed by the implementation of the Hudna, has an immediate impact on the perceived desire to avenge, which clearly begins to decline. Yet such a transformation is still difficult to accept for some of the victim's clan members, and they may look for rationalizations that will explain their progress along the Sulha path without forcing them (and the community) to view such progress as a weakness or a lessening of their retaliatory resolve. In the words of one informant: 'Sure we wanted revenge, but at the same time we felt we had no choice but to agree to a Hudna, or we would have insulted the *Jaha* and the entire community'.[53]

The data show that 36 per cent of the interviewees indicated that after receiving the Atwa and agreeing on a Hudna, they were very angry and wanted to take revenge. This is another marked decline compared with 54 per cent who indicated a similar sentiment in the previous stage of the process.

About 27 per cent of interviewees indicated disagreement with this sentiment, and 36 per cent expressed a neutral stance, marking a major shift to what may be looked at as a more ambivalent stance regarding revenge – not yet agreeing to remove revenge as a viable option but already committed (or reconciled) to the fact that an actual act of revenge may not materialize. These findings reveal the first significant change in attitudes on the part of the victim's clan.

WILLINGNESS TO FORGIVE

Willingness to forgive is not yet a publicly acknowledged sentiment with the victim's clan, but the data show that the realization is beginning to percolate, that the process is moving in this direction and that this may be a reasonably practical exit strategy from what appears so far as a bleak horizon of endless conflict. In the words of one informant: 'In my heart I didn't want to even think about forgiving them, but my head told me that we cannot go into another cycle of killings'.[54] Attempts at rationalization reflect this realization as expressed by another informant, who said: 'If we ever forgive them, it's going to be for the sake of our children, not theirs'.[55]

The collected data reflect a change towards greater ambivalence in that sentiment as well. About 45 per cent of interviewees disagreed with the statement that after accepting the Atwa and Hudna they were willing to forgive the victim's clan. This is a modest, yet visible, decline from 54 per cent. The neutral sector is growing consistently, now reflecting the sentiment of about 36 per cent of interviewees, while the same 18 per cent of interviewees indicated agreement to forgive.

Stage 5: Negotiations: determining culpability without dishonouring

Having succeeded in enfranchising the disputants publicly and formally to the transformative process and under the umbrella of the temporary truce, the *Jaha* is ready to begin moving the disputants the rest of the way to forgiveness and reconciliation.

The *Jaha*'s primary tool during this process is the private caucus, combined with liberal leveraging of honour-increasing moves. The committee members shuttle between disputants' representatives, interview witnesses and talk with just about anybody who they think may help them construct a successful conclusion.

There are two main reasons for the *Jaha*'s exclusive choice of a private caucus as the Sulha's main negotiating modality. The first is practical: the disputants' clans, despite the formal truce, are still emotionally and culturally committed to revenge and may be tempted to act if they find themselves in close physical proximity to the other side. Such an unfortunate event will surely scuttle the Sulha process, add significant complications to the dispute (by, among other things, adding another victim–perpetrator pair) and deal a severe blow to the honour of the *Jaha* by presenting the dignitaries as lacking social control and ability to guide the disputants. The second reason is that a private caucus allows the committee to reframe the disputants' narratives.[56]

Throughout the entire process, the *Jaha*'s goal is to nurture in the disputing clans a progressive sense of honorific added value in potential forgiveness, which will in due course lead to eventual reconciliation, and it creates this nurturing atmosphere through gestures and language. For example, the *Jaha* travels to the meeting place of the disputant's choice rather than inviting the disputants to appear before its members. This is a deliberate honouring mechanism using the reverse musayara approach whereby the dignitaries show excessive respect to those who, by cultural convention, should be honouring them.

This approach results in a reality in which the interveners find themselves on the road much of their time, travelling from village to town, spending hours on end, as well as considerable amounts of money. Some of the Sulha makers are well off; others have large families who support them and bask in the honour of having a *Jaha* member as part of the clan. Yet other *Jaha* members are retired and spend much of their limited income, and nearly all of their time, on facilitating reconciliation.

During these private caucus sessions the interveners behave like facilitators whose role is to ensure that a respectable resolution is crafted and presented to all involved. They listen very attentively as the disputing sides describe, often repeatedly and in excruciating detail, the injustice and damage to honour that were inflicted on them or that drove their clan member to behave violently. The *Jaha* members shy away from making harsh judgements or from engaging in extended arguments with the disputant representatives; they rarely raise their voice, and when they do so it is often a calculated behaviour designed to help facilitate movement, where they judge that the disputants are frozen in their positions and need a robust prodding.[57]

Yet these sometimes demure and attentive *Jaha* members gently but constantly remind the disputants of the social and personal cost of failing to agree, notably a continued threat of instability and violence to the affected community, accompanied by a significant loss of face to all – disputants and interveners alike. Gradually the disputants start to internalize the new 'menu' of options that is on offer through the process: revenge as 'instant gratification' leading to a possible restoration of honour but incurring a huge offence to all involved and leading to certain social displeasure and disapproval by the entire community (and the influential dignitaries of the *Jaha*), as opposed to forgiveness as the 'honourable' and religiously approved thing to do, hugely increasing the appreciation of all involved towards the forgiving side and enthusiastically supported by both community and dignitaries.[58]

Despite the fact that in order to start the Sulha process one side has to basically assume culpability (when it invites the Sulha committee to intervene on its behalf) and the other is marked as the victim (when it agrees to participate in the Sulha process), the committee is still charged with determining the level of guilt, magnitude of culpability and consequent liability and responsibility. These will be used later in the determination of the terms of the Sulha agreement, and within it the size of the compensatory payments (in the case of murder, such payment is called *Diya*).

There is no hard and fast rule about who the *Jaha* talks to first as it starts the shuttling process, but in line with its general attitude designed to gradually buttress the bruised sense of honour of the victim's family, it usually starts with them, demonstrating empathy and compassion, boosting the victim's sense of honour and getting the rival clan accustomed to its position as the offending side.

During the deliberations with each side, the *Jaha* members continuously describe to the disputants similar events from the past, providing detailed descriptions of the evolution of former disputes and their consequent resolution. Throughout these interactions, the committee always stresses that the traditional, obviously preferred direction was in the past, and by implication should be in this case as well, away from revenge and towards eventual forgiveness and reconciliation. The intended implication of this narration is to clarify to the disputants that moving the Sulha process forward will result in their attaining levels of honour and respect similar to those achieved by their 'predecessors'.

This repetitive narration of past Sulha stories is also designed to establish both a precedence and common ground and parameters of discussion.[59] Most of the information delivered during these exchanges comes from the collective memory of the *Jaha* members and their experiences over the years. This verbal repository of precedents is the *Jaha*'s main source of knowledge, and the members take great pride in their ability to recount and analyze many complex past Sulha stories.

One such example is the case of Faraj Khneifes, whose father, Sheikh Saleh Khneifes, was the head of northern Israel's Sulha Committee for the better part of thirty years. Serving for about fifteen years as his father's escort and driver, Faraj got to sit in during the committee's deliberations (without the right to contribute) and to listen and absorb the precedents and narratives of earlier generations. Faraj now constantly relies on and refers to this accumulated knowledge in his capacity as a member of the Sulha Committee.[60]

Having met with one disputant's group, the *Jaha* moves on to the preferred meeting place of the other group.[61] During these meetings its members use a variety of mediation tools to help restore (or maintain) the disputants' sense of honour and to steer them towards choosing forgiveness as the preferred option to restore their honour (in place of revenge).

One such mediating tool used extensively by the *Jaha* is reframing. In order to smooth out or skirt around honour-hurting, abusive and angry statements; aggressive gestures; and abusive utterances made by one side, committee members routinely isolate and highlight positive and/or conciliatory statements made by disputants to reinforce an increasing atmosphere of conflict resolution, while completely ignoring and avoiding any mention of the negative statements. For example, if one group describes historically good relations with earlier generations of the disputant's clan while arguing that the current generation lacks the social skills, the sense of honour and the willingness to behave like their predecessors, the members of the *Jaha* will most likely retell the story to the other side as an expression of respect by the disputing clan towards the shared history and the founding elders of the clan. The *Jaha* will use the narration of past amicable relations as proof of an existing history of peaceful collaboration between the clans, evidence that there exists a foundation of goodwill between the disputing clans and that this foundation could and should serve as a platform for the reconstruction of a future reconciliation agreement.[62]

Another tool that the *Jaha* uses extensively at this stage, and that is also used at times in Western ADR, is evaluating.[63] This practice consists of periodically highlighting to the disputants in vivid colours the advantages of reaching an agreed settlement, as opposed to the obvious disadvantages and dangers associated with a failure to reach such a solution. This mix of aggressive interventionist activism interspersed with gentle, modest posturing by the *Jaha* is designed to leverage all possible approaches: active and passive, gentle and harsh.

This shuttling process may take as little as a day and one meeting with each party or as long as several years and dozens of meetings with each side; it may consist only of meetings with the disputing clans or may include multiple meetings with witnesses, experts and any other party interested in contributing to the process. Often the *Jaha* meets with local religious leaders to brief them on the state of the dispute and to solicit from them advice regarding possible paths to reconciliation. Such meetings contribute to the process by increasing the clout of the local leaders, recruiting them as advocates for the ongoing Sulha process while at the same time enlisting them as possible leverage points on the disputants.

The main purpose of the negotiation stage is to help restore the sense of honour of the victim's clan by a process of consultation, active listening, effusive expressions of empathy and sympathy and a general effort to make the members of the

102   Sulha: structure and characteristics

victim's clan feel that their pain and sense of damaged honour are being attended to at the highest possible levels.[64]

At the same time, the *Jaha* has to ensure that the attention lavished on the victim's clan does not cause the perpetrator's clan to feel rejected or vilified by either the community or the dignitaries. To that end, *Jaha* members spend considerable time listening to members of the perpetrator's clan describe how their relative was provoked into an anfractuous, often violent, behaviour.

The disputants constantly try to bargain with the *Jaha*. This is not prohibited, takes place routinely and is expected by all parties involved, yet it is done discretely and behind the closed doors of the private caucus because, according to Sulha makers, it is necessary to maintain the appearance of continuity and progress; for if the community gets the impression that the process is stuck and that the disputants are not 'listening' to the *Jaha*, this may result in a significant loss of face to the *Jaha* members as individuals and to the committee as an institution, and all parties would like to avoid such a situation.[65]

Stage 5: data analysis

To measure the perspectives of victim's clan interviewees as the *Jaha* proceeds through the negotiation ritual, they were asked to respond to the following three statements:

- After meeting the *Jaha* several times, you felt you still wanted to take revenge.
- After meeting the *Jaha* several times, you were willing to forgive the perpetrator's clan.
- After meeting the *Jaha* several times, you still felt your clan's honour was hurt badly.

Table 4.5 and Figure 4.5 present the basic descriptive statistics derived from the aforementioned data.

Discussion

The negotiation part of the Sulha process provides both the space required for a shift in perceptions and perspectives and the vehicle needed to affect such a change. Sulha practitioners repeatedly reinforce the virtues of patience as they

Table 4.5 Stage 5: descriptive statistics – victim's clan

Median			Range			Average		
Revenge	Forgiveness	Honour	Revenge	Forgiveness	Honour	Revenge	Forgiveness	Honour
3.0	3.0	3.0	3.0	2.0	3.0	2.5	2.8	2.9

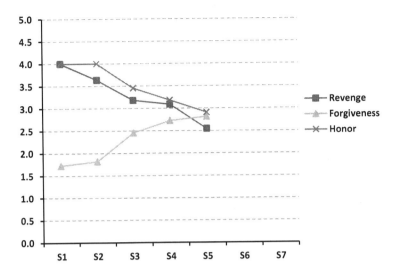

Figure 4.5 Stage 5: depicted averages – victim's clan

continue to prime[66] the disputing clans with reconciliation-promoting sentiments and examples.

Although the process may be fraught with crises and at times appear intractably stuck, the interveners continue to make their case for reconciliation, confident for the most part in their ability to succeed. In the words of Faraj Khneifes: 'Although sometimes it [the Sulha process] seems hopelessly stuck and even deteriorating back towards conflict, we have been there so many times, we know we will succeed in the end; we will resolve the conflict – but it will take a lot of patience'.[67]

PERCEPTION OF HURT SENSE OF HONOUR

At this stage in the process, the sense of hurt honour, while still evident with the victim's clan, is starting to show signs of a real shift. The combined restorative and supportive effort of both the *Jaha* and the community is beginning to have an impact. In the words of one informant: 'The *Jaha* really make you feel special'. Another informant commented about the support of the community and the sense of relief expressed when the victim's clan agreed to extend the Hudna.[68] In his words: 'People in the village were very relieved and grateful for the renewed Hudna, and we felt it's the right thing to do for everybody's sake'.[69] It seems that the cultural 'exchange' mechanism at this stage includes the victim's clan's increased sense of honour through the community's gratitude for the promise of continued cessation of hostilities. The community gets what it wants and needs – peace of mind – and the victim's clan gets what it needs – a restoration of its sense of honour by the community and the *Jaha*.

One cannot expect the shift from a sense of humiliation to a sense of restored honour to be immediate – it is reasonable to expect a gradual shift; and indeed, the data show that a solid majority of interviewees (about 63 per cent) are holding a neutral stance at this stage. The portion of interviewees who still feel that their clan's honour was hurt declines from about 36 per cent to some 18 per cent, whereas the portion of interviewees who do not view their clan's honour as damaged remains at about 18 per cent.

The direction and observed changes in all variables exhibit the characteristics predicted by RHC.

DESIRE FOR REVENGE

Indeed, the data show that the negotiation sessions have an impact on the perceptions of the victim's clan members regarding their approach to the dispute. Specifically, there is a marked decrease in the desire to avenge. Only some 9 per cent of interviewees indicated that after several negotiation sessions with the *Jaha* they were still very angry and wanted to take revenge.

About 45 per cent of interviewees reported a neutral stance towards the revenge sentiment at this stage, demonstrating yet again a significant shift from the decisive desire to avenge to a decidedly ambivalent state of mind. About 45 per cent of interviewees expressed disagreement with the desire to avenge, yet again indicating a strong distancing from that particular sentiment.

One of the informants provided the following explanation in an attempt to try to rationalize the shift in the desire to avenge. He said: 'They [the killer's family] moved out of town, so we did not see them all the time and could start thinking rationally'.[70]

WILLINGNESS TO FORGIVE

The willingness to forgive develops at a slower pace, 'lagging' as it were behind the change in the desire to avenge and the gradually restored sense of honour. In the words of one informant: 'I guess, as time passes, and life goes back to something like normal, you start understanding that maybe at some point you will be able to forgive them, but not now!'[71]

Apparently, affecting a change in the victim's clan's willingness to forgive requires significant work by the *Jaha*. But the change, though modest, is evident in the transition of about 9 per cent of interviewees from a disagreement with a statement regarding their willingness to forgive to a neutral stance. At this stage of the process, about 45 per cent of interviewees indicate a sense of neutrality: they are neither willing to forgive nor refusing to consider the option; this shift is attributed solely to a change of attitude from a refusal to forgive to a neutral stance. The proportion of those already willing to forgive remains similar to that of the earlier stage, at about 18 per cent, whereas a solid 36 per cent of interviewees still refused to consider forgiveness.

Stage 6: The Sulha agreement

Deciding the verdict

After listening to all involved parties, interviewing witnesses, visiting the site(s) of the event(s) and discussing all the issues among themselves, the *Jaha* decides a verdict, which it then puts down in writing.

The final verdict is discussed and crafted in total seclusion. Leading the process is the head of the *Jaha*, who asks committee members to speak and then synthesizes the necessary insights and formulates the evolving verdict. The basic building blocks of every Sulha verdict are earlier verdicts – precedents. Essentially, Sulha practitioners are human repositories of conflict and conflict resolution narratives. With each new conflict they try to resolve, they reach back and search for similar conflicts in the past, attempt to identify relevant precedents, examine their suitability to the conflict at hand and when they determine that a precedent provides the necessary response to a part of the current conflict, they 'mark' it (usually in memory alone, through discussion) and continue examining the next part of the conflict, comparing the next stage to known precedents and looking for similar or identical narratives.

When the entire conflict story is described through segments of precedents, each providing a solution to a relevant part, the Sulha makers know that they have a solution in hand. In the words of one Sulha maker:

> Not every conflict is the same, but many conflicts have similar stories and we use these to teach us what to do. For example, if a man was murdered in an argument over money, we look at past cases of arguments over money, or if we have a case where a woman was murdered by her husband, we discuss past cases of wife murders, and we find similar cases. From the verdicts in those past cases, we know what 'our' verdict should be. People don't change, conflicts don't change, and verdicts don't change.[72]

If there is a disagreement between Sulha practitioners about the suitability of a specific precedent segment, the *Jaha* leader calls for a vote. A simple majority suffices, but in most cases, the discussion continues until a large majority or a unanimous agreement is reached.[73]

Once the *Jaha* members agree on all the precedential components that are necessary to fashion a complete solution to the conflict at hand, there is no need to continue the discussion – a decision has been reached and it will be presented to the disputants as the unanimous decision of the *Jaha*.[74]

Confidentiality in these internal deliberations is crucial in such circumstances, primarily to avoid 'post factum' pressures and possible demonstrations of belligerency against members of the *Jaha* whose opinions and/or voting records may not have suited one or both disputants.[75]

The Sulha agreement concretizes and acknowledges the transformation of the victim's clan from a desire to avenge to a willingness to forgive. This transformation takes place mostly in the privacy of the disputants' deliberations with the *Jaha*, but the interveners are working towards a point in time where they feel that they can bring the revised attitudes of the disputants, as expressed in the Sulha agreement, to the public domain, where they strive to both receive public, quasi-official approval, endorsing the transformation on behalf of the entire community, and at the same time assure the community that the conflict is over. As Faraj Khneifes put it:

> The community is quite anxious to know that the situation has calmed down and there is no more risk of retaliations and more violence; the disputants very much need to hear the community telling them they did the right thing.[76]

Sulha verdicts usually include two parts: monetary and nonmonetary. This is in line with the basic elements of the Sulha, which are rights and honour. The honour part includes a formal assignment of guilt and liability, and the rights part includes the monetary and other considerations.

As noted earlier, in murder cases the monetary aspect of a Sulha agreement is called *Diya* (blood money), a determined compensation payment from the offender's clan to the victim's clan. In all other cases, the monetary part of the verdict is called *Taawir* (compensation).

Each geographic region in Israel (and also across the Middle East) has a *Diya/Taawir* 'menu' or 'price list' which determines the general amount of the compensation that would be considered proper. For example, in the north of Israel the *Diya* for a dead man is about 300,000 New Israeli Shekels (c. £55,000). In the centre and south of Israel, the *Diya* for a similar infraction may be about 250,000 New Israeli Shekels (c. £45,000). Similarly, there is a 'price list' for different levels of physical disability (*Taawir*), such as loss of limb, loss of mobility or loss of working ability.[77] Like everything else in Sulha, this is not a formal 'menu', and it is kept in the heads of Sulha makers.

The *Jaha* has a number of tools that allow it to modify the *Diya* and revise its size so as to fit the particular characteristics of each specific event and the economic realities of the disputants, as well as to accommodate other factors.[78] To that end, the *Jaha* recognizes three different levels of *Diya* depending on the severity of the offence and its resulting damage to the victim:

- *Diya (regular):* This is the 'standard' payment level for the type of offence at a given point in time.
- *Diya Mechafafa (Reduced Diya):* This is the traditional amount of blood money allotted to women.[79] Additionally, this reduced level of *Diya* is set in cases where there are extenuating circumstances, such as proof of extended aggravation or self-defence. The general level of compensation in this case is about half the standard *Diya* sum.
- *Diya Mezaraafe (Doubled Diya, sometimes also called Diya Mor'azala – 'double diameter' – alluding to the size of a tree branch or trunk):* This is an increased (sometimes doubled) *Diya* designed to compensate for particularly

offensive crimes, such as the killing of a pregnant woman, or for cases where extreme cruelty was exercised in the commission of the offense.

If the crime did not result in permanent handicap, the Sulha committee can determine that no or little *Taawir* will be paid. If the crime resulted in a physical handicap, the *Jaha*, occasionally, consults with professional experts (e.g. medical professionals) to determine the severity and impact of the handicap and uses such testimony to determine the consequent size of the *Taawir* – this in addition to heavy reliance on precedence.

When the *Jaha* members feel that they have assembled all the relevant parts of a solution, and with a draft solution in hand, they initiate a round of discussions with the disputing sides. Ostensibly, the determination of the verdict does not require the disputants' agreement and is given to the discretion of the Sulha Committee members who are playing the role of arbitrators by deciding the verdict and reporting it to the disputing parties. But the purpose of the verdict is to leverage the disputants' evolving and hopefully growing self-confidence and sense of honour towards a greater disposition to forgiveness and reconciliation, and to this end the verdict has to avoid aggravating any party or causing anyone to feel picked upon, singled out or overly burdened with a disproportional part of the guilt (and consequent 'punishment', with its accompanying loss of honour).

So, the members of the Sulha Committee also act as mediators; they present the evolving verdict to the disputants in separate private caucus sessions and solicit their support for it before it is cast in stone and declared a formal verdict. Every effort is made to avoid unfortunate reversals and relapses at this delicate and advanced stage of the process. In the words of *Jaha* member M'bada Naum (Abu M'bada):

> We don't want the sides to feel that we are punishing them more than they deserve, or that we are ignoring their arguments; we want them to feel that justice and honour walk together hand in hand within our verdict.[80]

The Sulha verdict along with its accompanying *Diya/Taawir* are binding on all sides to the dispute, and if one party refuses to accept it, the Sulha process effectively collapses, resulting in a grave loss of honour to the side that rejected the agreement and in a severe infraction of the traditional rules of the Sulha, together with an insult to the members of the *Jaha*. In rare cases, the disputants who reject a verdict may also lose the Atwa bond that they deposited when the Sulha process began as an indication of their willingness to abide by the *Jaha*'s verdict. In the words of Sheikh Rani: 'Even though we can, we never force the clans to accept the *Jaha*'s verdict against their will; it has to come from their hearts, otherwise it will not hold'.[81]

Still, despite its mediating posture, at this stage the *Jaha* sometimes exerts significant pressure on hesitating or reluctant clans, using extensive evaluative presentations, describing to the clan representatives in vivid colours what might happen if the Sulha process freezes or collapses.

Occasionally, the representatives of the victim's clan protest that the determined *Diya* is insufficient. In one case, the *Jaha* sat for six hours with the victim's clan, extolling them to accept the proposed *Diya* amount, explaining that the perpetrator's clan would not be able to raise more money and that it took weeks of pressure to get them to collect the proposed sum to begin with.[82]

Once the committee gets the impression that both disputing clans can and will abide by the determined verdict, they stop all shuttling and discussion activity and their verdict receives formal expression within the Sulha agreement, which is written by one of the *Jaha* members and is approved by all members.

The Sulha agreement

The Sulha agreement has both a formal and a symbolic meaning, and both are leveraged in support of the ultimate goal of restoration (enhancement where possible) of honour and of forgiveness (individual and communal). Its composition tries to balance the disputants' need to see both justice done and honour preserved and even enhanced with the community's need to see the dispute transcended so life in the community can proceed with a reasonable assurance of safety and harmony.

The Sulha agreement details the conditions under which the reconciliation takes place. It settles for the record (historical and formal) essential questions such as: Who is guilty, of what, and to what extent? Who pays whom and how much? When is payment to be made and in what currency? What other sanctions or steps accompany the agreement?

The Sulha agreement is considered binding, mainly because it has been hammered out by people of significant clout within the community, but also because the disputants know that their honour will greatly suffer if it is rejected; they may also feel that they must respect the Tafweeth (authorization) they gave the *Jaha* at the beginning of the process, and the perpetrator's clan may also loath the possible loss of the Atwa money.[83] From this perspective, the agreement appears to be more of an arbitration agreement, although, as we have seen, the process that brings it about includes elements of both mediation and arbitration. Copies of the written agreement are handed to the disputants' representatives at the end of the Sulha ceremony; they will be kept by the disputants and by the *Jaha* and will be referred to in the event of a dispute regarding the implementation of the agreement.[84]

When all elements of the proposed settlement are agreed upon, the *Jaha* sets a date for the Sulha ceremony; it also decides the exact place, the list of participants from each disputant's group and the list of invited community dignitaries. The dignitaries are invited to lend moral support and a seal of communal approval to the agreement.[85]

If a person was killed, the family of the victim has the right to determine the place of the ceremony. Also, if the Sulha is over a death, the agreement includes a specific ritual designed to officially mark the end of hostility and conflict between the disputant families.[86]

Stage 6: data analysis

To measure the perspectives of victim's clan interviewees as the *Jaha* formalized the Sulha agreement, they were asked to respond to the following three statements:

- After reaching a Sulha agreement, you felt you still wanted to take revenge.
- After reaching a Sulha agreement, you were willing to forgive the perpetrator's clan.
- After reaching a Sulha agreement, you still felt your clan's honour was hurt badly.

Table 4.6 and Figure 4.6 present the basic descriptive statistics derived from the aforementioned data.

Discussion

At this stage in the reconciliation process, the disputants have largely gotten used to the fact that their feud will be resolved through forgiveness rather than revenge. They actually feel pretty magnanimous and are 'pumped up' with

Table 4.6 Stage 6: descriptive statistics – victim's clan

Median			Range			Average		
Revenge	Forgiveness	Honour	Revenge	Forgiveness	Honour	Revenge	Forgiveness	Honour
2.0	3.0	2.0	2.0	3.0	2.0	2.2	3.5	2.2

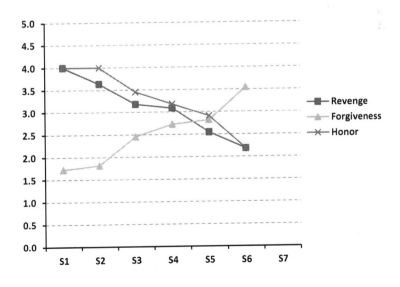

Figure 4.6 Stage 6: depicted averages – victim's clan

110 Sulha: structure and characteristics

honour-restoring and honour-sustaining gestures. They are ready for the final act: public forgiveness.

There is still reluctance by the disputants (particularly the victim's side) to talk openly about restored or preserved honour, probably because the feeling that if the Sulha process collapses or freezes at this stage a premature discussion of honour restoration will lead to a significant loss of face for the disputants.

But there is also very little talk about humiliation and loss of honour; the framework of the agreement responds to the major concerns raised by the victim's clan, though in most cases they do not get everything they wanted – notably the demand for the perpetual exiling of the offending clan. Yet although this demand isn't usually met, interim steps, such as several years of exile for the killer's immediate family, do routinely get incorporated into the agreement following extended discussion and negotiations between the *Jaha* and the two sides.

PERCEPTION OF HURT SENSE OF HONOUR

The shift towards a different perception of the victim's clan's state of honour appears to accelerate. About 72 per cent of interviewees stopped seeing their honour as hurt at this stage. About 27 per cent were still neutral (hesitating, uncertain), whereas none of the interviewees indicated an enduring sense of hurt honour.

As far as the victim's clan is concerned, the data indicate readiness to reconcile (in this case, go through the Sulha ceremony). In the words of one of the interviewees: 'At that point, we felt that finishing with all this is the only honourable thing to do'.[87]

DESIRE TO AVENGE

At this advanced stage of the process most of the victim's clan interviewees indicated a real distancing from a desire to avenge. The most striking sign of this transformation is demonstrated by the fact that none of the interviewees indicated at this stage that, with the Sulha agreement signed and sealed, they were still very angry and wanted to take revenge.

The portion of interviewees still holding a neutral stance has shrunk to about 27 per cent, exhibiting a significant shift away from the same sentiment expressed in stage 5 (about 45 per cent). At the same time, a large majority, about 72 per cent of the interviewees, expressed disagreement with the desire to avenge – signalling a major shift away from revenge. The revenge option may have finally left the table. In the words of one informant: 'I guess we'll not really avenge our loss. It'll just start a whole new cycle of horrible things'.[88]

WILLINGNESS TO FORGIVE

The proportion of interviewees indicating a willingness to forgive at this stage has more than doubled, from about 18 per cent to some 45 per cent. Yet the proportion of interviewees still undecided (expressing a sense of neutrality) remains at about

45 per cent. The transition is apparently from disagreement to agreement, from about 36 per cent who expressed disagreement with the thought of forgiving during stage 5, to just about 9 per cent remaining with this perception at this stage. This may reflect the passage of time, 'negotiation fatigue' or other reasons, but clearly merits further examination.

A clue to the rather confusing data at this stage may be found in the words of one of the interviewees:

> Now that we decided to forgive them we had to convince everybody in our clan that this is the best solution. The hardest [effort] to convince was his mother [the victim's mother]. It took us weeks to convince her that it is time to move on and that there is no moving forward without forgiveness. I don't think she'll ever really forgive, but she understands that this is best for the family.[89]

Stage 7: the Sulha ceremony: formalizing forgiveness

The Sulha ceremony formalizes the transformation from a desire to avenge to a willingness to forgive – in public and with the active endorsement of the community; local, regional and at times even state officials; and multiple dignitaries. The Sulha ceremony is rife with ritualistic and symbolic acts, gestures and protocols, providing the *Jaha* and the disputants with many honour-enhancing opportunities.

The ceremony binds together an elaborate set of related subrituals, which include the pre-ceremony preparations, the ceremony itself and a set of post-ceremony acts. All three elements are designed to build in the disputants and the community alike a critical mass of personal and communal commitment and goodwill that will hopefully help launch and secure the budding reconciliation.

Before the ceremony

The pre-ceremony ritual focuses primarily on the victim's clan. Now, after all the listening, discussions, negotiations, cajoling, coercing, reframing and other acts designed to build up the victim's clan's sense of honour, confidence and respect, it is essentially up to them to initiate and enable the practical act of forgiveness and conciliation out of their own free will (of course, with the help and accompaniment of the *Jaha* and other dignitaries).

To that end, on the ceremony's day, at an agreed time, the entire *Jaha* travels to the home of the victim's clan where they form a line in front of the residence awaiting the victim's family's representatives. When these appear, the Sulha makers greet them, thanking them for their honour and bravery in taking the last courageous step towards healing their painful wound.[90]

The leader of the *Jaha* then produces the yet disassembled parts of the *Rayah* – the Sulha flag. The *Rayah* will be used to provide security to the perpetrator's clan on its way to the Sulha ceremony. This rudimentary flag consists at this point of a simple wooden pole and a white linen sheet. The Sulha leader invites the most senior representative of the victim's family to tie the first knot, connecting the linen sheet to the wooden pole and thus creating the Sulha flag. This is a delicate moment in the proceedings because it is the first real test of the victim's family's actual willingness to go beyond declarations and carry out the act of reconciliation.

The *Rayah* flag is a curious cross between the universally acknowledged white flag of surrender – a distinct honour-reducing symbol (for the perpetrator's clan) and a demonstration of the offence-cleansing powers of the Sulha. Lang quotes a *Jaha* member, saying that '[t]he *rayah* is white and clean . . . the *rayah* has no spots – as if to show that the problem has been cleansed'.[91] This plurality of roles reflects the delicate dance that the *Jaha* performs throughout the Sulha process in its attempt to create the proper space for forgiveness by the victim's clan while at the same time avoiding acts that will damage the honour perception of the perpetrator's clan, thus causing them to resent the process.

The ritual of tying the first knot at the compound of the victim's clan embodies two distinct honour-related elements. The first is expressed in the *Jaha*'s invitation of the victim's clan to start the final forgiveness and reconciliation process, allowing them to gain additional honour by displaying magnanimity and concern for the general safety and welfare of the community at large.

The second, slightly masked, element is that in order to protect the honour of the *Jaha*, as well as that of the victim's family, this preliminary but essential ritual takes place in the privacy of the victim's compound, away from the eyes and ears of the community. This is to ensure that possible last-minute problems, such as outbursts by members of the victim's clan, hesitation or even outright refusal to tie the knot, will not affect the honour of the Sulha Committee or that of the disputants, as the damaging incidents would not have taken place in full public view. Furthermore, lack of publicity will give the dignitaries an opportunity to try to quietly repair the damage and put the process back on track.[92]

Having secured the victimized family's willingness to grant the offender's family safe passage to the Sulha ceremony under the *Rayah* flag, the retinue of *Jaha* members and local dignitaries proceeds to the home or gathering place of the offender's clan (at this point, still, far away from the victim's clan). A senior *Jaha* member hands over the *Rayah* to the leader of the perpetrator's clan, and a procession, including the perpetrator's clan leadership, dignitaries and *Jaha* members, forms behind the *Jaha* leader and the bearer of the *Rayah*. The procession then walks slowly towards the area selected (usually by the victim's family) as the site of the Sulha ceremony.

While the perpetrator's clan's procession forms up and slowly makes its way to the ceremony site, the victim's family's representatives arrive at the site and arrange themselves in a reception line. This will be the first time since the eruption of the conflict that the two disputing clans will face each other physically at close proximity.

The Sulha ceremony

The Sulha ceremony is the point when the process moves to the public domain and acquires a more pronounced communal character. It is no longer a ritual of conciliation between two clans, but rather between two elements of the same community, taking place under the sponsorship of the entire community.

The ceremony consists of three core rituals:

Musafacha: (public hand shaking): This is the first display of reconciliation between the families of the offender and the victim. In most conflicts, this is the first time that the disputing clans face each other at close proximity, and thus it is a real test of self-control, particularly for the victim's clan. Sulha makers dread this moment because of its potential volatility and therefore surround the disputants at the ceremony, helping to ease the sometimes awkward first encounters while constantly watching for signs of erupting tensions or even attempts to take revenge.[93]

If the killer's father and the victim's father are available, they shake hands first, leading their clans and providing the first tangible proof of the anticipated reconciliation. This is an act rife with emotion and eagerly watched over by the community. One by one, behind the *Rayah* flag, the representatives of the offending family walk past the reception line of the victimized family, shaking hands, exchanging sombre words of mutual consolation, encouragement and hope for a better future.

Having shaken hands and hopefully soothed each other's emotions with expressions of goodwill and reconciliation, the two clans move to the site of the final ceremony. The site, a large hall or an outdoor gathering place, is at this point populated by many men from the affected and neighbouring communities, laypersons and dignitaries (i.e. village heads, local religious leaders, leading businessmen, representatives of the police, members of parliament). Women are not allowed into the compound itself, but in many cases they throng the perimeter and witness the ceremony with much excitement mixed with occasional outbursts of either joy or agony.

Mushamacha (a declaration of forgiveness): Having successfully passed the first public ritual of the ceremony, the representatives of the victim's clan take their place behind a long table facing the gathered community, accompanied by members of the *Jaha*. The representatives of the perpetrator's clan sit in the front row, also flanked by *Jaha* members as well as the many dignitaries attending the ceremony.

The *Jaha* leader now reads the Sulha agreement. This is usually a fairly compact document outlining the infraction in general terms, recounting the sorrow of the offender's family, the suffering of the victim's family, the general terms of the verdict (monetary and otherwise) and an assertion that this agreement holds true for all members of the disputants' clans, past, present and future.

If the agreement includes the levying of a *Diya*, this is the time for the transfer of the funds. Representatives of the offending family approach the table and hand over the blood money, always in cash, to the most senior representatives of the victim's family.

This is one of the most emotional moments of the ceremony. The chosen victim's clan representative, having accepted the *Diya*, usually says a few words about the victim, extols the virtue of forgiveness as opposed to revenge and unambiguously declares that the offender and his clan are all forgiven.

This act of public forgiveness by the victim's clan is the true core of the Sulha ceremony. It is the functional enabler of reconciliation and is designed to maximize the honorific 'return on emotional investment' for the victim's family.

In some cases, the victim's family uses this part of the ceremony to further enhance their honour by handing the *Diya* back to the offender's family – in full view of the community. This is usually accompanied by an explanation that no money in the world will bring the victim back or undo the wrong and that the victim's family does not need the actual money as proof of goodwill, only the willingness to give it. Such a gesture is usually greeted with general approbation and applause by the gathered congregation.[94]

After the *Diya* is handed over and either accepted or returned, the senior member of the perpetrator's clan takes the podium and delivers an apology on behalf of his entire clan, extolling the virtues of reconciliation and expressing a hope for a brighter, conflict-free future.

This is a somewhat inverted process, where the declaration of forgiveness by the victim's clan precedes the expression of regret by the perpetrator's clan. The reason for this sequence is apparently anchored in the need to maintain the honour of the perpetrator's clan. Having handed over the *Diya*, the clan wants to witness firsthand a declaration of forgiveness by the victim's clan. Buoyed and reassured by the public forgiveness, they then feel that they can deliver an apology without losing their honour in doing so.[95]

With the public offering of the *Diya*, its public expression of regret, its apology and its unreserved acceptance of culpability and responsibility, the perpetrator's clan wins the community's respect and gets to maintain its perception of honour because it is seen as having agreed to put the interest of the community (resolving the dispute) before its own interest.

For its part, with the public acceptance of the *Diya*, the victim's clan expresses its final incorporation into the reconciliation process, its magnanimity in the face of a grievous injury to its person and honour and its willingness to let bygones be bygones – again, for the sake of the broader community.

Zero-sum arrangements are unthinkable in this context. In the words of Raymond Cohen: 'The appropriate response to the plea for pardon from the injured party, now in a position of moral superiority, is a magnanimous grant of forgiveness'.[96]

Having dealt with the monetary part of the ritual, and having successfully passed the delicate rituals of public apology and forgiveness, it is time for the disputants, the interveners and the attending dignitaries to sign the Sulha agreement in front of the community. This is usually an extended ritual because there are often multiple signatories to the agreement (sometimes more than twenty). This act serves a dual purpose: demonstrating the level of communal commitment to achieving and maintaining the Sulha, and constituting a public warning to the disputants – masked but universally understood – that should the idea of breaking the agreement ever cross their minds, they ought to remember that, by doing so, they would be causing a substantial loss of honour to many community, civic, governmental and religious leaders: an offence that is not likely to be taken without ramifications. In the words of Abu M'bada: 'They [the disputants] will think long and hard before they offend so many people in the community by backing out of the agreement'.[97]

Each signatory accompanies the signing of the Sulha agreement with a symbolic tying of a knot in the *Rayah* flag. As the process continues, the white sheet of the *Rayah* is gradually transformed into a line of knots around the flag's pole – a visual depiction of the transformation of the conflict as embodied by the flag of surrender into a line of knots, symbolizing the cohesiveness and unity of the community.

Most of the signing dignitaries use the occasion to say words of praise and encouragement for the process and the participating disputants, providing as it were the final gloss of honour on the already shining standard of reconciliation. Copies of the signed Sulha agreement are kept by the disputants and by the *Jaha*.

When the last dignitary has signed the agreement, tied the knot around the *Rayah* and said a few words of encouragement, the victim's family *always* gets to tie the last knot in the *Rayah*. There are symbolic and practical reasons for this. On the practical side, the first knot, also tied by the victim's family, was tied in the confines of the victim's family compound and not in the public domain, and certainly not before the community, dignitaries and all disputants. Tying the last knot gives the victim's family an opportunity to demonstrate its acceptance of the reconciliation principle in the broadest public forum. On the symbolic level, this is yet another opportunity to empower the victim's family with a sense of control over the proceedings: it gets to initiate the ceremony with the tying of the first knot and to close the proceedings and symbolically bring the conflict to its end by tying the last knot, almost the last ritual in the ceremony.[98]

Mumalacha (mutual breaking of bread): The Sulha ceremony must be sealed with a meal or an equivalent ritualistic act of 'breaking bread'. Traditionally the offender's family is responsible for inviting the victim's family to this ceremonial meal, or at least to a cup of bitter coffee.[99] The victim's family, for its part, is obliged to accept and cooperate by sitting down at the table and partaking in the proffered nourishment. If only coffee is offered, the victim's family is obliged to sip. Breaking bread in this context is seen by the disputants and the community alike as the ultimate symbol of conciliation and of termination of belligerence.[100]

The Sulha ceremony is predominantly a mediation-style process.[101] Despite the significant bargaining and negotiations, including coercive and evaluative acts by the *Jaha*, and despite the existence of the Tafweeth arbitration writ – acts that may be seen as far from a mediation practice, the culminating ritual does not contain any visible hint of coercion, as that might dilute the sense of reconciliation in the face of the community and dignitaries.[102]

After the ceremony: ensuring durability

With an agreement brokered by the *Jaha*, and following the Sulha ceremony, there still exists a concern that the budding, fragile reconciliation will not endure. Parties to the dispute, particularly within the victim's clan, sometimes feel coerced or tricked into an agreement that they do not see as equitable; both sides may feel that the Sulha Committee was biased against them, or some disputant's side may come to regret the agreement, usually as a result of input from other family members who did not participate in the negotiating team.[103]

Ensuring the durability of the Sulha agreement often falls to the womenfolk of the community and the disputing clans as men of the disputing clans approach the post-reconciliation stage gingerly. In the private sphere, soon after the ceremony, the senior members of the perpetrator's clan usually pay a visit to the victim's clan, where they exchange pleasantries and reaffirm their support for the reconciliation. In public, members of the disputing clans gradually resume sharing the same public spaces, coffee houses and communal rituals (e.g. religious rituals in mosques or churches, attending funerals, participating in celebratory marches). Post-Sulha reconciliation may take years, the ultimate sign of interclan reconciliation being the willingness to allow intermarriage.

Stage 7: data analysis

To measure the perspectives of victim's clan interviewees, after the conclusion of the Sulha ceremony, they were asked to respond to the following three statements:

- After participating in the Sulha ceremony you felt you still wanted to take revenge.
- After participating in the Sulha ceremony you were willing to forgive the perpetrator's clan.
- After participating in the Sulha ceremony you still felt your clan's honour was hurt badly.

Table 4.7 and Figure 4.7 depict the basic descriptive statistics derived from the aforementioned data.

Discussion

Having been persuaded, prodded, cajoled, coerced, tempted and occasionally almost bodily dragged into reconciliation, the disputing clans are faced with a united front of community and dignitaries whose sole message is 'Get it over with and let us all resume normal life'. This is a coalition that is difficult to resist. At this point, everybody is reasonably exhausted from the conflict, the process

Table 4.7 Stage 7: descriptive statistics – victim's clan

Median			Range			Average		
Revenge	Forgiveness	Honour	Revenge	Forgiveness	Honour	Revenge	Forgiveness	Honour
2.0	4.0	2.0	2.0	2.0	2.0	1.8	3.9	1.8

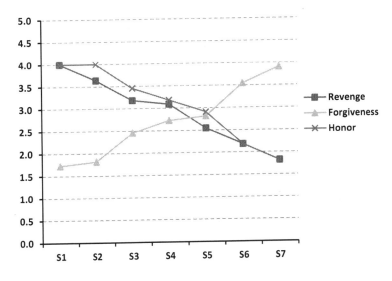

Figure 4.7 Stage 7: depicted averages – victim's clan

and the sense of precariousness and incipient danger that has pervaded the daily climate of the entire community since its eruption. With the passage of time, there are usually newer, sometimes more worrying conflicts to cope with, and a sense of ripeness envelops the conflict and its protagonists, prodding them towards resolution, acceptance and reconciliation.

PERCEPTION OF HURT SENSE OF HONOUR

As mentioned earlier, the Sulha ceremony is the grand opportunity for the victim's clan to demonstrate its magnanimity. In the words of one informant: 'Everyone saw that this is not about money. We gave back every Shekel. This is all about our family's honour and this was restored by the Sulha'.[104]

Furthermore, the ceremony is also an opportunity for the victim's clan to demonstrate the readiness to sacrifice its cultural prerogative (revenge) on the altar of communal peace, as expressed clearly by another informant: 'The community honoured us, and we honoured the community'.[105] All these gestures pay a handsome dividend in terms of a reconstructed sense of honour.

The numbers reflect the victimized clan's sense of reconstructed honour. Yet again, about 81 per cent of interviewees express disagreement with the statement regarding their hurt sense of honour; they now feel honoured again by the community, the dignitaries and the perpetrator's clan.

Here, too, there remain about 18 per cent of interviewees who express neutrality regarding their changed sense of dishonour, reflecting either a true sentiment or an inability – despite the ceremony and the passage of time – to publically take leave from the victim's posture.

DESIRE FOR REVENGE

The overwhelming sentiment at the end of a Sulha process is relief. In the words of one informant: 'The main reason for all of this is to make sure our kids, and their kids, know that there is no longer a need to take revenge and continue the dispute'.[106]

The end of the Sulha process finds its expression in the attitudes of the interviewees towards the need to avenge. About 81 per cent of interviewees now disagree with the statement that they would like to continue to pursue revenge. The remaining 18 per cent express neutrality on the subject. It is not entirely clear whether they are still committed to the concept of revenge but find it difficult to express such opinions in the overwhelming climate of reconciliation surrounding the Sulha ceremony, or whether they also gave up on the concept of revenge but find it difficult to express this sentiment.

What is clear, however, is that at the end of the Sulha process there are virtually no interviewees who clearly express a desire to avenge. One informant expressed the prevailing ambivalence in the following manner: 'We're still very angry and sad, but there is no more question of revenge. We don't need it now'.[107]

WILLINGNESS TO FORGIVE

After the Sulha ceremony the reported willingness to forgive has risen to an all-time high (about 63 per cent), yet there remains a good portion of interviewees (about 36 per cent) who report neutrality towards this sentiment. This enduring ambivalence may demonstrate that although people adopt positions for a variety of reasons (social pressure, sense of inevitability), their emotional universe changes more gradually, pointing towards the importance of the post-ceremony process – the period during which the strength of the achieved reconciliation is tested on the ground.

Not surprisingly, the act of forgiveness itself is used to further reinforce the victimized clan's sense of honour as it is translated into magnanimity. In the words of one informant: 'We showed everybody how big our hearts are, big enough to forgive, even after what they did to us'. Yet another informant expressed this enduring ambivalence in the following words: 'We'll never forget what they did to us, but for the sake of the community, and for the sake of future generations, we are willing to forgive'.[108]

All-process analysis

Having examined each particular stage of the Sulha, this section examines the survey's findings as they reflect on the entire process as a whole.

Table 4.8 presents the aggregate calculated averages for all the measured variables throughout the entire Sulha process.

Observing the aggregate table of averages for the entire process (seven stages, three variables), the most obvious finding is the almost symmetrical inversion of

Table 4.8 Descriptive statistics (averages): victim's clan – all stages, all variables

Perception	S1	S2	S3	S4	S5	S6	S7
Revenge	4.0	3.6	3.2	3.1	2.5	2.2	1.8
Forgiveness	1.7	1.8	2.5	2.7	2.8	3.5	3.9
Honour	4.0	4.0	3.5	3.2	2.9	2.2	1.8

S = Stage

sentiments. From an average of 4.0 at S1 for the desire to avenge and the sense of hurt honour and an average of 1.7 for the willingness to forgive, when the process culminates at S7, the picture is virtually inversed: now the desire to avenge and the sense of hurt honour average 1.8 each, and the willingness to forgive averages 3.9.

Discussion of survey results: *aggregate observations*

Looking at the entire process, it is possible to make the following observations:

- At the start of the conflict the desire to avenge is very high and the willingness to forgive is very low. Respondents indicate a strong sense of hurt to the clan's sense of honour.
- When the dignitaries first approach the victim's clan, there is an indication of some decrease in the desire to avenge and a smaller increase in the willingness to forgive, but the sense of damage to the clan's honour remains high and unchanged compared with that measured at the eruption of the conflict, when it was expected to be at its highest.
- With the signing of the Tafweeth by the victim's clan following its earlier signing by the perpetrator's clan, there are clear indications of a reduction in the sense of damage to the victim's clan's honour, along with a concurrent decline in the desire to avenge and a marked increase in the willingness to forgive.
- The payment of the Atwa and signing of Hudna (stage 4) come very soon after stage 3 (hours to a few days), yet they achieve a significant change in the perceptions of the victim's clan. The overall trend remains consistent: the willingness to avenge continues to decline, the willingness to forgive continues to increase and the sense of hurt honour continues to weaken.
- As negotiations and discussions with the *Jaha* proceed, the trend continues in the same direction, with a marked decline in the desire for revenge, probably attributable to several reasons, including the passage of time (this stage can take months, even years), the impact of the *Jaha*'s efforts to 'reduce the flames' of the conflict by buttressing the victimized clan's sense of honour and restoring their sense of security and self-confidence. Concurrently, the measured willingness to forgive continues to show improvement.
- As the *Jaha* reaches its verdict, there is a marked progress in the victim's clan's sense of honour; by now, the committee demonstrates to them that it

120 Sulha: structure and characteristics

has received some (if not all) of their demands. They know that the community will greet with relief and approval the knowledge that an agreement is imminent and that the victim's clan has demonstrated concern and responsibility for the community's sense of security and confidence, and for preserving the public peace. This overall sense of relief is amply reflected in the marked measured increase in the willingness to forgive by the victim's clan and the corresponding decline in the victim's clan's desire to avenge.

- As the disputants and the community gather to seal the reconciliation agreement with an elaborate ceremony, the measured desire to avenge is at its lowest throughout the process, at about the same level the willingness to forgive was at the start of the process; by contrast, the willingness to forgive is at its highest point, very near where the desire to avenge was at the eruption of the conflict, and the victim's clan's sense of hurt honour is at its lowest, indicating a restored sense of honour – the assumed key to the success of the Sulha process.

T tests: examining the statistical significance of the change between Sulha stages

To determine the statistical significance of the changes between each stage and its preceding stage, a set of six T tests was performed on paired samples (correlated groups) across each of the three examined variables (revenge, forgiveness, honour).

Desire to avenge

Table 4.9 presents the calculated statistical significance for each stage of the Sulha process compared with its preceding stage.

The analysis of the data shows that the reported level of change in the perception of the desire to avenge between stages is *not* statistically significant, except

Table 4.9 T test analysis: desire to avenge – all Sulha stages

Measured Stages		Mean	Std. Deviation	t	df	Sig. (1-tailed)
R1–R2	R1	4.00	1.00	1.789	10	0.052
	R2	3.64	1.12			
R2–R3	R2	3.64	1.12	2.887	10	0.008
	R3	3.18	1.08			
R3–R4	R3	3.18	1.08	.559	10	0.294
	R4	3.09	0.83			
R4–R5	R4	3.09	0.83	2.631	10	0.012
	R5	2.55	0.82			

Sulha: structure and characteristics 121

Measured Stages		Mean	Std. Deviation	t	df	Sig. (1-tailed)
R5–R6	R5	2.55	0.82	1.789	10	0.052
	R6	2.18	0.60			
R6–R7	R6	2.18	0.60	2.390	10	0.019
	R7	1.82	0.75			

R = Desire to take revenge
Number = Stage of process (e.g. R2 denotes calculated desire to avenge after stage 2)
Minimum accepted level of significance (one-sided test) α = 0.01
Note: Because of the small sample size, the selected level of confidence was very high.

for the change between the mean of stage R3 compared with stage R2. This is consistent with the earlier discussion, suggesting the signing of the Tafweeth is a very influential stage, central to edging the victim's clan towards the recognition that revenge is no longer the only option. As the process evolves, changes in attitudes are more subtle and gradual.

WILLINGNESS TO FORGIVE

Table 4.10 presents the calculated statistical significance for each stage of the Sulha process compared with its preceding stage.

Just like the gradual change in the desire to avenge, the analysis of the data for the victimized clan's willingness to forgive shows that the reported level of change in this perception is not statistically significant between most of the stages. The exception is the difference between stage 5 and stage 6, which *is* significant and occurs fairly late in the process – towards its conclusion. The reason is very likely a reflection of the difficulty of the victim's clan to internalize the need to actually forgive the perpetrator.

The measured difference in the evolution of the perception of desire to avenge and the willingness to forgive may also suggest that the changes in the emotions of anger (revenge) and acceptance (forgiveness) follow different mental paths.[109]

Another observation that may shed light on this process takes into account the actual length of time associated with the process. Whereas the first four stages occur in quick succession, allowing little time for the slower emotional adjustment of forgiveness (but stopping an immediate rush to revenge), negotiations can take weeks, months, even years, a time that may allow for the acceptance or forgiveness to emerge.

Sense of damage to the perception of state of honour

Table 4.11 presents the calculated statistical significance for each stage of the Sulha process compared with its preceding stage.

The RHC paradigm suggests that the variables of desire to revenge and sense of hurt honour should be closely related, which is clearly demonstrated by the

Table 4.10 T test analysis: willingness to forgive – all Sulha stages

Measured Stages		Mean	Std. Deviation	t	df	Sig. (1-tailed)
F1–F2	F1	1.73	0.79	−1.000	10	0.170
	F2	1.82	0.87			
F2–F3	F2	1.82	0.87	−2.283	10	0.023
	F3	2.45	1.04			
F3–F4	F3	2.45	1.04	−1.936	10	0.041
	F4	2.73	0.79			
F4–F5	F4	2.73	0.79	−1.000	10	0.170
	F5	2.82	0.75			
F5–F6	F5	2.82	0.75	−5.164	10	0.000
	F6	3.55	0.93			
F6–F7	F6	3.55	0.93	−2.390	10	0.019
	F7	3.91	0.83			

F = Willingness to forgive
Number = Stage of process (e.g. F2 denotes calculated desire to avenge after stage 2)
Minimum accepted level of significance (one-sided test) $\alpha = 0.01$

Table 4.11 T test analysis: sense of damage to honour – all Sulha stages

Measured Stages		Mean	Std. Deviation	t	df	Sig. (1-tailed)
H1–H2	H1	4.00	1.10	0.000	10	0.500
	H2	4.00	1.10			
H2–H3	H2	4.00	1.10	3.464	10	0.006
	H3	3.45	1.21			
H3–H4	H3	3.45	1.21	1.150	10	0.138
	H4	3.18	0.75			
H4–H5	H4	3.18	0.75	1.936	10	0.041
	H5	2.91	0.83			
H5–H6	H5	2.91	0.83	2.185	10	0.027
	H6	2.18	0.60			
H6–H7	H6	2.18	0.60	2.390	10	0.019
	H7	1.82	0.75			

H = Perception of damaged sense of honour
Number = Stage of process (e.g. H2 denotes calculated desire to avenge after stage 2)
Minimum accepted level of significance (one-sided test) $\alpha = 0.01$

data. Damage to honour follows closely the statistical progression of desire for revenge, as the reported level of change in the perception of the damage to the sense of honour is not statistically significant *between* the stages. The similarity extends to the only pair that *does* show early significant change, between stages 2 and 3, just as it did with the revenge variable, as the signing of the Tafweeth is accomplished via first a request for Sulha from the offending clan as a significant reversed honour (musayara) activity by the *Jaha* dignitaries.

Table 4.12 summarizes the total or cumulative effect of the stages in bringing about the overall attitudinal change by looking at the aggregate statistical significance for each measured variable throughout the entire Sulha process.

Table 4.12 T test analysis: revenge, forgiveness, honour – start and end of Sulha process

Variable	Stage	Mean	Std. Deviation	df	t	Sig.
Desire to Avenge	Start	3.82	1.01	10	4.90	0.001
	End	2.00	0.63			
Willingness to Forgive	Start	1.77	0.82	10	−6.12	0.000
	End	3.77	0.85			
Perception of Damage to Honour	Start	4.00	1.07	10	6.05	0.000
	End	2.00	0.63			

Discussion of statistical findings

The calculated statistical significance between S1 and S7 is so much higher (0.000 and 0.001) than the measured level of statistical significance between any two individual stages during the Sulha process. *This may suggest that the statistical tests mirror closely the proposed thesis of this exploration, namely, that the power of the Sulha is in its logical and chronological progression, in which each stage plays a small but crucial role in enabling the change in attitudes (and its attendant behaviour).*

We may thus conclude that even if changes between stages are not all significant, they do accumulate, making it eminently clear that the overall change is unlikely to occur by random chance and can therefore only be the result of the gradual progression of the process.

Another aspect worth noting is that with the desire to avenge and perception of hurt honour, significance is observed between stages S2 and S3, whereas the willingness to forgive shows significance between S5 and S6, later in the process. This may allude to different mental and/or social processing of the different variables and requires additional research, both of the specific phenomenon and of each individual stage of the Sulha.

Looking at the entire process, it is possible to observe that it appears that the willingness to forgive increases only slightly from the start of the conflict through the recruiting of the victim's clan (S2), where there is a sharp increase, probably due to the emotional reaction associated with the formal joining of the process, whose major goal is to facilitate forgiveness. During the negotiation stage (S4, S5), the rate of increase in willingness to forgive tapers off as the victim's clan faces the reality of having to reconcile with people whom they see as having done them a terrible wrong, both physically and emotionally. But as the Sulha process enters its last phase, the work of the *Jaha* shows its effect on the victim's clan with their willingness to forgive rising sharply (S5).

The data and the results of the analysis support the RHC assumptions in many ways. At the start of the process, the desire to avenge is at its highest, the willingness to forgive is at its lowest and the indication is that the victim's clan feels that its honour was hurt badly. As the process moves forward and key events take place, there is consistent evidence of a continuing monotonic trend with respect to all three indicators: the desire to avenge declines consistently, the willingness to forgive increases steadily and the sense of hurt honour declines persistently.

Looking at the honour perception, it is interesting to note that, according to RST, acceptance of responsibility and an apology by the offender serves to defuse the offender's shame, whereas in RHC, acceptance of responsibility and an apology by leaders of the offending clan infuses the victim's clan with a sense of restored honour, a central enabler of reconciliation.

Another obvious conclusion is that the stages of the Sulha process are unidirectional and monotonic. A visual inspection of the data and the resultant graph confirm this observation. At no stage of the process does there appear to be a change in the direction of the variables.

These findings may lead to the conclusion that the Sulha works on two levels: an adjustment of attitudes (honour, forgiveness) that may eventually lead to an adjustment to action (decision to not take revenge). It can be surmised that the less dishonoured the victim's clan feels, the less inclined it is to avenge and the more inclined it is to forgive.

Notes

1. McCullough, *Beyond Revenge*, p. 39.
2. Lang, Sulha Peacemaking, p. 54.
3. The author identified thirty-eight disputes that reached a resolution within the decade preceding the interviews to ensure reasonably fresh memory by interviewees. Out of this population, the author interviewed all those who agreed to be interviewed (eleven persons), regardless of their attitude toward Sulha because they had actively participated in the process.
4. This demand for anonymity seems to be consistent with reports by Lang, who writes: 'In consideration of requests for anonymity, the names of Palestinian informants quoted throughout this article are not cited; most locations, likewise, are kept intentionally vague' (Lang, *Sulha Peacemaking*, p. 65.)
5. Rensis Likert, 'A Technique for the Measurement of Attitudes', *Archives of Psychology*, Vol. 140 (1932), pp. 1–55. See also Mark S. Rye, Dawn M. Loiacono, Chad D. Folck, Brandon T. Olszewski, Todd A. Heim and Benjamin P. Madia, 'Evaluation of The Psychometric Properties of Two Forgiveness Scales', *Current Psychology*, Vol. 20, No. 3 (2001), pp. 260–77.

6 Lawrence Sanna and Edward Chang (eds.), *Judgement Over Time: The Interplay of Thoughts, Feelings and Behaviours* (Oxford: Oxford University Press, 2006), Chapter 15.
7 *Ibid.*, p. 272.
8 Linda Levine, 'Reconstructing Memory for Emotions', *Journal of Experimental Psychology: General*, Vol. 126, No. 2 (1997), p. 165.
9 For example, the statement referring to a pre-Sulha stage and to a revenge sentiment was coded '1a'; the statement referring to forgiveness sentiments during the negotiations stage was coded '5b'.
10 Jabbour, *Sulha*, p. 33.
11 Stages 1 and 2 can be viewed as a single stage (recruiting the disputants), but to facilitate analysis it was divided into two separate substages, thus allowing a more accurate examination of the different tools used to recruit the perpetrator's and victim's clans.
12 Although much of the analysis in this chapter focuses on the victim's clan, recruitment of the offender's clan is a necessary condition for launching the Sulha process.
13 Author interview with Jabbour, 4 March 2009.
14 Author interview with Khneifes, 2009.
15 Jabbour, *Sulha*, p. 27. The author witnessed several such instances and can confirm that the perpetrator's clan representatives use similar texts.
16 Author interview with Khneifes, 5 July 2012.
17 Jabbour, *Sulha*, p. 27; personal observation by author.
18 Author interview with Khneifes, 2012.
19 *Ibid.*
20 *Tarhil* is also called sometimes *Jala*, Arabic for 'departing under duress'.
21 Author interview with Khneifes, 2007.
22 Occasionally, members of the victim's clan try to set fire to vehicles and/or property belonging to members of the perpetrator's clan.
23 Based on multiple observations by the author.
24 Identifying details of the informants and the conflict were omitted at their request.
25 Hand shaking (*Musafacha*) is one of the core elements of the Sulha ceremony, and one of the ultimate signs of forgiveness. See further discussion in stage 7 later.
26 Author interview with Khneifes, 2007.
27 Lang, *Sulha Peacemaking*, p. 55.
28 Jabbour, *Sulha*, p. 32.
29 The author witnessed several such instances.
30 Lang, Sulha Peacemaking, p. 55. In a somewhat strange twist of cultural norms, the more the members of the Sulha Committee allow themselves to be abused in this role-reversal ritual, the more honour and respect they gain – essentially, they gain honour by losing it.
31 Jabbour, *Sulha*, p. 29.
32 Author interview with Rani, 16 October 2012.
33 Author interview with M'bada Naum, 13 November 2011.
34 Only men can be *Jaha* members or give evidence before it.
35 Lang, *Sulha Peacemaking*, p. 54.
36 Author interview with Rani.
37 Author interview with Khneifes, 2007.
38 *Ibid.*
39 Author interview with Shtewe.
40 *Ibid.*
41 Conversation with author on condition of anonymity.
42 *Ibid.*
43 *Ibid.*
44 Author interview with Khneifes, 2007.
45 *Ibid.*

46 Author interview with Shtewe.
47 Author interview with Khneifes, 2007. According to Khneifes, discussions about the length of the Hudna that will go into effect immediately following the Atwa ritual take place constantly in the background between the dignitaries and the victim and perpetrator clans.
48 Author interview with M'bada Naum, 2011.
49 Author interviews with Sheikh Shtewe and Khneifes, 2012.
50 Author interview with Khneifes, 2007.
51 Based on the author's personal observation of several instances.
52 Conversation with author on condition of anonymity.
53 *Ibid.*
54 *Ibid.*
55 *Ibid.*
56 See a detailed description of reframing further on in this chapter.
57 Author's personal observations; author interview with Rani.
58 Author interview with Khneifes, 2007.
59 *Ibid.*
60 *Ibid.*
61 The Jaha often meets with only one side on any given day. This is mostly because each such session takes at least four hours, including the ceremonious session of small talk and the consumption of proffered fruit, cake, coffee and sometimes whole meals.
62 Author's personal observations.
63 Joseph B. Stulberg, 'Facilitative Versus Evaluative Mediator Orientations: Piercing the "Grid" Lock', *Florida State University Law Review*, Vol. 24 (1997), pp. 985–1003.
64 Mneesha and Vuinovich, 'From Sulha to Salaam', p. 140.
65 Comments by Sulha practitioners to author on condition of anonymity.
66 See the section 'Possible directions for future research'.
67 Author interview with Khneifes, 2007.
68 At this stage of the conflict, several months after its eruption, the first Hudna has probably expired and the disputants have to agree to an extension – usually for another short period of three to six months. This process may recur several times because a Sulha may take years to conclude.
69 Conversation with author on condition of anonymity.
70 *Ibid.*
71 *Ibid.*
72 The Sulha maker who provided this description insisted on anonymity.
73 Author's participant observations.
74 Author interview with Khneifes, 2007.
75 Jabbour, *Sulha*, p. 37.
76 Author interview with Khneifes, 2007.
77 Author interview with M'bada Naum, 2011.
78 *Ibid.*
79 Reduced *Diya* is still the norm in some Arab/Muslim countries, as can be seen from the following quote (Published Sunday, 11 September 2011, on *Emirates 24/7 News* – an online news service): 'Saudi Arabia has decided to triple diya, the money paid by a killer to the victim's relatives under Islamic law, but kept the sum for female victims at half that for male victims, newspapers in the Gulf Kingdom said on Saturday', www.emirates247.com/news/region/saudi-arabia-triples-blood-money-to-sr300–000–2011–09–11–1.417796 (accessed 24 January 2014)
80 Author interview with M'bada Naum, 13 November 2011.
81 Author interview with Rani, 16 October 2012.
82 Author's personal observation.
83 Author interview with Khneifes, 2007.

84 See a sample Sulha agreement (original and translation) in Appendix 1.
85 Jabbour, *Sulha*, p. 51.
86 *Ibid.*, p. 52.
87 Conversation with author on condition of anonymity.
88 *Ibid.*
89 *Ibid.*
90 Author's personal observations.
91 Lang, *Sulha Peacemaking*, p. 58.
92 Author interview with Khneifes, 2007.
93 Author's personal observations.
94 According to several informants, such acts are at times prompted by tacit 'refund' agreements prior to the Sulha ceremony; yet all interviewed Sulha makers claimed that the victim's family is always entirely free to do with the money as it sees fit and can never be coerced into paying it back if it does not want to do so.
95 Author interview with Khneifes, 2007.
96 Cohen, 'Language and Conflict Resolution', p. 41.
97 Author interview with M'bada Naum.
98 Author interview with Khneifes, 2007.
99 The scope of the ritualistic meal spans from a cup of coffee or a symbolic offering of fruits to an elaborate, catered meal, depending on the economic status of the perpetrator's clan and the sense of true reconciliation felt by the disputants and the Jaha, whose role is to 'calibrate' the interaction between the newly reconciled clans, to provide a public demonstration of reconciliation without 'stretching' the goodwill and restraint of the newly reconciled parties.
100 Author interview with Jabbour, 2009.
101 Shapiro, 'It's Sulha Time', p. 437; Lang, *Sulha Peacemaking*, p. 52.
102 Author interview with M'bada Naum, 2011; author's personal observations.
103 Author interview with Khneifes, 2009.
104 Conversation with author on condition of anonymity.
105 *Ibid.*
106 *Ibid.*
107 *Ibid.*
108 *Ibid.*
109 See the section 'Possible directions for future research'.

5 Sulha and gender

The Sulha process takes place in a strictly patriarchal setting without the formal physical participation (or even presence) of women. Sheikh Abu Riad Ali Shtewe, the current acting head of northern Israel's Sulha Committee, was quite clear about the reigning perspective regarding the place of women in this process: 'Sulha is men's work; there's no place for women in it'.[1]

There is a significant amount of literature on various aspects of the lives of Arab women in Israel, including the duality of subordination and empowerment.[2] These studies use different approaches, from comparison to Western feminist models, to a cultural-relativistic approach, to a linkage between familial, community and state patriarchal agencies of oppression, to highlighting women's 'creative forms of resistance'.[3]

Yet none of the existing works examines the interaction between women and traditional conflict resolution processes in general, or the agency of Sulha in particular. This may partly be the case because literature examining Sulha *in general* is sparse and focuses mostly on a general comparison between Sulha and Western ADR[4] or on other gender-related issues, such as honour killings.[5] A salient exception to this pattern is a chapter in Elias Jabbour's study of Sulha that deals with 'Women in the Culture of Sulha: Arab Traditions and Values'.[6] Yet despite its suggestive title, the chapter focuses on the general place of women in Arab culture and contains no examination or analysis of Sulha's impact on women and/or the female role within this practise.

Thus, to the casual observer, it may indeed appear that women do not have an impact on the process, its progression, outcome and durability. Yet an examination of conflicts and their associated Sulha processes reveals that women are at the same time one of the most severely affected populations in such situations and, furthermore, that despite their disenfranchised status in Sulha, women do exert significant influence on the process, duration and outcome.[7]

Conflict and patriarchy

Israel's Arabs (Muslims, Christians and Druze) are part of the broader Arab culture, and their habits and customs, including customary justice practices, draw, with local variations, on the wider Arab/Muslim culture of the Middle East that is predominantly based on patriarchal values and norms. Within this framework, women in Israel's Arab community function within the prevailing social framework of their clan, which is patriarchal by organization and exerts significant internal and external power and control on all members and which 'have retained much of their power and political significance'.[8]

This social reality affects all aspects of life for women, including conflict resolution. Although there is scant, uncorroborated evidence of women playing a formal role as mediators and in some instances in the pre-Islamic Middle East,[9] today the Sulha in general, and in Israel in particular is, at least formally, an exclusive male domain,[10] employing a strictly male cast of third-party interveners; disputants' representatives are all males, and only males are allowed to act as witnesses in front of the *Jaha*. The only formal access women have to the *Jaha* – and through it to the Sulha process – is through their agnate relatives (father, brother, son).[11]

Although women are excluded from formal participation in conflict resolution processes, conflicts and their management and resolution influence their lives in multiple ways. Their husbands and sons of all ages, including babies in cribs, become potential targets of revenge killings, and women and their families are sometimes exiled from the conflict zone to help reduce friction, resulting in economic, social and cultural dislocation for them and their families.

The impact of interclan conflicts on women

Conflicts within Israel's Arab community, particularly blood conflicts (those involving death or severe injury), have a significant impact on the immediate and extended family of the perceived perpetrator. Intraclan bonds, which Jabbour calls 'circles of loyalty/responsibility'[12] and Ginat terms 'co-liable',[13] along with the traditions of conflict management in this region, decree that the male members of the victim's clan have a cultural obligation to restore the lost honour of their clan by avenging the death/injury of their clan member.

Sometimes, in an attempt to both protect the perpetrator's clan from a precipitous revenge attack by members of the victim's clan and to try to reduce friction in the hope that it will lead to the diminution of accompanying anger and frustration, the *Jaha* commands the extended family of the perceived perpetrator (sometimes more than one nuclear family), including – in many cases – dozens of women and children, to relocate en masse after the eruption of a conflict and go into a temporary, extended and sometimes permanent exile (*Tarhil* in Arabic) in another village or town, away from the victim's family. Abu M'bada says about this practice: 'We must do this [command an exile] to let passions cool down and avoid further killings'.[14] The authority of the *Jaha* in this case is informal, but it is rarely, if at all, rebuffed.

In a clan-based rural culture, such as that of northern Israel's Arabs, people often live all their lives next to their kin group, and lifelong social networks are a centre of people's economic, social and religious lives. Transplanting a family into a new environment causes a major loss of social network, particularly for women, at times coupled with the loss of mobility and economic well-being. Whereas in their permanent place of habitation women may have held a job outside the home to help with the family's finances, in the new place, because of their 'foreigner' status and unfamiliarity with the new human and economic environment, women are often prohibited by their male kin from leaving the house, except for shopping in nearby stores. This represents a significant burden on the family's female members, who shoulder most of the caring for the children, elderly, health care, feeding and many other family and clan-related activities – activities that rely heavily on the support of a social network.[15]

The impact of conflict-related exile on women: a case study

On 20 July 2007 the Sulha Committee instructed Mrs. Rym Musa, along with seventy family members, including nine women and forty-three children under the age of eighteen, to leave their home village of Dir al-Assad in northern Israel. The order came two days after two members of the clan were detained by police on suspicion of killing thirty-five-year-old Amar al-Indi.[16] Since then, the exiled family has been living in rented accommodations in the nearby Arab town of Sachnin and other villages in the area.

The forced exile resulted in the dispersal of a close-knit family, along with the removal of several dozen children from their schools (they remained at home with their mothers, greatly hampering the family's women's ability to carry on with their extensive domestic workload). A newspaper article described the situation as follows:

> Some of the family's children still do not have an organized educational venue. Dozens live in crowded rooms without minimal conditions . . . The family's women are isolated and find themselves far away from the homes that they established with hard work over the years.[17]

This case highlights the extensive impact of forced relocations on the exiled women. There is a direct impact when these women are removed from their homes; their daily routine is disrupted, as they are disconnected from the network of family and friends with whom they lived, and they are cast into an isolated setting where they have little or no social contacts, and are sometimes looked upon as 'relatives of criminals'. It is no wonder, then, that many women are resentful of the forced exile practice. Rym said in an interview with an Israeli newspaper: 'We understand the pain of the murdered man's mother. He is her only child. But why do we have to pay for this by being exiled from our homes? I do not understand the logic of this'.[18]

This interview is the first time Israeli Arab women have come out publically using a national media platform (a broadsheet, and in Hebrew to boot) to voice opposition to the practice of forced exile. In the context of the strictly patriarchal practices of Israel's rural Arab community, and within the tendency of Israeli Arabs to 'launder their dirty laundry at home and not outside', this is quite a daring and unusual move and, if repeated, it will probably attract the attention of the patriarchal leadership, both within the Arab communities and the Sulha Committee. Yet measured against the threat of a retaliatory revenge attack by the victim's family, it appears likely that the practice will continue, though Sulha practitioners are said to 'do their best to avoid sending families into exile'.[19]

This specific conflict was resolved in July 2011. Yet according to the Sulha agreement, the exiled members of the Musa clan must remain in the town of Sachnin until the summer of 2016, when they will be allowed to return to Dir al-Assad.

It is doubtful whether opposition by women to forced exile will bear fruit, but in a strict patriarchal society, even the fact that women are publicly airing their grievances is highly significant and has made Sulha makers, as noted earlier, more conscious of the disruption caused by exile. This may, in turn, lead to greater restraint on their part before imposing exile, though it is clear that the practice will not stop in the foreseeable future.

The impact of women on Sulha

This section discusses the influence of women on the process of Sulha with a view to demonstrating that, despite the informal nature of this influence, women's impact on the process and its outcome is significant and material.

Women's influence on pre-Sulha stages[20]

Multiple interviews held by this author with women and Sulha practitioners provide clear evidence of female participation in the Sulha process as early as the pre-deliberation stages.[21] Such participation takes place at several points, including:

- Venting (mostly by the victim's family side).
- Deciding on the makeup of the *Jaha*.
- Agreeing to enable the formal Sulha process to start by allowing their male kinfolk to deal with the Atwa and Hudna (a token of goodwill and a truce, respectively).

Venting

Venting is a necessary condition to enable the victim's family to subscribe to a nonviolent attempt at conflict resolution – and women are the main participants in this stage. After the offender's family's representatives sign the Tafweeth (writ of authorization) document – authorizing and enabling the initiation of the Sulha process and requesting the *Jaha* to contact the victim's side – the dignitaries approach the victim's clan for the first time. They stand at the doorway and say: 'We were sent and are authorized as *Jaha* by the killer's clan, and we invite you to consider us'.[22]

At this preliminary stage, often the women and youngsters of the victim's clan may be allowed to vent their frustration on the dignitaries of the *Jaha* by abusing them verbally and physically, sometimes to the extent of even lobbing fruits and vegetables at the dignitaries. This is a totally unacceptable behaviour that deviates sharply from all accepted norms, those of treating strangers, visitors, dignitaries and men with respect. Yet it is allowed, even encouraged, by the dignitaries in order to provide the women of the victim's clan with a significant (and public) outlet for their rage and sense of helplessness, together with an acknowledgment of their suffering and sympathy with the clan's collective sense of lost honour.[23]

This is the first contact between the victim's clan and the dignitaries who represent what may later become the formal Sulha Committee (*Jaha*). This is also the *only* part of the Sulha where women's participation is recognized (even somewhat encouraged). The dignitaries know very well that without the women's support, the nascent Sulha process has little chance of making any significant progress; hence, within the limits of the patriarchal structure, they create the space to enfranchise the women into the process.

Determining the Jaha's makeup

With the two disputing clans' signatures on the Tafweeth, the formal Sulha process gets underway, and its first order of business is deciding the makeup of the *Jaha*. This task incorporates ritualistic elements and behind-the-scene negotiations and bargaining with the representatives of the disputing clans. At this stage, the involvement of women in the process moves to the backdrop, where it will stay until the Sulha ceremony – a public ritual.

The makeup of the *Jaha* changes from case to case, with the number of its members ranging from one to 'about [twenty]'.[24]

Although the offending and victimized clans are not allowed to stipulate conditions for the operation of the *Jaha*, they do have some input regarding its makeup. For example, the disputants may veto the participation of individual *Jaha* members.[25]

At this stage, women stay in their homes. Their husbands, brothers and uncles represent the entire family. They negotiate with the temporary *Jaha* and report to their respective clan about the proposed makeup of the permanent *Jaha*. On occasion, a woman objects to a proposed *Jaha* member because of past conflicts or because she thinks that the particular person is negatively disposed towards the family, hamula or the family's religion (*Jaha* members tend to be from more than one denomination). If a woman succeeds in convincing her male relatives of the need to exclude and/or include a specific *Jaha* member in the group, the men will return to the dignitaries and convey the point, either disclosing the women's objections or, more likely, presenting the objections as their own. At this preliminary stage, the *Jaha* tends to accept such objections.

Interviewed Sulha practitioners indicated that in many cases women play an active role in determining the composition of the *Jaha*. 'Without the tacit agreement of women-folk, no *Jaha* will start operating', said one practitioner, who refused to be named. Several women informants also corroborated that perspective, indicating that, in general, men, despite their outward display of dominance, listen very carefully to what the female members of the clan say.[26] This is yet another example of the centrality of women in the process despite their formal exclusion, as well as an indication that both the clans' menfolk and the *Jaha* members recognize this centrality and accommodate it, albeit informally and anonymously.

Initiating the hudna

The Sulha process cannot move forward in earnest without a formal truce agreement (Hudna) between the disputing clans because in its absence, the threat of retaliatory revenge attacks will virtually paralyze the entire community. This makes the reaching of a Hudna an urgent priority of the *Jaha*, and, indeed, as soon as the Sulha process begins (in many cases even beforehand), the *Jaha* members start negotiating the details of the Hudna agreement.

Testimonies of both women and Sulha makers indicate that in many cases the women of the victim's clan argue forcefully with their male relatives to postpone agreement to initiate a Hudna. The women are said to do so in part for emotional reasons when they feel unable to accept a formal – though temporary – abdication of their clan's right to avenge the dishonour and the loss of life (of a son or a husband, in some cases).

There is also a practical aspect to the pressure exerted by the victim's family to postpone agreement to the initiation of a Hudna. Israeli law obliges the courts to examine substitutes to jail detention (e.g. house arrest) if it is possible to determine that the offender is not a danger to himself or herself or to society. Postponing the Hudna agreement denies the offender and his or her clan the opportunity to appear in court and to claim that a Sulha process is in progress and that a Hudna agreement is in force, and thus to evade detention.[27]

Whereas men tend to see the Hudna agreement as an organic part of the ongoing reconciliation process, women are said (by men mostly, but also by some women) to have greater difficulty accepting the fact that the offender will not remain under lock and key for the duration of the formal legal proceedings and for the duration of the Sulha process.[28]

Women's influence on Sulha deliberations

Throughout the deliberations of the Sulha Committee, women have no formal access to it and no formal influence on the process. Women, including mothers and wives of victims or offenders, and, of course, female witnesses to the events, are not eligible to testify formally in front of the *Jaha* and are not allowed to participate in its meetings as members of the disputants' family groups.

Yet women apparently do participate in Sulha deliberations informally. In an author's interview with Faraj Khneifes, he indicated that women are often involved indirectly: 'The men go home and come back to us the next day with a completely different idea or attitude, and we know that they had a discussion with their wives, and are now actually representing them in the discussion'. He added: 'Of course, a man would never admit that the idea is not his but his wife's, but we can already distinguish between them'.[29]

A perpetrator's mother interviewed by the author on condition of anonymity said that she received no information about the Sulha process from her husband, who was part of the family's delegation, but that she regularly contacted members of the *Jaha*, mostly at night, and that she heard from them about the evolution of the process.[30] A member of the *Jaha* who conducted the Sulha in which the woman's son was involved corroborated her claim. He also indicated that this was not a unique instance of informal contact between womenfolk and *Jaha* members.[31]

Such input allows women to convey their attitudes and desires to the *Jaha* and even, as will be shown later, exert some influence over the process of the Sulha, albeit indirectly, through the *Jaha* member they are in contact with – all without breaking any patriarchal taboos.

Women's influence on Sulha agreements

After hearing the disputants and consulting extensively with them, interviewing all available witnesses (male only), discussing the subject at length and examining Shari'a precedence and the unique aspects of the case on hand, the *Jaha* finally nears the end of its deliberative stage. The end product of the entire process is the Sulha agreement, a concise and ritualistic document that encapsulates tradition, reality, economics, emotions and, most of all, a view to the future.

Women are formally excluded from negotiating with the *Jaha* about the composition of the Sulha agreement. But informally, it appears from information gathered from women, men and *Jaha* members that they do make a significant contribution to the crafting (and later the execution) of this agreement.

Fairouz Yassin from the village of Arabe, a university-educated accountant (Muslim) and member of the board of the city of Acre Women's Association Pedagogical Centre, described a conflict she was familiar with between two parts of the same *hamula*. The conflict involved a cousin murdering his uncle during a property-related argument. Because both families lived literally in the same building (a common situation in Israel's Arab community), the *Jaha* instructed the alleged murderer's family to leave the village immediately and take up residence in another village.

Through male relatives, the victim's widow conveyed to the *Jaha* that she would not accept any Sulha agreement that allowed the murderer's family to return to the village – ever. Her argument was that the presence of this family in close proximity to hers would both be a permanent reminder of her misfortune and serve as a constant irritant to her children as they grew up, perhaps even leading to revenge attempts. The *Jaha* agreed informally because doing so formally would erode its position significantly and instructed the murderer's family to relocate permanently to another village.[32]

Here we have a salient example of the indirect, yet highly significant, influence of a woman on the Sulha's resultant agreement. Although the *Jaha* did not hear the widow in person, her representation by her male relatives was sufficient to make a major impact, all the more so given the growing inclination by Sulha makers to reduce the frequency of forced relocations, let alone permanent exile, by members of the offending clans.

It is highly likely that the widow's male relatives supported her position. Often, male relatives are reluctant to be perceived as compromising their traditional, dominant posture by appearing to allow any input by womenfolk or 'complicating' the pending agreement, in the words of one interviewee, who insisted on anonymity. The informant further explained that men often support their women's positions and that had they not supported a woman's position, there would have been no reason for them to present her conditions to the *Jaha* and to negotiate successfully for the acceptance of these terms.

Faraj Khneifes described a situation where the *Jaha* initiated an indirect and informal consultation with a victim's widow in order 'to ensure that her sons do not grow up feeding on her resentment and hiring an assassin as soon as they come of age and have the money to do so'. In practice, what took place according to Khneifes is that the *Jaha* consulted a male relative of the widow regarding the evolving format of the agreement. Only after the widow reportedly gave her blessing to the tentative agreement did the *Jaha* proceed to finalize it.[33]

Women's influence on post-Sulha reconciliation

Apart from the pre-Sulha venting stage, the only other stage where women have a quasi-formally recognized role in the Sulha is in the post-Sulha reconciliation. After a Sulha agreement and ceremony, it is time for the disputants' clans to start building a post-conflict relationship, essentially reconstructing the fabric of cooperation and neighbourliness that may have existed before the conflict. This is a crucial element in the lives of many Arab communities, who reside in crowded conditions, and must be able to sustain, at a minimum, a modicum of civil communal relations if they want to successfully coexist in the same town or village after a conflict.[34]

For women, the centres of social networking are their respective homes, as well as the homes of female blood relatives, who may at times be married into the disputant's family, and the homes of other female relatives and friends, who may be associated with their clans through blood, friendship, commercial or marriage relations. The clans and the entire community expect women to use these social skills to start and maintain an initial healing process between the disputant families, first through small-scale meetings between formerly belligerent female clan members, and later by bringing their children to start resocializing with the 'other side'; still later on, the clans' menfolk will pick up on such nascent social interactions and use them to gradually expand the scope of communications to facilitate meetings, celebrations, ritual meals and other traditional and/or commercial events such as religious feasts, ceremonies to celebrate births of new family members and business meetings to help re-establish business relationships that may have existed before the conflict.

This reliance by the *Jaha* and clan leaders on women to actively re-establish the broken relationships between clans in the aftermath of a resolution clashes with the insistence of many Sulha practitioners that women are, almost always, obstacles to reconciliation because of what they see as women's 'emotional' perspective on life and the attendant desire to see the perpetrator's family suffer the consequences of the deed.

A possible explanation to this tension between the attitude of the *Jaha* and that of the community at large is the practical need to reconcile patriarchal taboos with communal realities. The 'disruption' narrative supports the former, whereas the recruitment of women for post-Sulha reconciliation reflects the latter need.

Yet, as shown in this chapter, notwithstanding longstanding social and cultural obstacles, women play a central *informal* role in interclan reconciliation process – from the pre-Sulha stage of venting, to the determination of the *Jaha*, to behind-the-scenes involvement in the deliberations, to indirect influence on the evolving Sulha agreement, to the important task of assisting the disputing clans to heal the rift after the completion of the formal reconciliation process.

Notes

1 Author interview with Sheikh Abu Riad Ali Shtewe, 16 October 2012.
2 See, for example: Orna Cohen and Rivka Savaya, 'Reasons for Divorce among Muslim Arabs in Israel', *European Societies*, Vol. 5, No. 3 (2003), pp. 303–25; Yvette Batrice, *al-Mar'a al-Filastiniyya fi Isra'il: Waqi wa-Tahaddiyat (The Palestinian Woman in Israel: Reality and Challenges)* (Haifa: Self-published, 2000); Joseph Ginat, *Women in Muslim Rural Society: Status and Role in Family and Community* (New Brunswick: Transaction Books, 1982); Naomi Levy-Weiner, 'I am Like a Bird That Hasn't Flown Yet: Life stories of Druze Women Who Pursued Higher Education', PhD Thesis, Hebrew University of Jerusalem, 2003; Michael Gorkin, *Three Mothers, Three Daughters: Palestinian Women's Stories* (Berkeley: University of California Press, 1996); Khawla Abu Baker, '"Career Women" or "Working Women"? Change Versus Stability for Young Palestinian Women in Israel', *Journal of Israeli History*, Vol. 2, No. 1–2 (2002), pp. 85–109.
3 Sa'ar, 'Feminine Strength', pp. 397–430.
4 Abu-Nimer, 'Conflict Resolution Approaches'; Irani, 'Islamic Mediation Techniques for Middle East Conflicts'; Lang, Sulha Peacemaking, pp. 52–66.
5 Hasan, 'The Politics of Honour'.
6 Jabbour, *Sulha*, Chapter 6.
7 This chapter is partially based on Pely, 'Women in Sulha'.
8 Amalia Sa'ar, 'Contradictory Location: Assessing the Position of Palestinian Women Citizens of Israel', *Journal of Middle East Women's Studies*, Vol. 3, No. 3 (2007), p. 49.
9 Jane Smith, 'Women, Religion and Social Change in Early Islam', in Elison Findly and Yvonne Haddad (eds.), *Women, Religion, and Social Change* (Albany: State University of New York Press, 1985), pp. 19–37.
10 The terms 'formal' and 'informal' as used in this chapter are researcher generated, but are directly related to Jaha-associated definitions of 'formal' and 'informal' parts of the process. The term 'formal' in the context of this chapter, therefore, denotes those aspects and stages of the Sulha process that are proscribed by its practitioners

as necessary for the application to be considered complete and binding, culturally and within Shari'a. This includes all designated rituals, meetings and deliberations between the Jaha and the disputants' representatives (e.g. the Sulha ceremony). Everything else is informal (e.g. communication of women with individual Jaha members – not with the Jaha as a quasi-formal body).

11 Author interview with Khneifes, 2007. This was corroborated by Sheikh Abu Riad Ali Shtewe in an interview with author, 16 October 2012.
12 Jabbour, *Sulha*, p. 73.
13 Joseph Ginat, *Blood Disputes among Bedouin and Rural Arabs in Israel: Revenge, Mediation, Outcasting and Family Honor* (Pittsburgh: University of Pittsburgh Press, 1987), p. 21.
14 Author interview with M'bada Naum, 13 November 2011.
15 Rachel Hertz-Lazarowitz and Tamar Shapira, 'Muslim Women's Life Stories: Building Leadership', *Anthropology and Education Quarterly*, Vol. 36, No. 2 (2005), pp. 51–67.
16 Author interview with Khneifes, 15 July 2011.
17 Fadi Ayadat, 'A Man Charged With Murder and His Entire Family is Exiled From the Village: Because of Tradition', *Haaretz*, 30 December 2007.
18 *Ibid.*
19 Author interview with Khneifes, 2011.
20 For a detailed description of the Sulha stages, please see Chapter 4.
21 Most women insisted on anonymity as a condition for discussing their involvement in Sulha. Wherever possible, women informants are identified.
22 Jabbour, *Sulha*, p. 32.
23 Author interview with Khneifes and author's personal observation.
24 Jabbour, *Sulha*, p. 28.
25 Author interview with Sulha practitioner Sheikh Mahmud Abu Saaluk, 12 July 2007; author interview with Khneifes.
26 Author interview with anonymous informants (male and female).
27 Criminal Due Process Regulations (Enforcement Authority – Detention), 1996, New Section: 338 (translated from Hebrew).
28 Author interview with anonymous informants (male and female).
29 Author interview with Khneifes, 2007. This was corroborated by M'bada Naum in an interview, 13 November 2011.
30 Author interview, 3 June 2009 (all possible identifying details were removed intentionally).
31 This informant (who arranged the interview) insisted on anonymity. Interview conducted with author, 10 June 2009.
32 Author interview with Fairouz Yassin, 5 June 2009.
33 Author interview with Khneifes, 14 June 2009.
34 *Ibid.*

6 Sulha and Western ADR

In his discussion of the similarities and differences between Muslim and Western conflict resolution approaches, Muhammad Abu-Nimer argues that '[c]onflict resolution processes exist in every society. However, a comparison between Western and Middle Eastern procedures of dispute resolution processes reveals that different assumptions underline each approach'.[1] Paul Salem adds to the differentiation argument by suggesting that '[t]he Western community of conflict resolution theorists and practitioners operate within a macro-political context that they may overlook, but which colors their attitudes and values'.[2]

Much of our understanding of the Sulha emanates from the ability to locate, describe and analyze the place in this process of mediation and arbitration practices – two of alternative dispute resolution's (ADR's) ubiquitous and universally acknowledged applications.[3] Yet although universally acknowledged, these practices and their frame of reference are Western, and although the similarity in reference and nomenclature often creates a sense of familiarity, as well as a sense of identity of perception and practice, this is not always the case. In fact, when comparing similar Muslim/Arab and Western ADR practices, it is possible to identify both similarities and significant differences.

According to Ramahi, Westerners and Arabs differ in both their philosophical and functional attitudes to dispute resolution, with the former emphasizing 'the primacy of law' and the latter 'the primacy of interpersonal relationships', and she leaves little doubt as to which approach she deems more effective: 'the Eastern party has an intrinsic community and a collective attitude to conflict whereas the Western party is individually minded and procedurally orientated, thus causing friction between the two sides'.[4]

In this context, it is important to note that such a cross-cultural exploration may not always be necessary or productive. In Salem's words:

> One must make clear from the beginning that any attempt to make broad generalizations about two diverse and loosely defined cultural and social groupings as 'the West' and 'the Arab world' is fraught with dangers of reductionism, essentialism, and simplification, to say nothing of Orientalism.

Yet he concludes that despite the potential pitfalls: 'The effort of finding general cultural patterns and tendencies . . . is, I think, well worth the risk and the effort'.[5] Thus, for example, an examination of mediation and arbitration practices in cross-cultural contexts shows that contrary to the evolution of Western ADR – where mediation and arbitration practices morphed over the years into distinct applications that fill up the conceptual and functional gaps between formal adjudication and violent self-administered justice – the practice of Sulha has always made, and continues to make, interchangeable use of both mediation and arbitration elements.[6]

Western and Muslim/Arab conflict resolution assumptions

Before analyzing the actual use of specific ADR elements and the manners of their use, it is important to identify and explain the relevant Western and Islamic/Arab central conflict resolution assumptions. As far as the Western approach to conflict resolution is concerned:

- Individualism and individual affiliation and responsibility are the basis of the conflict and its resolution.[7]
- The conflict resolution approach is mostly interest based and tends to advocate a collaborative process aimed at reaching a consensus.[8] Essentially, this perspective is reflected through the interest-based relational (IBR) approach, whose major tenets call for separating people from the problems, paying particular attention to the interests of the disputants rather than their positions and/or postures and seeking an integrative, win-win solution through a mutual exploration of possible options.[9]
- Emotions and values, though important, rarely help promote a resolution. Because these traits are defined as 'irrational', although Western ADR strives to perform a 'rational' service, the expression of emotions beyond confined venting rituals (mostly at the start of the process) is discouraged. In the words of Dutch cultural anthropologist Niko Besnier: 'Ethnographic work on emotions has shown that the opposition between cognition and emotion is a Western construct'.[10]
- Provision of mediation and arbitration services has largely become a paid career – a profession. Trained professionals provide dispute resolution services. People train to become mediators or arbitrators, then seek employment in organizations that provide such services in the private and public sectors. This trend has resulted in the development of varying degrees of certification requirements and regulations. In the words of Irani and Funk: 'Western practitioners of mediation are expected to be formally certified professionals'.[11]
- Third-party interveners must be completely neutral and play a facilitating role, rather than an active guiding role, letting the disputants reach a resolution by themselves. As political scientist Anthony Greco put it: 'Western ADR seeks to find impartial advisers to negotiate and mediate settlements

between two parties'.[12] Legal scholar Baruch Bush and communications professor Joseph Folger, leaders of the transformative school of Western dispute resolution, define mediation as 'an informal process in which a neutral third-party with no power to impose a resolution helps the disputing parties try to reach a mutually acceptable settlement'.[13]

- Civic legislation (secular) is the foundation of Western ADR. Following the evolution of Western law as a separate branch of ethics not directly resting on religious jurisprudence, Western ADR followed pretty much the same path. Law professor Stephen Subrin called ADR a 'new ideology of civil litigation'.[14]
- Conflicts are not always bad; they can actually benefit the disputants and the community. In the words of business professor Gupta Lovleen: 'However, the conflicts are not always bad, rather they help in creating [a] healthy and vibrant environment. The conflicts introduce competition'.[15]
- Direct contact between the disputants (face to face) is, by and large, a preferred method of negotiation. This is seen as a format conducive to enabling the sides to experience firsthand the anger, frustration and indignation of the other side and to come to terms with the lack of exclusivity of their pain and hurt.[16]

By contrast, in the Muslim/Arab conception:

- Dispute resolution mechanisms are religiously based, with Qur'anic roots and Shari'a expression. It is important to note, however, that despite its Islamic roots, Christian and Druze Arabs participate in this ADR process as well. This phenomenon is intriguing, but beyond the scope of this work.
- Conflicts are intractable, require extended management and are essentially a negative experience because they threaten the stability of the community.[17]
- Due to prevailing cultural structures, notably the primacy of social groupings such as family, clan and tribe, although individuals may start a conflict, it immediately expands to engulf related families, clans and associated communities. In Ramahi's words:

> Dispute resolutions in the Middle East are guided with an overarching principle of collective interests of the family, the tribe, the community and the country. The Arab's Islamic and tribal history places collective interest as the highest principle in a hierarchy of values in both dispute resolution and everyday dealings.[18]

This perspective is at variance with the individualistic perspective that characterizes most Western dispute and dispute resolution perspectives.

- Competition over physical resources and/or security and safety needs may cause a conflict, but resolution will not occur unless reference is made to core values such as honour, revenge and forgiveness and the inevitable victim–perpetrator pairing. In the words of Irani and Funk, 'many of the world's most

intractable conflicts involve age-old cycles of oppression, victimization and revenge. These conflicts, which can have dangerous and long-lasting political repercussions, are rooted in a psychological dynamic of victimization'.[19]
- Third-party intervener(s) should be unbiased but are not expected to be neutral in the same sense as Western ADR practitioners are expected to be. In the Muslim/Arab world, the interveners often know the disputing sides well and are occasionally their neighbours, yet are obliged to make every effort to present an unbiased approach. Failing to do so may result in losing their public standing in the community, effectively terminating their 'career' as an intervener.
- Interveners generally avoid assembling the disputing clans for face-to-face neg.otiations.

Sulha mediation elements vs. Western-style ADR mediation elements

Western-style mediation is essentially a voluntary process requiring the agreement of the disputants for it to take place (in some countries, there is court-mandated mediation under certain conditions, but even there disputants can terminate the process at any point prior to a signed agreement).[20] Mediators in the West are seen as essentially facilitators; they do not 'own' the process, but are charged with helping the disputants – the formal 'owners' of the dispute – explore ways to manage and reconcile their conflict. Disputants who find mediation unsuitable for any reason can opt for other practices, such as arbitration or adjudication.[21]

A widely held Western perspective of mediation considers it a 'narrow', problem-solving, functional process, designed to help solve a technical problem (e.g. 'who pays how much to whom').[22] Other perspectives of Western-style mediation propose a 'broad' definition, assuming that the parties want to move beyond the technicalities to a process of reconciliation that includes such practises as victim-offender mediation programs (VOMPs), also known as victim-offender reconciliation programs (VORPs), and even transformational processes.[23] Law professor Dwight Golann demonstrates how mediators tend to move between different mediation descriptions, making a clear, precise definition of a process difficult, if not impossible. Still, he argues, such movements take place *within* the accepted definitions of mediation and do not extend to other ADR applications, such as arbitration.[24]

The Sulha, in most instances, aims at providing a solution that is more similar to the 'broad' definitions of Western-style mediation, in that the disputants are seen as striving for full-fledged reconciliation and termination of the state of conflict. With Sulha, *Musalaha* (reconciliation) is a core principle, so much so that Sulha is sometimes called *Musalaha*.[25] According to Sulha maker Ibrahim M'bada Naum, *Musalaha* is sometimes called 'Sulha Light' because 'it is less rigidly anchored in Shari'a, yet aims to achieve the same broad goal – intra and inter communal reconciliation'.[26]

Like Western-style mediation, Sulha is also a voluntary process, except that with this practise the voluntarism aspect is strictly limited; the offender's family is *expected* to approach the interveners and ask them to initiate the process. In Khneifes' words: 'They often come to us in the middle of the night, banging on the door, demanding that we come and take charge'.[27]

The victim's family, on the other hand, is *asked* by the interveners to join the process. But as shown elsewhere in this book, once the disputants join the process, they give it a formal dimension by signing the Tafweeth (writ of authorization), through which the process acquires a binding arbitration dimension that locks the disputants into it. The Tafweeth is a written obligation by the disputants' clans (first the perpetrator's and later the victim's) to join the Sulha process and accept whatever verdict the *Jaha* decides. With the inclusion of the T*afweeth*, the Sulha cannot be seen as a purely mediation-based process.

Furthermore, unlike Western-style mediation-based procedures, Sulha makers often push the disputants quite vigorously to join the process in order to be able to rapidly mitigate against a potential cycle of counter-revenge and retaliation. In the words of Sulha maker Abu M'bada: 'If they [the offending clan] do not move fast [to join the Sulha], we warn them there's going to be trouble and they should think about it'.[28]

As shown in Chapter 4, once the Sulha process begins, the interveners stop being just facilitators and formally become part-owners of the process through the arbitrative powers given them by the Tafweeth. Disputants cannot really stop the Sulha process once it has started, though they can certainly slow it down by various tactical manoeuvres. As Khneifes explains: 'Sometimes, they do things to avoid giving an advantage to the other side'.[29]

Some of the mediation practices used in Sulha are also different from those in Western-style mediation. For example, in Western-style mediation disputants often conduct face-to-face meetings facilitated by the interveners. Such meetings allow each side to become familiar with the sense of victimization and the anger felt by the other side.[30] In Sulha, the process involves exclusively private caucus meetings between the *Jaha* and each of the disputant's representatives. In fact, the disputing clans completely avoid meeting each other during the process. This is because with the very high commitment to retaliation and the equally high level of frustration and anger, particularly within the victim's clan, there is a real danger that a face-to-face meeting between disputing clan members will degenerate to violence.

Furthermore, the exclusive private-caucus format of the Sulha gives the *Jaha* the opportunity to reframe, rephrase and on occasion even creatively invent disputants' narratives when reporting to the other side; this way the interveners can remove potentially inflammatory narratives and retain those parts that are conducive to fostering a climate of reconciliation. According to Sulha maker Abu M'bada, the *Jaha* often goes beyond reframing to 'manufacturing' positive messages and narratives designed to help reduce negative feelings between disputants.[31] On the other hand, the lack of joint meetings denies disputants the possibility of witnessing firsthand the frustration, sense of victimization and perception of injustice felt by the other side.

Western-style mediators often use a tool called 'comparing alternatives', in which they present the disputants with the (sometimes unsavoury) consequences of *not* reaching an agreement.[32] *Jaha* members also make extensive use of blunt alternative-comparison techniques, sometimes painting the alternatives to no agreement in very dire but realistic terms. Often *Jaha* members adopt an aggressive evaluative stance, cajoling, threatening and coercing the disputants to reach an agreement. The instruments of coercion in the case of the Sulha are mostly social.

Khneifes describes a meeting of the *Jaha* with a victim's clan, where the *Jaha* head painted in vivid colours what may happen if the victim's clan resorts to a revenge killing and the perpetrator's clan retaliates in kind. 'He said to them', Khneifes recalled, 'move as fast as you can towards an agreement. They [the victim's clan] are all killers; before you know it, your clan will be bathing in blood'.[33] This is a prime example of a combination of alternative comparison and evaluative approaches.

In the West, using evaluative practices as part of a mediation process is often frowned upon and considered unwanted and unnecessary. In a paper titled 'The Top Ten Reasons Why Mediators Should Not Evaluate', law professor Lela Love writes: 'The role of mediators is to assist disputing parties in making their own decisions and evaluating *their own* situations'.[34]

Another significant difference between mediation elements in Sulha and Western-style mediation is the place and use of honour. In the Western context, the term honour is usually evoked in its 'folkloristic' form. It is important, but not crucially so.[35] In Muslim/Arab societies, by contrast, honour is not only central to life in general, it is central to dispute resolution because in many cases the perception of lost honour fuels the eruption of the conflict, and the perception of restored honour is a crucial component of the resolution and the reconciliation process. In the words of Abu M'bada: 'That's the Arab culture; Muslims, Christians, Druze, if you hurt their honour, they get very angry and can do terrible things'.[36]

Arbitration elements in Sulha and Western-style ADR

In addition to the mediation-style tools discussed earlier, Sulha employs several arbitration-style applications interspersed within the mediation-style practices and designed to achieve specific goals throughout the process.

Arbitration is a form of ADR designed to facilitate dispute resolution outside formal courts. In Western-style arbitration, disputants negotiate with each other and with the intervener the terms of the arbitration process to ascertain prior agreement on its scope and purpose. There are several similarities and several differences between Western-style binding arbitration contracts and the arbitration elements of Sulha, including in the way they are obtained, the ways the disputants view them and the way they are used throughout the process.

One of the central arbitration-style elements within the Sulha process is the signing of the Tafweeth – an irrevocable written commitment to participate in the process and to abide by the *Jaha*'s verdict. This means that, like Western-style arbitration, the Sulha process does not start before both sides are committed in writing to the process and to its results. Yet the path to this commitment in Sulha differs from that taken before the launch of a Western-style arbitration process.

In Sulha it is the perceived offending side that must appeal to the interveners to initiate the process. Once the offender's side signs the Tafweeth, the dignitaries appeal to the victim's side to join the process. If they (the victim's clan) agree, they also sign the Tafweeth, and the Sulha becomes a formal process (formal in the sense that all sides and the community see it as such; the state, of course, accords no such status to the process).

In Western arbitration, the process can be voluntary (entered into voluntarily by the disputants) or mandatory (entered into by legal direction of the court). In either case, the proposed arbitrator(s) negotiates simultaneously with *all* parties to the dispute, determining the terms of the arbitration contract. Once disputants agree on the scope of the arbitration (e.g. binding or nonbinding) and on the rules of engagement (e.g. the allotted period, the type of evidence allowed), all parties sign the resultant arbitration contract and the process gets underway, sanctioned formally by the law of the land (or by international law).

Having agreed to participate in a binding arbitration process, the disputants sign a binding arbitration agreement, and their commitment to abide by the arbitrator's ruling is enforced rigidly. Essentially, this commitment is the core component of the arbitration process. For this reason, in many instances an arbitration ruling has the power of a court ruling.[37] As law professor Paul Rice noted: 'If the parties fail to reach [a] settlement, the arbitrator has the authority, consented to beforehand by the parties, to impose a solution upon them'.[38]

Because the Sulha is an informal customary justice process, the enforcement mechanisms are similarly informal, yet they are no less binding than formal mechanisms in Western-style practices. In a tribal society, honourable status is crucially important to the clan's standing within the community, as well as to the clan's political and economic well-being, and clan elders will think long and hard before refusing to abide by a *Jaha*'s edict, a step that will damage the standing and respectability of the entire clan in the community. So the twin threat of being shamed and of shaming the *Jaha* dignitaries is a potent one. Abu M'bada reinforces this sentiment when he says: 'We [the *Jaha*] don't have police or prisons, but we have quite a lot of power, and we have to be very careful about using it for good'.[39]

Confidentiality, venting and neutrality in Sulha and Western ADR

The following section presents an analysis of the similarities and differences between the concepts of confidentiality, venting and neutrality as applied within Sulha and Western-style mediation and arbitration processes.

Confidentiality

Practitioners of Western-style mediation are obliged to maintain confidentiality from public disclosure regarding the content of discussions that take place within the mediation process.[40] One of the main reasons for this confidentiality is to help disputants feel that they can express themselves freely in front of the mediator and confide in her or him details and arguments they may not be so eager to discuss otherwise for fear that the other side may use them as leverage during the negotiation process.[41] Yet the understanding is that disputants may expressly allow intervener(s) to share specific information with the other side.

Jaha members share this reasoning, albeit with some local variants. They will not reveal to the other disputant(s) information and/or remarks made by the other party in private caucus, unless the disputing side agrees *or* – and this is a major difference – if the *Jaha* members decide that the disclosure will help the conciliation process. The main reason for this 'selective confidentiality' practice is the *Jaha*'s desire to increase harmony and decrease possible friction points between the disputants.

Consequently, on occasion, the *Jaha* takes rather broad poetic license with the confidentiality rule and reframes – and sometimes even invents – the statements of one group in private caucus, again in the service of furthering reconciliation. Describing this practice, M'bada Naum said: 'Conveying positive messages does not require permission. Sometimes, we even "manufacture" positive messages – more than "sometimes" '.[42] This rather 'creative' approach to confidentiality by the *Jaha* shows a similarity of general reasoning, but a definite divergence of particular applications between Western mediation and Sulha.

There are several additional junctures where the concept of confidentiality within Western-style mediation expresses itself. For example, if a mediation process ends without an agreement, the conflict may revert to a court, and the mediator, in such an eventuality, is obliged to keep confidential all information regarding the (failed) process, both from the public at large and from the subsequent formal adjudicator. One of the main reasons for this, in the words of Lawrence Freedman et al, is that '[i]n mediation, unlike the traditional justice system, parties often make communications without the expectation that they will later be bound by them'.[43]

Of course, if an agreement is reached in Western-style mediation (in arbitration, a decision is *always* made by the arbitrator, so an agreement of sorts is always achieved), the mediator or arbitrator is obliged to reveal the agreement's particulars, at least to the judge in court-mandated mediation, but the events leading to the agreement (e.g. evidence heard, exchanges between disputants) still remain confidential.[44]

Some of the differences between confidentiality in Western-style mediation and Sulha arise from differences in the general context within which Sulha and Western-style ADR function. For example, in Israel, the Sulha process takes place in many instances *alongside* a formal legal process (e.g. the formal courts adjudicate between the state's prosecution and individual defendant(s)); on the other hand,

Western-style ADR processes such as mediation and arbitration take place *instead of* formal legal processes.

The differences in application reflect on the perception and uses of the confidentiality principle in both Sulha and Western-style ADR. In Sulha, much like in Western-style mediation and arbitration processes, *Jaha* members are obliged to maintain strict confidentiality with respect to information they collect as they make their rounds, visiting and interviewing witnesses, members of disputants' clans and other interested parties, unless explicitly postulated otherwise by the originator of the information.[45] All such encounters take place in the seclusion of private caucuses. Discretion, in such cases, is essential to obtaining the cooperation of the people the *Jaha* or the Western mediators seek to interview.

However, because Sulha often takes place *alongside* (as opposed to *instead of*) a related formal legal proceeding, this confidentiality obligation gets tested in situations that are completely alien to, and different from, those potentially and practically affecting Western ADR interveners. For example, *Jaha* members may be summoned to a formal state court to testify about a Sulha agreement they have obtained. This happens mostly when the state prosecutes the alleged offender and the defence lawyers ask a *Jaha* member to testify on behalf of the defendant about a Sulha agreement that may have been reached while the court was in session – adjudicating between the state and the alleged perpetrator in the case that created the need for the Sulha process in the first place. Sheikh Abu Riad Shtewe said in this regard: 'The police don't really call us in [to testify in court] but the killer's lawyers, under pressure of the family, sometimes ask us to help'.[46]

Because the Sulha does not have a formal standing in Israel, there is no legal barrier to the mixing of the formal process and the customary process and to the summoning of *Jaha* members to court. But over the years, the established convention is that summoned *Jaha* members testify only about the Sulha agreement proper; that is, they testify to the fact that the process resulted in an agreement, not about the process itself, and certainly not about deliberations among themselves, or between them and the disputants, or about testimonies heard by the *Jaha*. The exception is that a *Jaha* member may agree to testify about the 'positive' (non-incriminating, reconciliation-promoting) aspects of the testimonies and deliberations. In Shtewe's words: 'If we come to court, it is *only* to help with reconciliation. We don't help the police and we never tell them what takes place in the Sulha'.[47]

But complications may arise when a judge requests to see the Sulha agreement prior to a court's relevant decision (e.g. detention, verdict or punishment). This agreement might contain potentially damaging information, such as tacit admission of culpability, or other evidentiary facts, which may influence the court's decision. Sociologist Nurit Tsafrir writes in this regard: 'In the eyes of the court, the Sulha may express the accused admission of having committed those deeds . . . Furthermore, the Sulha agreement presented to the court sometimes contains details of the injury caused by the accused'.[48]

In order to protect the confidentiality of the Sulha against such eventualities, Sulha agreements nowadays tend to be very brief (half a page in many cases) and contain mostly vague, ritualistic language about 'a sorrowful event'.

Another aspect of confidentiality that has more relevance for Sulha than for Western-style mediations has to do with the decision-making process of the *Jaha* as it contemplates the verdict. Because it is reasonable to assume that different *Jaha* members may have (and may express) different opinions as the process evolves, it is crucial to maintain confidentiality about the committee's internal deliberations and its members' positions and opinions so as to minimize their exposure to possible pressures and/or retaliation following a verdict that may be perceived as unfair by one or more disputants. In the words of Abu M'bada:

> We never tell stories from inside the deliberations. If people ask, we just say that everything is fine. If, however, someone from the *Jaha* spills information about *Jaha* deliberations, it's a big shame, and he gets kicked out of the *Jaha*.[49]

Venting

Venting is a recognized and well-described practice in some mediation applications in the West, as well as in the Sulha process.[50]

In Western-style ADR, venting (where it is accepted as a legitimate tool of mediation) serves a dual purpose: it allows the parties to vent their anger and frustration, and it allows each party to become exposed to the realization that the other party also feels similar anger and frustration. At times venting is even seen as a therapeutic process.[51] Both purposes coalesce into one single super-purpose – helping the parties become emotionally 'unstuck' as a prerequisite to starting a move towards a possible solution. Working towards this goal is possible because, in many cases, at least part of the venting process takes place when the two parties are in the presence of each other, usually during the early stages of the mediation process.

It is also important to note that there is a strand in Western mediation called transformative mediation, where conflict is viewed *not* as a problem but as an opportunity for growth and transformation, and where anger and venting are seen as contributing to empowerment, recognition and the making of outcome-related decisions.[52]

However, venting is not universally accepted as a legitimate and/or constructive tool of conflict resolution within some strands of Western ADR. In the words of law professor Trina Grillio: 'I believe that uncontrolled venting of anger, at least in the presence of the other party, is of little use and can be frightening to all present'.[53] Mediator Christopher Moore is similarly blunt in his opposition to venting, arguing that 'face-to-face expression of emotions can also damage relationships so that no agreement can be reached'.[54]

The similarity between venting in Sulha and in Western ADR is in that both approaches see this phenomenon – under certain conditions – as a potentially useful path maker on the road to reconciliation because it helps the disputants get beyond the immediate grief, anger, sense of victimization and frustration and helps them agree to give reconciliation a chance.

Indeed, in Sulha, venting is an acknowledged and frequently used part of the process. Elias Jabbour writes: 'Grief work, in many cases, must be enabled by the *Jaha* to make way for peace'.[55] *Jaha* member M'bada Naum provides a more specific description of the place and use of venting when he says: 'Many times we face bad language and insults from women when we come to talk to the victim's clan. It's not nice, but we understand'.[56]

In the Sulha process, venting is important for the *Jaha*'s ability to recruit the victim's side to the process. But unlike Western-style mediation and/or arbitration where disputants meet face to face (accompanied by the third-party intervener), in Sulha they never meet during the process. In fact, the families meet for the first time after the eruption of the conflict only during the Sulha ceremony, and even then only under strictly regulated, formalized and ritualized terms. Abu Riad says: 'We don't allow the disputants to have any [direct] contact before everything is ready, because one word [between the disputants] can ruin a year of careful work'.[57]

The venting ritual in Sulha is designed to start the process of channelling the victim's family away from the desire for revenge to the communally preferred option of conciliation and ultimate forgiveness – something that may appear to be unthinkable at the early stages of the conflict but still figures in the *Jaha*'s grand scheme of things. In one of the venting situations that the author witnessed, women, including the victim's mother, screamed abuse at the *Jaha* and the process from within a darkened room, next to the room where the committee and the victim's clan delegation were meeting. The male clan members and *Jaha* all waited in silence until the screaming and abuse came to a halt, whereupon they recommenced the discussion in quiet, subdued voices.[58]

Neutrality

Third-party neutrality (sometimes defined as impartiality, objectivity and maintaining equidistance from disputants) is as central to the Sulha process as it is central to Western ADR.[59] In the words of Kevin Gibson et al.: 'Most observers view neutrality as a critical component of mediation'. So much so, that the authors go on to stress that '[n]eutrality is so central to the mediation literature that mediators are commonly called "neutrals"'.[60]

Yet despite its seeming centrality, neutrality remains very much a debated and controversial concept. Janet Rifkin et al. shed light on some of the controversy surrounding the place of neutrality in Western ADR when they write:

> In mediation, neutrality has often been treated both as a means to an end, and as an end in itself. As a means, it is seen as the necessary step toward problem resolution; as an end, it is viewed as the necessary quality that the mediator must possess to ensure a fair and just process.

They further focus on the difficulties associated with the concept and practice of neutrality, pointing out that 'neutrality, as it is often understood, leads to problems for mediators in constructing agreements'.[61] This position is reinforced by Gibson et al., who claim that '[t]hough it is an intuitively appealing concept, neutrality is also ambiguous', stressing that 'there are practical difficulties with the concept of neutrality. The goal of neutrality provides the mediator little guidance about whether to intervene in the negotiation, and the nature of any such intervention'.[62]

In Sulha the requirements for neutrality are sometimes difficult to uphold. Specifically, in the case of the Sulha in Israel, the fact that the country's Arab community is small and lives in concentrated areas is at times a source of difficulties because it is likely that the *Jaha* members come from the same geographic area as the disputants and are involved in the life of the community, its commercial, territorial, professional, political and even personal disputes. This involvement may touch directly or indirectly on members of the disputants' clans, making it difficult for *Jaha* members to be neutral or appear to be neutral.

This is why members of the *Jaha* spend their lives constructing a public persona that projects an unbiased, even-handed approach to disputes; their desire (and need) to maintain such a posture in the eyes of the community is the best incentive to maintaining neutrality, or to at least making a visible effort to do so. In the words of Sulha practitioner Sheikh Hamis Mahmud: 'We know everybody and everybody knows us. This is why it is doubly important that we live a life of total honesty and fairness'.[63]

Furthermore, because in the end the *Jaha* actually imposes a settlement on the disputants, it is crucial that all sides to the dispute feel that it is completely neutral in its approach to and handling of the dispute. Otherwise, the reconciliation agreement will be tarnished by the resentment of at least part of the disputants, and there is a danger that it will collapse under the pressure of displeasure or disagreement by one or both sides.

To pre-empt the potentially damaging perception of the interveners' lack of neutrality, the Sulha process allows disputants to have a significant say in the makeup of the committee. If a clan suspects the impartiality of a specific *Jaha* member, it can cast a veto on his participation and this veto is accepted by the *Jaha*, which is obliged to remove the vetoed member and replace him with another.[64]

This veto power is similar to the veto rights available to disputants in a Western-style mediation and arbitration. Here, too, disputants may refuse to participate in a process they deem to be prejudicial to their cause for a variety of reasons, including the choice of mediator(s) or arbitrator(s). The system is normally trusted to provide a suitable and acceptable substitute.

Another specific aspect of neutrality that finds its expression in Sulha is known as 'location neutrality'. The *Jaha* makes sure to always meet for its deliberation at neutral venues – locations which are not associated with any of the disputants' clans or that could be construed by either side as giving even the appearance of advantage to one of the disputants. This is not always easy in a community where everybody knows everybody else and family relations are widespread and wide ranging, but the interveners are aware of such potential difficulties and do their utmost to avoid them. One common solution is to meet at the local council chambers.[65]

The issue of remuneration is another aspect that might put a strain on the appearance of neutrality in dispute resolution practices. In Western-style mediation and arbitration, paying the interveners for services rendered is considered acceptable, indeed necessary, in many situations.

With the Sulha, however, the situation is different: in northern Israel the issue of remuneration is a taboo; committee members do not ask and never accept payment, gifts or anything that might be construed as such for services rendered – doing so will sully them permanently in the eyes of the community and would be the cause for a professionally crippling loss of honour. As a result, they perform their work voluntarily, sometimes sustaining significant expenses and loss of income. Faraj Khneifes described the financial burden shouldered by his father, the late Sheikh Saleh: 'In the case of one Sulha, my father drove the 40 kilometres (24.8 miles) from his home in Shefa'amer to Dir al-Assad, more than 50 times, paying for fuel out of his own pocket'.[66]

It is important to note that Sulha processes elsewhere in the Muslim/Arab world, including the Bedouin Arab community in southern Israel, sometimes include financial remunerations for the intervener(s), as corroborated by veteran Sulha practitioner Sheikh Hamis Mahmud Abu Saaluk: 'In Jordan and in the south of Israel this is the custom'.[67]

It seems that the different assumptions, as well as the different practices observed in key applications of mediation and arbitration elements, within Western ADR and Sulha reflect functional responses to differing cultural landscapes, which give rise to different, localized solutions. Conversely, the similarities between the practices and their applied elements reflect the common foundations of customary justice, regardless of the specific cultural location.

Notes

1 Abu-Nimer, 'Conflict Resolution Approaches', p. 35. In this context, it is worth noting that most, if not all, of the currently published research comparing Sulha to other ADR practices compares it to Western ADR practices, regardless of the cultural origins of the authors (e.g. Malaysia, Saudi Arabia, Lebanon, Israel). This is probably because most authors and researchers completed at least part of their education in Western academic institutions and were exposed primarily to narratives exploring, analyzing and comparing Western ADR practices.
2 Salem, 'A Critique of Western Conflict Resolution From a Non-Western Perspective', p. 1.
3 ADR is a generic term referring to a collection of various means of settling disputes outside the courtroom, such as conciliation, facilitation, negotiation, neutral evaluation, mediation and arbitration, among others.
4 Ramahi, 'Sulh', p. 1.
5 Salem, 'A Critique of Western Conflict Resolution From a Non-Western Perspective', p. 1.
6 Jeromme Barrett and Joesph Barrett, *A History of Alternative Dispute Resolution* (San Francisco: Jossey-Bass, 2004), Chapter 1; Jabbour, *Sulha*.
7 Robert N. *Bellah*, Richard Madsen, William M. Sullivan and Steven M. Tipton, *Habits of the Heart: Individualism and Commitment in America* (New York: Life Harper and Row, 1985).

8   Ramon Hollands, Iyad Rahwan, Frank Dignum and Liz Soneberg, 'An Empirical Study of Interest-Based Negotiation', *Autonomous Agents and Multi-Agent Systems*, Vol. 22, No. 2 (2011), pp 249–88.
9   Roger Fisher and William Ury, *Getting to Yes* (New York: Penguin, 1991).
10 Niko Besnier; 'Language and Affect', *Annual Review of Anthropology*, Vol. 19 (1990), p. 420.
11 Irani and Funk, 'Rituals of Reconciliation', p. 61.
12 Anthony P. Greco, 'ADR and a Smile: Neo-Colonialism and the West's Newest Export in Africa', Pepperdine Dispute Resolution Law Journal, Vol. 10, No. 3 (2010), p. 658.
13 Baruch R. Bush and Joseph P. Folger, *The Promise of Mediation: Responding to Conflict through Empowerment and Recognition* (San Francisco: Jossey-Bass, 1994), p. 2.
14 Jeffrey W. Stempel, 'Reflections on Judicial ADR and the Multi-Door Courthouse at Twenty: Fait Accompli, Failed Overture, or Fledgling Adulthood', *Ohio State Journal on Dispute Resolution*, Vol. 11. No. 2 (1996), p. 311. See also Sally Merry, 'Mediation in Nonindustrial Societies', in K. Kressel and D. Pruitt (eds.), *Mediation Research* (San Francisco: Jossey-Bass Publishers, 1989), pp. 68–90.
15 Gupta Lovleen, 'Regulating the Regulator: The Need for a Super Regulator', *International Journal of Business Economics and Management Research*, Vol. 2, No. 4 (2011), p. 223.
16 Fisher and Ury, *Getting to Yes*.
17 Salem, 'A Critique of Western Conflict Resolution From a Non-Western Perspective'.
18 Ramahi, 'Sulh', p. 2.
19 Irani and Funk, 'Rituals of Reconciliation', p. 56.
20 The American Bar Association and American Arbitration Association and Association for Conflict Resolution, 'Model Standards of Conduct, 2005', states: 'Mediation is a process in which an impartial third party facilitates communication and negotiation and promotes voluntary decision making by the parties to the dispute', www.mediate.com/articles/model_standards_of_conflict.cfm (accessed 9 June 2013).
21 Janice Roehl and Royer Cook, 'Issues in Mediation: Rhetoric and Reality Revisited', *Journal of Social Issues*, Vol. 41, No. 2 (1985), pp. 161–78.
22 Leonard L. Riskin, 'Mediator Orientations, Strategies and Techniques', *Alternatives to the High Cost of Litigation*, Vol. 12, No. 9 (1994), p. 111.
23 Bush & Folger, *The Promise of Mediation*, p. 46.
24 Dwight Golann, 'Variations in Mediation: How-and Why-Legal Mediators Change Styles in the Course of a Case', *Journal of Dispute Resolution*, Vol. 1/41 (2000), pp. 41–63.
25 Jabbour, *Sulha*, p. 56.
26 Author interview with M'bada Naum, 13 November 2011.
27 Author interview with Khneifes, 2007.
28 Author interview with M'bada Naum, 2011.
29 Author interview with Khneifes, 2011.
30 Harold I. Abramson, *Mediation Representation – Advocating in a Problem-Solving Process* (Louisville: NITA, 2004), p. 77.
31 Author interview with M'bada Naum, 2011.
32 David Matz, 'Notes Towards a Mediator's Theory of Mediation' (1996), p. 3 (unpublished paper, on file with author).
33 Author interview with Khneifes, 2011.
34 Lela Love, 'Top Ten Reasons Why Mediators Should Not Evaluate, *Florida Law Review*, Vol. 24 (1997), p. 939 (emphasis in original).
35 Umi Wikan, 'Shame and Honour: A Contestable Pair', *New Series*, Vol. 19, No. 4 (1984); Margaret S. Herrman (ed.), *The Blackwell Handbook of Mediation – Bridging Theory, Research and Practice* (Oxford: Blackwell Publishing, 2006), pp. 237–38.
36 Author interview with M'bada Naum.

37 Edgar L. Warren & Irving Bernstein, 'The Arbitration Process', *Southern Economic Journal*, Vol. 17, No. 1 (1950), p. 16; also see, Jacqueline M. Nolan-Haley, *Alternative Dispute Resolution in a Nutshell*, 4th ed. (St. Paul, MN: West Wadsworth, 2008), pp. 153–214.
38 Paul R. Rice, 'Mediation and Arbitration as a Civil Alternative to the Criminal Justice System – An Overview and Legal Analysis', *American University Law Review*, Vol. 29 (1979–80), p. 21.
39 Author interview with M'bada Naum.
40 Baruch Bush, 'The Dilemmas of Mediation Practice: A Study of Ethical Dilemmas & Policy Implications', *Journal of Dispute Resolution*, Vol. 1 (1994), pp. 400–1.
41 Christopher Honeyman, 'Confidential, More or Less', *Dispute Resolution Journal*, Vol. 5, No. 12 (1998), p. 12.
42 Author interview with M'bada Naum.
43 Lawrence R. Freedman & Michael L. Prigoff, 'Confidentiality in Mediation: The Need for Protection', *Ohio State Journal on Conflict Resolution*, Vol. 2, No. 1 (1986), p. 38.
44 Scott Hughes, 'A Closer Look: The Case for a Mediation Privilege Still Has Not Been Made', *Dispute Resolution Magazine*, Vol. 5, No. 2 (1998), p. 14.
45 Jabbour, *Sulha*, p. 37.
46 Author interview with Shtewe, 16 October 2012.
47 *Ibid.*
48 Tsafrir, 'Arab Customary Law', p. 88.
49 Jabbour, *Sulha*, p. 37; Author interview with M'bada Naum.
50 Matz, 'Notes', p. 9; Tricia S. Jones & Andrea Bodtker, 'Mediating With Heart in Mind: Addressing Emotion in Mediation Practice', *Negotiation Journal*, Vol. 17, No. 3 (2001), pp. 207–44.
51 Susan Silbey & Merry Sally, 'Mediator Settlement Strategies', *Law and Policy Quarterly*, Vol. 8, No. 1 (1986), p. 19.
52 Bush & Folger, *The Promise of Mediation*, pp. 46, 59.
53 Trina Grillio, 'Respecting the Struggle: Following the Parties' Lead', *Conflict Resolution Quarterly*, Vol. 13, No. 4 (1996), p. 281.
54 Christopher W. Moore, 'The Caucus: Private Meetings That Promote Settlement', *Conflict Resolution Quarterly*, Vol. 1987, No. 16 (1987), p. 88.
55 Jabbour, *Sulha*, p. 47.
56 Author interview with Abu M'bada, 2011.
57 Author interview with Sheikh Abu Riad, 2012.
58 Author's participant observation at a Jaha meeting with a victim's clan, Deer al-Assad, 2 August 2010.
59 Jabbour, *Sulha*, pp. 38–9. See also Bush, *The Dilemma of Mediation*, p. 385.
60 Kevin Gibson, Leigh Thompson & Max H. Bazerman 'Shortcomings of Neutrality in Mediation: Solutions Based on Rationality', *Negotiation Journal*, Vol. 12, No. 1 (1996), pp. 69–70.
61 Janet Rifkin, Jonathan Millen & Sara Cobb, 'Toward a New Discourse for Mediation: A Critique of Neutrality', *Conflict Resolution Quarterly*, Vol. 9, No. 2 (1991), pp. 151–52.
62 Gibson et al., 'Shortcomings', p. 70. See also Suzanne Mccorkle, 'The Murky World of Mediation Ethics: Neutrality, Impartiality, and Conflict of Interest in State Codes of Conduct', *Conflict Resolution Quarterly*, Vol. 23, No. 2 (2005), pp. 165–83.
63 Author interview with Sheikh Hamis Mahmud Abu Saaluk, 12 July 2007; Jabbour, *Sulha*, p. 39.
64 Author interview with M'bada Naum.
65 Jabbour, *Sulha*, p. 38.
66 Author interview with Khneifes, 2007.
67 Author interview with Abu Saaluk, 2007. Abu Saaluk is active in the Bedouin communities of southern Israel, as well as in the Palestinian Arab communities in the West Bank, and lives in the Israeli town of Kafr Qassem.

7 Sulha and Israel's legal system

In the state of Israel, Sulha is practiced throughout the country's Arab community, though specific details and rituals differ between regions.[1] For example, in the centre and south of Israel, the Sulha process follows more 'judicial' (*Quthat al-Shari'a*) rules: the intervener gets paid, leads the process and 'tells' disputants what will happen, whereas in northern Israel the process follows a more 'traditional' path where interveners do not get paid and disputants have a major say in the process.[2]

Regardless of the 'flavour' of Sulha practiced, Israel's formal legal system does not accord the practise official recognition of any kind, nor does the state have an official or even quasi-official policy designed to deal with the Sulha and its interaction with the formal system. Yet, court records and other available evidence show that despite its lack of formal standing, the Sulha does play a role and *is* taken into consideration within Israel's formal judiciary system.[3]

This 'official ambivalence' results in an inconsistent approach to the Sulha by the courts, affecting the relationship between the practices and their practitioners, generating friction between the systems and leaving both sides unsure about the place of Sulha within or alongside the formal law of the land.

As we shall see, Sulha differs from Israel's formal legal system in many ways, including its underlying principles, practice and goals. This chapter employs interviews, analysis of legal decisions and existing literature to consider the most significant differences between Sulha and Israel's formal legal system, to locate and examine the relationship and interaction between them and to demonstrate its resultant, symbiotic reality. The insight gained from this exploration contributes to clarifying the place and function of Sulha, and may help understand and predict its future evolution.

The differences between the Sulha and Israel's legal system

Israel's formal legal system draws its definitions of the Sulha's core concepts – mediation and arbitration – from different sources.

The legal foundation of Israeli mediation rests on the 1984 Law of Mediation.[4] Recent legislation (2008) mandates mediation as a first step, before adjudication for all civil cases above £9,320 (US$15,000).[5] But the concept itself is predicated on individual autonomy as elucidated in Hebrew law and the desire that people arrive at solutions without external intervention.[6]

The legal foundations of arbitration in Israel are anchored in Turkish (Ottoman) legal code, the Mejelle,[7] were transferred to British code[8] and in 1968 converted to Israeli legislation by bringing in aspects of Hebrew law.[9]

The main difference between Israel's formal legal system and the Sulha is that the former is the law of the land, applicable to all citizens and residents of the country, whereas the latter has no official recognition or standing and is practiced exclusively by and within Israel's Muslim/Arab population.[10]

The second major difference between Israeli law and the Sulha rests in the way the two systems categorize crimes: Israeli law sees infractions that involve the infliction of damage either on the property or the body of a person as criminal offenses, the handling of which is the domain of the state.[11] Consequently, *individuals* who commit such offenses should be prosecuted by the state according to its laws. Of course, the state may decide not to prosecute for a variety of reasons, but then again, the decision is up to the state legal system, not the victim, the community, local dignitaries and definitely not the offending party.

A criminal prosecution by the state is thus an act of significant symbolism for members of a culture that has central institutions of governance (particularly such that have the trust of the constituencies). A criminal conviction is a 'mark of Cain' that the community puts on the individual, a mark that remains, with variations, for life (e.g. criminal record, sex offender registrar, parole restrictions, ex-convict lifelong restrictions). In a very practical sense, the slate is never really 'wiped clean', so the community not only remembers the pain of the offense but also does not really forgive the criminal.

The Arab community in Israel, on the other hand, sees the same infractions that are classified as criminal offenses by the country's legal system as tort (a civil wrong that can be redressed through compensation) rather than a crime.[12] The view of the Sulha is that '[a] man's blood must not be spilled for nothing'.[13] Furthermore, the responsibility for such offenses and for redressing them rests with the offender's entire clan; they are communally responsible for the offense and should undertake the prescribed actions to atone for it and resolve the dispute. Such cases, classified as infractions between people (as opposed to offenses of people against Allah) do not end up in front of a Muslim religious Shari'a judge (*Qadi*) but are dealt with by Sulha practitioners.

Sulha and the courts

One of the most prominent areas of interaction between the Sulha and Israel's legal system is in the country's judiciary system. A demonstration of the complex relations between formal courts and the Sulha can be seen in a sentencing decision by Supreme Court Justice Elyakim Rubinstein in its appellate capacity as a Supreme Court of Appeals, which displays a positive disposition towards Sulha and its role. In his words: 'We should encourage the making of peace through a Sulha agreement, particularly where we deal with large groups – families, and extended families – which in the absence of Sulha, based on age old traditions, might deteriorate to continuous bloodshed'.[14]

Yet alongside this apparent inclusive attitude, Justice Rubinstein makes it clear that there are strict limits to this inclusiveness. Again, the justice initially strikes an inclusive tone, but it is followed by sharp assertion of the court's absolute supremacy. Justice Rubinstein writes: 'The Sulha institution is honourable and should be honoured. Furthermore, we should encourage the making of peace by Sulha'. This is followed by a sharp qualifier: 'It is important that those involved in making Sulha agreements be aware that in both criminal and civil matters the Sulha does not act as substitute to legal proceedings'.[15]

Yet again, towards the end of his summation, Justice Rubinstein presents a more inclusive posture, writing: 'And of course, each issue will be considered on its own merits, and questions such as the amount of the real damage against the amount set in the Sulha agreement, and other circumstances, will be examined as necessary'.[16]

This example demonstrates how, under certain circumstances, the courts allow Sulha to play a role that has a direct bearing on the outcome of legal proceedings; in this case, when setting damages, the court accepts as legitimate the possible inclusion of Sulha agreement sums in the overall consideration of damages (civil in this case).

Another example highlights a situation where the court rejects any linkage between a Sulha agreement and the consideration of the verdict. On 24 February 1993 the Supreme Court of Israel, sitting as the country's highest criminal court of appeal, published its decision to accept the state's appeal against the 'lightness' of the sentence meted out by the municipal court of Tel Aviv on 12 June 1992 against Rifaat Masrawa, convicted of assault and battery with intent to cause severe bodily harm and sentenced to seven months imprisonment and twenty-four months suspended sentence.

When responding to the defendant's arguments as presented in the appeal, Justices Meir Shamgar, Eliezer Goldberg and Mishael Hashin wrote:

> The learned advocate for the respondent claimed that the court should take into consideration, with a view towards reducing the punishment, the fact that in the meantime a Sulha agreement was arranged between the respondent and his family and the victim and his family. We do not see in the Sulha an element that should influence the determination of a proper punishment as indicated by the circumstances of this case; this is because the determinant in this case [is] not the relations between the relevant families but the level of danger to the public at large from the violent, unbridled behaviour of the respondent, who in one instance stabbed a man just because he was a member of a family, one of whose members stabbed the respondent a year earlier. This time the respondent broke both arms of the father of the plaintiff, a man who has done nothing to offend the defendant. This means that if the respondent is furious, he is willing to hurt whoever is in his way. It is suitable, then, that he would be punished in such a way that will constitute

another attempt to educate him to behave in a more restrained manner and to avoid violence.[17]

It seems that the justices ignored or were unfamiliar with the position and role of Sulha in Arab society, as well as the relationship between the events examined in the decision and the traditional dispute behaviour of the disputants, as reflected in the pre- and post-Sulha actions taken by the disputants. The justices do not take into account the fact that although, formally, the court may consider *only* the defendant, in reality, the circle of disputants in this case is by no means confined strictly to the victim and perpetrator, but encompasses entire clans. In the words of Sulha maker Elias Jabbour: 'The collective responsibility of the extended family (*hamula*) in Arab culture toward all its members is one of the main factors that makes Sulha work'.[18]

Indeed, the pattern of violence described by the justices as unrelated to the case (and, of course, unjustified in their opinion under any circumstances) reflects the traditional 'retaliatory revenge' attack profile that characterizes the kind of 'tit-for-tat' behaviour that Sulha agreements are specifically designed to mitigate against. In this case, there was no direct 'danger to the public' as the court indicated; the danger was ostensibly confined (and indeed occurred) exclusively to the circle of the disputant's extended families.[19]

Another court decision, this time by Israeli Supreme Court Justice Armand Levi, demonstrates an attitude that, contrary to the former decision, *does* recognize the Sulha agreement as a central consideration in the decision to accept the defendant's appeal against what he perceived as the harshness of the sentence and to effectively reduce the sentence from imprisonment to community service. Justice Levi wrote:

> I will not hide [the fact] that deciding in this case caused me no small amount of hesitation. The violence meted out by the appellants on their victims, including children, was harsh, and after they left the apartment, they left behind a scene of severe damage to property. These are deeds that under regular circumstances necessitate a severe punishment with twin purposes: to repay the perpetrators for their deeds, and to try to decrease as much as possible the disease of violence that infected Israeli society. On the other hand, this is a long running family feud between relatives, some of whom are 'first degree' relatives; and it is just possible that the last events, and the criminal proceedings that followed, gave all involved pause to understand that there is no substitute to peace and reconciliation, since the other way might lead to destruction and loss. Therefore, many dignitaries from the Bedouin community, and some police officers, including the Chief of the Northern Command, took it upon themselves to try to bring the feuding sides to negotiations. It seems that these efforts bore fruit, as evidenced by the Sulha agreement that was signed on June 2004.

Against this backdrop the justice concluded that '[f]urthermore, since the violent events in Bir al-Maksur, in 1999, five-and-a-half years have passed without a repeat of such events, and this too may point to the possibility that a lesson was learned by all involved'.[20]

Judge Nava Appel-Danon of the Nazareth Municipal Court in northern Israel addressed the lack of formal policy regarding Sulha agreements in court considerations. 'There are conflicting decisions regarding the ramifications of Sulha agreements in the case of defendants accused of violent crimes', she wrote in a detention appeal decision, before adding that in this particular case 'it is certain that the fact that the disputing clans in this case reached a Sulha agreement serves as a new circumstance, justifying a complete re-evaluation of the decision to detain the defendants until the end of the process or to find a substitute to detention'.[21] In these particular circumstances, Judge Appel-Danon ordered the defendants to be released from detention in favour of a house arrest.

Is the Sulha agreement admissible evidence?

The mere simultaneous (though informal) cohabitation of Sulha with Israel's formal legal system, as described earlier, gives rise to some interesting dilemmas facing the disputants, Sulha practitioners and the country's formal legal system.

One such dilemma that perhaps symbolizes the complex relations between courts and Sulha in Israel comes to the fore when a defendant submits a plea of 'not guilty' to the court as a formal part of the legal proceedings, yet at the same time presents the court with a Sulha agreement that contains implicit admission of guilt, including assumption of responsibility and expressions of regret.

Such a situation highlights two significant dilemmas: one is that of the court, which has to decide which submission of the defendant is relevant (if any) and, if so, what part of either (or both) should affect the court's decisions and how. The other dilemma is on the part of the defendant who also has to decide in advance whether submitting a Sulha agreement is advantageous to his case or not.

From the court's perspective, a Sulha agreement may add information that could influence its decision in two directions. For one thing, the fact that the disputants' families reached a Sulha agreement may drive the court towards leniency when considering a variety of actions, such as detention, sentencing or appeals. For another, the very same agreement, designed to encourage the court to look more favourably on the defendant, might collide head-on with the defendant's 'not guilty' plea – and possibly with other formal utterances of innocence – by providing a de facto admission of guilt, which may result in the court meting out an even less favourable decision (e.g. longer punishment, detention instead of a house arrest, refusal to release on parole). Nurit Tsafrir, one of the few scholars to pay attention to this possible discrepancy, writes:

> In the eyes of the court, the Sulha may express the accused admission of having committed those deeds . . . Furthermore, the Sulha agreement presented to the court sometimes contains details of the injury caused by the accused . . . Consequently, the Sulha may lose its value as a reason for releasing the accused from detention.[22]

An even larger dilemma for the courts in general is that if they accept Sulha agreements as facts and consider the statements included in them, no one in the Arab community will ever bring such agreements to court, which may in turn weaken the status of the Sulha, a change that in the current sociological state (clan-based culture) will leave the Arab community with a weakened dispute resolution tool – an outcome that both sides (the community and the state) are probably loath to face.

One reference to a Sulha agreement that contradicts the defendant's claims is mentioned in the court's response to an appeal of a detention order where the judge, Justice Itzhak Cohen, wrote:

> In the preamble to the Sulha agreement it is written: 'Due to the severe case of assault on the minor Suhad Ahmed Salame by Mr. Atef Hussein Fuaz and another man from the village Arab al-Heyab, on 16.09.2006' and further: 'The Fuaz family from [the] Ilabon [village] admits assaulting the minor and inflicting on him a severe physical and mental damage'; and even further: 'In exchange for this confession and the agreement to pay compensation, the plaintiff's family obliged itself to cancel the complaint only against the respondent. The Sulha agreement was signed by the respondent, the plaintiff, his father and two members of the Sulha Committee'.[23]

So here, according to the judge, is a confession for all intents and purposes. The judge, thus, continues: 'Why then, if the respondent admitted to an assault [in the Sulha agreement], did he move to nullify the complaint against him, claiming that there was no factual truth behind the complaint?' And the judge continues to wonder:

> If the respondent is not responsible for assaulting the plaintiff and causing the bodily damage done to the plaintiff, why did he go about explicitly admitting the assault in a signed and sealed Sulha agreement, one that also sets the duty of paying compensation?[24]

In his verdict, perhaps reflecting the complexity of the issue and the judicial inability to simultaneously accommodate formal and informal processes, the judge completely ignored the questions that he himself had raised. Furthermore, the verdict demonstrated a clear preference to ignore the explicit admissions made in the Sulha agreement (and referred to by the judge), as it, somewhat surprisingly, decided in favour of a house arrest as a substitute for detention.

In another instance, the court explicitly touched upon the core of the dilemma. Judge Erica Priel of the Haifa Local Court noted in her verdict that despite the fact that a Sulha agreement was reached between the plaintiff's family and the defendant's family, the agreement was not an indication of admission of guilt of any kind. In the judge's words:

> Whether the defendant participated in the Sulha (personally) or not, it [the Sulha agreement] is not to be seen as an admission on his part of the

commission of the offence, since like in the case of arbitration, the Sulha process is designed to settle a conflict by reaching a compromise.[25]

This case represents a curious attempt by the judge to accommodate the informal and formal processes by insisting on referring to the facts of the matter (admission of guilt) and immediately relegating them to an informal place where they would not 'confuse' the court. The problem here is that in the real world, an arbitration process would not have found its way to a consideration by a court of law (except to ratify the arbitration decision); neither would the court have become privy to information collected in the process of arbitration in the event that the arbitration ends up being decided in court instead of by the arbitrator.

Furthermore, the judge in this case took the opportunity to leverage the Sulha agreement in the 'opposite' direction (away from possible admission of guilt) when she wrote:

> A Sulha took place between the sides, as expected in the Druze community; the plaintiffs received monetary compensation, and from the words of the defendant it appears that he will ensure not to repeat his actions in the future. It is true that the mere fact of a Sulha agreement cannot serve as an excuse for not prosecuting a criminal offense and its influence [the Sulha's] is apparent mainly in arguments to sentencing. But under the current circumstances, the Sulha serves as another supporting argument to reach the conclusion that we have here a case that under the circumstances had not justified the initiation of a criminal prosecution.[26]

Consequently, the court acquitted the defendant of all charges despite the Sulha agreement with its explicit admission of guilt. The judge did not give any reason for her decision beyond the early indication that the explicit admission in the Sulha agreement was not admissible by reason of being similar to arbitration.

From the defendant's perspective, the dilemma is that presenting the court with a Sulha agreement (assuming that courts delve into the details of the agreement and incorporate its elements into their decisions) implies a level of culpability and responsibility that weakens the defendant's ability to plead 'not guilty'. If courts insist on taking the language of Sulha agreements literally, then the admission of guilt in these agreements collides directly with the not-guilty plea in court. Moreover, until the rendering of a decision, the defendant never knows which part of the Sulha agreement the court decided to incorporate into its formal decision. As Khneifes commented: 'In some cases defendants are afraid that the Sulha agreement will be used to incriminate them and they demand a separation of the processes'.[27]

How do the Sulha and Israel's formal legal system complement each other?

The core area where the Sulha and Israel's formal legal system complement each other is in that the Sulha, from its inception, was designed to provide an answer to the unique issues that arise from the centrality of the extended clan-based family unit (*hamula*) in the life of both related individuals and their community, whereas Israel's legal system, indeed Western legal systems in general, although acting on behalf of the community and for its general good, revolve around the concept of individual personal responsibility.[28] Together, the two systems cover a fuller spectrum of human interactions and relations than each covers by itself – from the individual through to the entire community and its building blocks (the clan and the tribe in this case). Thus, Israel's formal legal system accommodates the individual responsibility side of the equation, and the Sulha addresses the communal side.

In a decision pursuant to civil appeal on payment of punitive damages following a criminal conviction, Justice Rubinstein of Israel's Supreme Court (sitting as the country's highest court of appeal) highlighted one such accommodation when he wrote:

> I re-read and reconsidered the lower court's sentence and verdict, and also the Sulha agreement and the letters of recommendation that were presented on behalf of appellant No. 1 in particular. I am indeed aware that we have here appellants without a prior criminal record. There is certainly public interest in bringing peace between members of belligerent families, and in re-affirming the Sulha agreement that was reached with the plaintiffs, in a way that will contribute to future stability.[29]

In this case, the lower court decided, and the Supreme Court affirmed the decision, that the payment to the plaintiff made under the Sulha agreement was part of the punitive damages and satisfied the 'communal' element of the case. Beyond that, the court allowed the plaintiff to claim additional damages based on the medical evidence of the bodily damage that was inflicted on him; apparently, this, in the court's eyes, will have satisfied the 'private' (individual) part of the case. Thus, in practice, the court was careful to chart a path that left both institutions and practices actively and practically engaged in terms of authority and clout.

Furthermore, this was a case where the criminal part required a formal legal system whereas the resultant interclan conflict necessitated the Sulha system. Here, again, 'bridging' the remaining gaps between the areas covered by the formal criminal system and those covered by the Sulha necessitated the introduction of a civil authority, which took into consideration the monetary compensation of the Sulha agreement. As such, this case encompassed the utility of all available conflict resolution/management frameworks.

Ron Shapiro, a municipal judge and a lecturer at the Haifa University Law School, stressed the fact that '[l]aw enforcement is not a task assigned exclusively to the courts'. He added that

> [g]iving status to community institutions, and giving status to the social uniqueness and otherness, in the course of conflict resolution process, contributes to reducing social tensions and to changing the focus to maintaining harmony between the components of a multi-cultural society.[30]

It seems that the reason the two systems (Sulha and Israel's formal legal system) can coexist is precisely because they are so different in philosophy and practice, that they are not likely to compete with each other and thus may be referred to and utilized in ways that are complementary rather than contradictory. Yet despite their complementary characteristics, the coexistence between the two systems is by no means assured and/or easy. This is because integrating them requires each side to give up some of its autonomy, perhaps even authority, and to walk an uncertain path of informality, the kind that frees both sides from the need to commit themselves to a rigid and uniform course of action vis-à-vis the other system. The formal legal system, thus, has the necessary flexibility to use Sulha as a consideration whenever it sees fit, yet to reject it (as a consideration) whenever it does not want to let it have an influence (e.g. appeals). Tsafrir highlights this freedom by writing:

> Thus, recognition by the court of the Sulha can have ramifications that may not be to the court's liking. At the same time, total rejection of Sulha agreements as an argument in court, because of their problematic aspects, may also not be desirable.[31]

It appears that the only functional solution recognizing and responding to the coexistence of diverse social and legal structures (Muslim/Arab vs. Jewish/Israeli/Western, and customary justice vs. formal justice), as well as to the differences in philosophy and application between them, is the path of ambiguous collaboration. A formal recognition of Sulha by the courts will most likely lead to a collision rather than to collaboration/cooperation because, despite the unique ways in which the two systems complement each other, they clearly emanate from different competing sources and operate in different modes – different enough so that if they cohabit a formal space, they will inevitably pull in different, conflict-creating directions that would make their coexistence unlikely.

As for the Muslim/Arab side, recognizing Israel's formal legal system as the only dispute resolution/management 'player' will deprive this minority community of an essential, traditional, and long-practiced peacemaking tool without providing any socially or legally functional substitute. This might be a costly loss because in the absence of any conflict management/resolution mechanism that will deal with extended inter- and intraclan disputes, it is likely that such disputes will not reach a final resolution at the clan level, leading to consequent cycles of retaliation and revenge.

Sulha's place within Israel's judiciary system: a quantitative perspective

A quantitative examination of Sulha-related court decisions was undertaken in order to try to identify and measure significant trends and patterns in the Israeli courts' attitudes towards Sulha agreements. This exploration also set out to locate and understand how Sulha processes and agreements are viewed by Israeli courts during different stages of the (legal) litigation, such as detention decisions, sentencing, verdicts and appeals.

Data sources

The court decisions used for this sample were taken from a national computerized database of court records, called Takdin.

At the time of the data collection (summers 2007–11), the database contained 322,549 distinct records of court decisions and actions. The court decisions examined were those made by municipal courts and by the Supreme Court.

Of the total database, there were 1,066 court decisions that referred to Sulha, of this a mere 27 decisions (~ 2.5 per cent) dealt with Sulha agreements made by Jews, and those were removed from the sample.[32]

Assuming that Arabs are represented in court proceedings in Israel in a way that is about equal to their proportion in the general population (~20 per cent), the percentage of court decisions containing reference to a Sulha agreement was very low (~ 1039 * 100/(322,549/5) = ~1.6 per cent.

This is an unusually low proportion. One explanation for it may be that formal courts rarely consider it. Another explanation may be that significant Sulha agreements, those involving either death or a grievous injury, account for only a small portion of the total adjudicated case load in Israeli courts.

Yet another explanation of this phenomenon may be found in interviews with Sulha practitioners and judges who indicated that many Sulha negotiations take longer than criminal proceedings to reach an agreement and that only a final Sulha agreement stands a chance of affecting the judicial process through its inclusion in the courts' major or minor considerations. Informants added that many victimized clans slow down the Sulha process deliberately so as to deny the offending side the opportunity to use the Sulha agreement as an element in a plea for leniency from the courts.[33] Furthermore, as we shall see, it may be that because Sulha agreements may indirectly provide the courts with evidence, many defendants choose to avoid presenting them to the courts so as to avoid self-incrimination, thus keeping the two processes – formal and informal – completely separate, from start to finish.[34]

Sulha: sample size

For the quantitative sample in this work, 123 court actions were randomly selected out of the total population of 1,039 decisions mentioning Sulha (approximately every eighth court record).

Total Sample Size (TSS) = 123

The 123 cases were divided into the following five categories:

1. Plea Bargain (PB) – Cases where there was reference to Sulha in relation to the plea bargain = 19 = (15.4 per cent of TSS).
2. Appeal on Verdict (A) – Cases where there was reference to the Sulha in relation to the appeal on verdict = 17 = (13.8 per cent of TSS).

3   Detention (original decision) (D) – Cases where there was reference to the Sulha in relation to detention (original decision) = 23 = (18.6 per cent of TSS).
4   Appeal on Detention (AD) – Cases where there was reference to the Sulha in relation to the appeal (on detention) = 15 = (12.2 per cent of TSS).
5   Sentencing (S) – Cases where there was reference to the Sulha in relation to sentencing = 49 = (39.8 per cent of TSS).

Table 7.1 presents the data described earlier in a tabulated format.

Hypothesis (for all categories and for cumulative results)

Hypothesis (H_0) = P = 0.50: It is assumed that normally, if a court has to select between accepting or rejecting Sulha agreements as a consideration, the probability for a decision to go either way is a random 50 per cent (even). Court decisions can therefore be modelled as a binomial distribution with p = 0.5.

Alternative Hypothesis (H_1) = P > 0.50: The proportion of acceptance or rejection is larger than 50 per cent.

The test here is for the presence of a systematic pattern in the courts' decisions.

Examination of each category

Plea bargain (PB)

Within the first category, Plea Bargain (PB) Court Decisions = 19 (15.4 per cent of TSS), the decisions were classifiable into two general sections:

- Court considers Sulha positively for the purpose of the plea bargain = 13 (68.4 per cent of PB, 10.6 per cent of TSS).
- Court rejects/ignores Sulha for the purpose of the plea bargain = 6 (31.6 per cent of PB, 4.9 per cent of TSS).

Using the normal approximation to the assumed binomial distribution of court outcomes (npq > 3), the standard score (Z) for the plea bargain court decisions is 1.606 (see the following equation and computation).

$$Z = \frac{x - np}{\sqrt{nqp}}$$

where:
x = sample proportion
n = sample size
p = population proportion (H_0) = P = 0.50

Table 7.1 Tabulation of quantitative data and analysis for courts' Sulha-related decisions

Court Action	Court Attitude*	Number per Attitude	Total Number	Percentage of TSS	Percentage of Action	Percentage of TSS
Plea Bargain (PB)	Positive	13	19	15.4 per cent	68.4 per cent	10.6 per cent
	Negative	6			31.6 per cent	4.9 per cent
Appeal (Verdict) (A)	Positive	3	17	13.8 per cent	17.6 per cent	2.4 per cent
	Negative	14			82.4 per cent	11.4 per cent
Detention (original decision) (D)	Positive	12	23	18.6 per cent	52.2 per cent	9.8 per cent
	Negative	11			47.8 per cent	8.9 per cent
Appeal on Detention (AD)	Positive	2	15	12.2 per cent	13.3 per cent	1.6 per cent
	Negative	13			86.7 per cent	10.6 per cent
Sentencing (S)	Positive	19	49	39.8 per cent	38.8 per cent	15.4 per cent
	Negative	30			61.2 per cent	24.4 per cent
Totals	NA	123	123	99.8	NA	**100 per cent**

Total Sample Size (TSS) = 123
* Legend (court attitude):
Positive = Court considers Sulha positively
Negative = Court rejects/ignores Sulha

$$q = 1 - p$$

$$Z = \frac{13 - (19 \times 0.5)}{\sqrt{19 \times 0.5 \times 0.5}} = 1.606$$

Using a standard normal probability table, we find that the area to the left of the Z score (1.606) is 95.15 per cent.

That means that the area to the right of the Z score is 4.85 per cent, which is more than the 2.5 per cent required for a one-sided test of significance.

Conclusion: The acceptance/rejection rate of Sulha agreements in a population of plea bargain court decisions is *not* significantly different than random.

Note: For reasons of space conservation, this section presents the entire reasoning process for the first category. The other four categories show only the main Z calculation and the resulting conclusion(s), without the computations, which are identical to those of the first category.

Appeal on verdict (A)

Within the second category, appeal (verdict) (A) = 17 (13.8 per cent of TSS), the decisions were classifiable into two general sections:

- Court considers the Sulha positively for the purpose of appeal (on verdict) – = 3 (17.6 per cent of A, 2.4 per cent of TSS).
- Court rejects/ignores the Sulha for the purpose of appeal (on verdict) = 14 (82.4 per cent of A, 10.8 per cent of TSS).

Standard score calculation for second category

$$Z = \frac{14 - (17 \times 0.5)}{\sqrt{17 \times 0.5 \times 0.5}} = 2.66$$

Conclusion: The rejection rate of Sulha agreements in a population of appeal (on verdict) court decisions is statistically significant (larger than can be expected at the 2.5 per cent one-sided test).

Original detention decision (D)

Within the **third category, detention (original decision) (D) = 23 (18.6 per cent of TSS)**, the decisions were classifiable into two general sections:

- Court considers the Sulha positively for the purpose of the detention decision = 12 (52.2 per cent of D, 9.8 per cent of TSS).
- Court rejects/ignores the Sulha for the purpose of detention decision = 11 (47.8 per cent of D, 8.9 per cent of TSS).

Standard score calculation for third category

$$Z = \frac{12 - (23 \times 0.5)}{\sqrt{23 \times 0.5 \times 0.5}} = 0.208$$

Conclusion: The acceptance or rejection rate of Sulha agreements in a population of detention court decisions is *not* statistically significant (not significantly different than a random decision, or p = 0.50 in the population).

Appeal on detention decision (AD)

Within the fourth category, appeal on detention = 15 (AD) (12.2 per cent of TSS), the decisions were classifiable into two general sections:

- Court considers the Sulha positively for the purpose of appeal on detention = 2 (13.3 per cent of AD, 1.6 per cent of TSS).
- Court rejects/ignores Sulha for the purpose of appeal on detention = 13 (86.7 per cent of AD, 10.6 per cent of TSS).

Standard score calculation for fourth category

$$Z = \frac{13 - (15 \times 0.5)}{\sqrt{15 \times 0.5 \times 0.5}} = 2.84$$

Conclusion: The rejection rate of Sulha agreements in a population of appeal on detention court decisions is statistically significant (significantly larger than random).

Sentencing decision (S)

Within the fifth category, Sentencing (S) = 49 (39.8 per cent of TSS), the decisions were classifiable into two general sections:

- Court considers the Sulha positively for the purpose of sentencing = 19 (38.8 per cent of S, 15.4 per cent of TSS).
- Court rejects/ignores the Sulha for the purpose of sentencing = 30 (61.2 per cent of S, 24.4 per cent of TSS).

Standard score calculation for fifth category

$$Z = \frac{30 - (49 \times 0.5)}{\sqrt{49 \times 0.5 \times 0.5}} = 1.57$$

Conclusion: The acceptance or rejection rate of Sulha agreements in a population of sentencing court decisions is *not* statistically significant.[35]

In general, the sample's results are as follows:

Court considers Sulha positively /TSS = 49 cases (39.8 per cent)
Court rejects/ignores Sulha/TSS = 74 cases (60.1 per cent)
Total = 99.9 per cent

When all rejections are added to the sample (74 out of 123), we get a **Z score** of 2.25, resulting in 98.78 per cent of the area left of the normal curve and 1.22 per cent to the right. This in turn means that the overall (cumulative) rejection rate of Sulha agreements in court decisions is statistically significant.

Discussion

The main conclusion arising from the previous discussion is that, statistically, courts tend to *systematically reject/ignore Sulha agreements* as a consideration in their overall decisions.

Regarding the individual groups of court decisions as presented in this analysis, it is possible to say that they exhibit a mixed approach to the Sulha process and agreements as a significant consideration. In some categories (e.g. plea bargain and sentencing), courts' decisions are not statistically significant (compared with a random decision); for other categories (e.g. appeal on detention and appeal on verdict), courts' decisions are statistically significant.

In addition, it is possible to say the following about the way courts relate to Sulha agreements in their decision process:

- Courts relate to Sulha agreements most positively as a consideration during *plea bargain* agreements.
- Courts are at their most adamant in rejecting the introduction of Sulha as a consideration during *appeals*, on either sentencing or detention.
- Courts are split about the question of accommodating Sulha as part of the arguments for (original) *sentencing* and/or (original) *detention* decisions.
- In the case of *primary detention decisions*, courts are almost evenly split between accepting and rejecting Sulha agreements as a positive consideration. It is likely that at this stage courts are not familiar with the nuances of the cases in front of them, testimony and evidence are just starting to accumulate and decisions by the courts are probably affected by the personal familiarity of the presiding judge with Muslim/Arab dispute resolution. Likewise, the Sulha process is not likely to have started in earnest at this early stage and it is unlikely, therefore, that the Sulha would play a significant role in the communication between the prosecutorial and/or defence representatives and the courts. Indeed, the previous analysis shows that at this stage of the (legal) process, there is no statistically significant difference between Sulha-related decisions and a random decision in the courts.

- In the case of appeals on detention decisions, courts tend to reject the inclusion of Sulha as a positive consideration by a statistically significant margin. Here, too, it seems that at this early stage of the legal process courts are loath to give Sulha a place in their considerations. The rather determined tendency to reject consideration of Sulha in court decisions at this stage may also reflect the fact that the defence teams, almost reflexively, bring up the Sulha question as part of their appeal strategy, forcing courts to relate to the subject, but achieving the opposite effect from that desired by the defence teams.
- In the case of plea bargain agreements, courts appear to embrace the inclusion of Sulha as a significant element contributing to the decision to accept plea bargain agreements by a margin of almost 7:3 (see Table 7.1). Yet statistically, it is not a significant deviation from a random decision. Such attitudes probably reflect the courts' more conciliatory attitude as they enter the plea bargain process, when all parties (court, prosecution and defence) know that they will not have to face a protracted and sometimes contentious adjudication process and are, therefore, probably more disposed to consider positively extenuating circumstances that lend credence to court decisions as they proceed toward what will most likely be a less harsh punishment (compared with one that will follow a full trial process). It may also be that the courts actually *want* to use the Sulha process argument to help explain the plea bargain in general and what may be perceived by the victim's clan and the community at large as a relatively lenient outcome.
- In the case of sentencing decisions, the courts tend to reject Sulha as a positive contributing element, but the rejection is *not* statistically significant. The influence of Sulha is at its most prominent during this stage of the formal legal process. Although judges reject Sulha by about a third more than they allow it to influence their considerations, there is still a good number of decisions where Sulha plays a prominent role in judges' considerations. Because the sentencing phase takes place usually several years after the conflict's eruption, there is a better chance that the customary process has played its course and that the interclan dispute has been resolved. Under such circumstances, the victim's clan is much less likely to object to the judge's inclusion of the Sulha agreement as part of the considerations. Conversely, it is reasonable to assume that judges will have a more positive view of the Sulha process if told by both sides (victims and perpetrators) that the dispute has effectively been resolved at the clan level.
- In the case of appeals on sentencing decisions, courts reject the inclusion of Sulha as a positive contribution by a statistically significant margin. Here, too, it seems that the court, having made up its mind regarding the case, is reluctant to allow an external process (possibly even viewed as competing) to sway its opinion significantly. If the judge rejected Sulha as a consideration during the sentencing phase, it is unlikely that the appellate court will introduce a new element at such a late stage in the legal proceedings.

- The earlier statistical examination of the cumulative results (acceptance vs. rejection) of Sulha as a consideration in court decisions shows that courts tend to reject the Sulha agreements by a statistically significant margin. Still, it is quite apparent that a large minority of the judges do allow Sulha in their decision making throughout the process.

Possible reasons for the mixed approach

There are several possible reasons for the mixed attitude that Israeli courts exhibit towards the Sulha:

- The absence of an official policy, combined in some cases with a lack of clear understanding by the judiciary of the role of Sulha in Arab culture in general, and in dispute resolution in particular. Judge Aharon Aminof, vice president of Israel Nazareth Municipal Court (a court that adjudicates a majority of Arab-Arab cases) was quite blunt about it, saying: 'Most judges don't really know much about the institution of Sulha, how it takes place and what are the ramifications'.[36] Other judges and Sulha committee members voiced similar sentiments independent of each other.
- Changes in attitude towards Sulha, resulting from an evolution of attitudes towards victim rights in Israel, in both legislation and court behaviour.
- Evolving attitudes of Israeli society and courts towards the country's Arab community.[37] A mixed approach makes functional sense. Lack of policy may sound confusing, but in reality it creates flexibility and does not force to the fore a potential confrontation between the informal Sulha and the formal legal system, allowing both sides to make use of Sulha agreements whenever desired and to ignore them whenever they see fit. Of course, the same flexibility also allows expressions of anti-Arab bias to be expressed where they exist.

A relevant demonstration of what Judge Aminof referred to may be seen in a decision (CRP, 373/93) where three justices of the Supreme Court wrote that 'the determinant in this case is not the relations between the relevant families but the level of danger to the public at large from the violent, unbridled behaviour of the respondent'.[38] This is significant because the facts of the case demonstrated that the only violence ever to take place in this dispute was between members of two families as part of an interclan dispute, which is *exactly* what Sulha is designed to handle.

Another issue worth considering in this respect is the evolution of the inclusion of the victim as an element in the court's consideration of punishment. Traditionally, this was not an element of the sentencing decision in Israeli courts, which concentrated centrally on punishing the guilty/offending party, but were less interested in either considering or promoting conciliation between the disputants (other than through the tool of court-awarded compensation), or in the fact that the victim could participate in the process by, for example, arriving at an agreement with the offending party that included forgiveness (as is the case with Sulha).[39] Actually, the legal system acted *counter* to the Sulha process by removing the conflict from the offender–victim arena and placing it in the offender–state arena (i.e. the State vs. John Doe), marginalizing the victim from the outset of the legal process (detention) to the end (sentencing).

But this situation is now changing. Specific victim's rights legislation was enacted in Israel (2003) alongside a larger general trend towards increased individual rights and a specific reference to victim's rights that were set in one of Israel's quasi-constitutional laws, 'Basic Legislation: Human Honour and Liberty', which contains a specific clause instructing courts to guard the victim and her or his rights.[40]

Every Sulha process, and its resultant agreement, includes a direct, central reference to the will of the victim and his or her family. In view of this, it may be reasonable to assume that with the general change of attitude towards greater reference to victim's rights there may be growing realization within the Israeli legal community that Sulha, with its victim's inclusiveness (victim and her or his family) may include proper enough considerations to merit references within the court's decision. Such a change will probably have to find its balance with the legal system's official role in preventing and deterring future and further violence, and with its attendant concern to remove the perpetrator(s) from the vicinity of the victim in particular and from society in general. These assumptions require additional research.

Another possible explanation of the way Israel's legal system treats Sulha may be found in the general relationship between the Israeli legal system and the country's Arab population. This relationship has been marked over the years by several characteristics, including a lack of will by the legal system to accord the Arab population recognition as anything other than a religious community, on top of their recognition as individuals. Official Israel, including the courts, go to great lengths to look at Arabs only as individuals, sparing the country the obligation to accord them rights inherent in their being a community in several aspects (e.g. political, cultural, agrarian). In the words of Haifa University law professor Gad Barzily: 'The state did not tend to recognize several identities of the [Arab] community, since these disturbed the legitimacy of Zionism by postulating alternate modes of political leadership'.[41] Shapiro adds that

> [t]he law in Israel gives equal rights to all the state's citizens. In the area of protection of rights of the individual, the law and the courts protect the rights of the Arab citizens. But the legal authorities do not recognize the Arab community [in Israel] as a separate community of a minority deserving of collective rights.

He adds: 'The allocation of a high priority to establishing Israel as a Jewish state created inequality in dealing with problems of the Arab community'.[42]

Conversely, these particular issues (a sense of discrimination and inequality) are reflected in the attitude of Israel's Arab community towards the courts. Referring to several studies of the relations between the Arab community and Israel's formal legal system, Barzily writes:

> My research confirms some of the central findings in these studies. Firstly, Israeli Palestinian Arabs trust the judiciary less than Israeli Jews. Secondly, the minorities do not experience an atmosphere of legitimacy in the legal system at the same level as the Jewish majority; and thirdly, the minority feels that it is getting the short end of the stick.[43]

Distinct minority groups in Israel, including ultra-orthodox Jews, as well as the Christian, Druze and Muslim communities, have the legal right to maintain a separate (but officially recognized, sanctioned and financed) judicial system dealing mostly with family and personal matters. So, for example, Jews in Israel must marry and divorce in rabbinical court in front of Dayanim (Hebrew for religious judges), whereas Muslims adjudicate family matters in Shari'a court (sanctioned by the state) led by a Qadi.

Such courts do not adjudicate according to the state's legal system, but rely on religious legal codes, and their rulings are recognized by the state. All other legal matters are dealt with by the state's official legal system or are handled clandestinely by rabbis or Qadis within the community, without the knowledge or sanctioning of the state and its legal system. This happens quite often, and when it becomes public (particularly where a violent crime is involved), the state's legal system tends to intervene and take charge of the process.

But the Sulha is different from both the formal and informal ethnic/religious meta-legal setups in Israel. It serves Muslims, Christians and Druze, and it covers areas of dispute resolution that are left entirely untouched by the formal legal mechanisms (i.e. inter- and intraclan disputes). When it comes to relations between Israel's formal legal system and the informal Sulha, it appears that the lack of official policy actually makes sense – for all sides. Israel's formal legal system is comfortable with its relationship with the Sulha and its practitioners. On the one hand, the formal system gets to use the informal, yet proven, peace-making services of the Sulha; on the other, the state can choose when to take the Sulha into consideration and to what extent and when to ignore it, as judges often do.

For its part the Sulha, through its practitioners, seems to find the complex informality a satisfactory arrangement that gives it the necessary space to deal with what it does best: mend relations within the community while leaving the guilt-assigning work to the state.

All in all, it appears that the complexity of the considerations as they appear in Israeli courts' Sulha-related decisions is affected by the issue's central dilemma: if the Sulha is an institution and a practice that contributes to peace making and public safety, and as such serves the obvious interests of both the state and the community, courts will probably want to encourage and advocate it. Yet the very same Sulha has no official standing. So by advocating it or by giving it a significant weight in legal decisions, the courts – representatives of the state's official legal system – may be indicating (however indirectly) to the Sulha makers and the Sulha-using population that the institution has a quasi-official status within Israel's legal system.

Such a perception may collide head on with the 'equality before the law' principle, which is central (certainly at the declaratory level) to Israel's legal system, because the Sulha is not available routinely to the Jewish part of the population. So there is an apparent conflict here between the interest of the state to promote communal tranquillity and peace making in a minority part of the general population while presenting the law of the land as the single equitable reference point for the entire population – binding equally and inclusively all communities, without exception.

Notes

1. Author interview with Abu Saaluk; Irani, 'Islamic Mediation Techniques for Middle East Conflicts', p 8; Said, Funk & Kadayifci, *Peace and Conflict Resolution in Islam*, p. 182.
2. Author interview with Khneifes, 2011; Ginat, *Blood Disputes*.
3. Shapiro, 'It is Sulha's Time'.
4. Section 79c, Courts of Law Legislation, 1984 (translated from Hebrew).
5. Amendment to Courts of Law Legislation, Chapter G1, Section 99, 2 March 2008/
6. Rabbi Yosi Shar'abi, JD & Dr. Yuval Sinai, Mediation in Civil and Family Courts in Israel – Sources in Hebrew Law, Center for Application of Hebrew Law, Netanya Academic College, 29 November 2006. (Translated from Hebrew), www.netanya.ac.il/ResearchCen/JewishLaw/AcademicPub/FamilyLaw/Documents/opinion_29112006.pdf (accessed 19 October 2014).
7. Islamic Law Texts, Ottoman Civil Code Ottoman Civil Code, An English Translation of the Complete Turkish Text, Based on the Work of C.A. Hooper, Article 1850, p. 288, http://majalla.org/books/2003/mejelle.pdf (accessed 19 October 2014).
8. Robert H. Eisenman, *Islamic Law in Palestine and Israel* (Leiden: E.J. Brill, 1978), p. 126.
9. Hok Haborerut (Hebrew, "Arbitration Law"), 535 S.H. (1968), at 184, *reprinted in* 1 Dinim 631, *translated in* 3 International Commercial Arbitration IV Israel, at 1–17 (Kenneth A. Simmonds ed., 1992).
10. As indicated, although the Sulha is Shari'a based, non-Muslim Arabs (e.g. Druze, Christians) practice it as well.
11. Gad J. Bensinger, 'Criminal Justice in Israel', in Robert Freedman (ed.), *Crime and the Criminal Justice System in Israel: Assessing the Knowledge Base Toward the Twenty First Century* (Albany: SUNY Press, 1998).
12. Tsafrir, 'Arab Customary Law', p. 78. See also Cornell University Law School, *Public Access Law Dictionary*, www.law.cornell.edu/wex/index.php/Tort) (accessed 31 July 2013).
13. Jabbour, *Sulha*, p. 41.
14. CP (Civil Petitions) 621/04, Ali Asaad v. Amal Kablan (2005) Taqdin Elyon, 2005, Vol. 4, p. 3 (translated from the original Hebrew by the Author).
15. *Ibid.*
16. *Ibid.*

17 CRP (Criminal Petitions) 373/93, State of Israel v. Rifaat Masrawa (1993) Taqdin Elyon, Vol. 93(i) (translated from the original Hebrew by the author).
18 Jabbour, *Sulha*, p. 69.
19 Occasionally unrelated bystanders become victims of violent retaliation and counter-strikes between disputing clan members. Such occurrences give rise to new interclan conflicts.
20 CRP (Criminal Petitions) 7126/04, Ahmad Gadir, Abed Elgabar Gadir, Abed Elkahar Gadir, Abed Elsatar Gadir, Muhammad Gadir v. State of Israel (2005) Taqdin Elyon, 2005(2) (translated from the original Hebrew by the author), p. 3.
21 DA (Detention Appeal) 1842/02, Mursi ben Muhammad Arshid et al v. State of Israel (2002) (translated from the original Hebrew by the author), p. 2.
22 Tsafrir, 'Arab Customary Law', p. 88.
23 DA (Detention Appeal) 2797/06, State of Israel v. Ataf ben Hussein Fuaz, Municipal Court, Nazareth (2006) (translated from the original Hebrew by the author).
24 *Ibid.*
25 CC (Criminal Conviction), 10544/99, Haifa District Attorney v. Marwan Wahabi, Peace Court, Haifa (2004) (translated from the original Hebrew by the author).
26 *Ibid.*
27 Author interview with Khneifes, 2007.
28 Robert N. Bellah, Richard Madsen, William M. Sullivan, Ann Swidler & Steven M. Tipton, *Habits of the Heart: Individualism and Commitment in America* (New York: Harper and Row, 1985).
29 Civil Appeal 621/04, p. 3.
30 Shapiro, 'It's Sulha Time', p. 448.
31 Tsafrir, 'Arab Customary Law', p. 97.
32 Although Jews in Israel use the same term 'Sulha' to denote a reconciliation process, the actual meaning of the term in this context is reconciliation between individuals, not clans; furthermore, the process that Jews call Sulha is not governed by the rules of the Muslim/Arab Sulha, and is similar to it only in name.
33 Author interview with Khneifes, 2007.
34 Author interview with Abu Saaluk.
35 This particular finding contradicts Tsafrir's assertion that '[o]nly rarely does a judge reject the Sulha as a mitigating factor in sentencing' ('Arab Customary Law', p. 94). It should be noted that Tsafrir brings no reference to any statistical sampling or any other sampling that she has undertaken or is quoting from, so it is impossible to ascertain on what she based her previous comment.
36 Author interview with Judge Aharon Aminof, 15 July 2007.
37 Shapiro, 'It is Sulha's Time' pp. 440, 449. See also Gad Barzily, 'Arabs? Only in Singular', *Mishpat Nosaf* (Hebrew), Vol. 1 (2001), p. 55.
38 CRP (Criminal Petitions) 373/93, State of Israel v. Rifaat Masrawa (1993) Taqdin Elyon, 93(i) (translated from the original Hebrew by the author).
39 Shapiro, 'It Is Sulha's Time', p. 437.
40 *Ibid.*, p. 441.
41 Barzily, 'Arabs', p. 55.
42 Shapiro, 'It Is Sulha's Time, pp. 449–50.
43 Barzily, 'Arabs', p. 58.

8 Sulha case study

There are some descriptions of Sulha ceremonies in the literature, but there is no comprehensive description and analysis of the entire Sulha process from infraction to ceremony. The reason is simple: Sulha processes may take years to conclude, and while they proceed, all interactions between the *Jaha* and disputants, witnesses, local dignitaries and other affiliated persons are strictly confidential and barred to outsiders.

Sulha ceremonies are the only part of the process that is opened to the public at large. Yet, although ceremonies are important and worthy of studying, they provide only a partial perspective on the process. A thorough understanding of the process requires examining it in its entirety from inception to conclusion.

This chapter includes detailed description and analysis of one Sulha process, from the infraction that created the dispute through the progression of events all the way to the dispute's resolution and the Sulha ceremony that marked that resolution.[1] Note: Pictures from the Sulha ceremony are interspersed throughout this chapter; they relate only to the ceremony.

Murder in A'eblin

The dispute ensued on the early afternoon of Thursday, 23 July 2005, when the sixty-six-year-old Tawfiq Farhuni murdered Dr Nasser Nur Salman, a same-age gynaecologist – both residents of the village A'eblin, near Shefa'amer, in the lower Galilee region. Following a trial at the Nazareth Municipal Court, Farhuni was convicted of first-degree murder (with reduced sentence for borderline legal responsibility for mental health reasons) and is currently serving a twenty-year sentence in a local prison; Tawfiq's son, Osama Farhuni, who assisted his father in the murder, was found guilty of first-degree murder and is currently serving a life sentence.

Dispute's origin

Osama Farhuni, a twenty-three-year-old career criminal and member of A'eblin's 'criminal' family 'burned rubber' with his newly acquired BMW in front of the home of Dr Salman, who had returned a month earlier from an extended stay in the United States.

Sulha case study 175

Figure 8.1 Getting ready for the Sulha ceremony

The reason Osama chose this particular spot to, literally, spin his wheels is because this is one of the few places in the village where the road is wide enough to allow for such practices.

After suffering through half an hour of unrelenting noise and the stench of burning rubber, Dr Salman came out of his home and asked the young man to leave and stop being a nuisance. Osama responded by asking: 'Do you know who I am?' Salman answered something like: 'Yes, I know you, and I know your father. We went to school together, where I used to beat him up every intermission'.

Osama was gravely offended. He returned to his father's home, where he supposedly reported the exchange with Salman. Father and son descended down the hill together later that afternoon; they went to Salman's home, where Osama held the family at gunpoint using a stolen AK-47 Russian assault rifle. The father, Tawfiq Farhuni, walked up to Salman and said: 'So you're bragging that you beat me in school? I'll show you beating me.' Whereupon, Tawfiq shot Salman with a pistol he was holding – one shot to the heart – killing him instantly.

Tawfiq and Osama then ran away, but were arrested within twenty-four hours.

Ostensibly, this would have been the end of the story. The police investigated the murder and arrested suspects; the state prosecutor's office prepared indictments; both Farhunis were remanded in custody without bail pending trial.

Yet, as shown in this book, in the cultural context of Israel's Arab community, the dispute was not between individuals but between clans, and under the traditional, unwritten, yet almost universally acknowledged rules of the clan's mutual responsibility pact, all of its male members, without exception, are held responsible for each infraction committed by every member of the clan (male or female). Furthermore, every male member of every clan is obliged to avenge every infraction committed against any member of his clan. A dispute, personal, familial and tribal, cannot, therefore, be resolved until the interclan dispute is settled, not least because there is currently no known social, cultural, formal or informal mechanism designed for and capable of resolving interclan-level disputes other than the Sulha.

Who started the Sulha process and why?

Traditionally, the leaders of the perpetrator's clan are supposed to initiate the Sulha process. In this specific dispute, although a revenge attack did not take place or was at all expected, the Farhuni clan wanted to start a Sulha process, not so much because they felt threatened by the Salman clan, but because they felt that they were seriously wronged by the state with the detention of their father and brother and hoped to be able to leverage an ongoing Sulha process to influence the police investigation, the prosecutorial process and, if possible, the judicial process (e.g. in the case of remand decisions).[2]

Yet despite their interest in starting the Sulha process, the Farhuni clan was in such disarray and dysfunctionality that it failed to initiate the first contact with the representative of the Sulha Committee. As a result, the actual initiator of the Sulha process was the former head of the A'eblin municipal council, Saleh Murshid Salim – a respected member of the community, a former member of parliament and a person of official capacity within the village. Salim took the initiative because he was afraid that the Farhuni family, which in Khneifes' words, was considered 'insane and dysfunctional', would decide to attack the Salman clan again to avenge the arrest of Tawfiq and Osama. According to Khneifes, Salim approached him (he resides in the neighbouring town of Shefar'am) with the request to assemble a skeleton Sulha Committee and begin the Sulha process by approaching the Farhuni clan.[3]

What did the Sulha Committee do immediately after the dispute started?

Upon receiving the call from Salim, Khneifes gathered two additional committee members (Ibrahim Naum and Sheikh Fathi Hatib), and the trio drove to A'eblin and met two members of the Farhuni clan at Salim's home, with the participation of the latter, who acted as a kind of an intervener between the Sulha Committee and the Farhuni family representatives. This was an unusual practise: traditionally the members of the Sulha committee meet the perpetrator's clan representatives at the residence of one of the clan's leaders. But the Farhuni clan was so dysfunctional that it was potentially dangerous to meet them at their home, so the committee preferred to meet them at the home of a local dignitary.

What did the perpetrator's clan do/say?

True to their volatile nature, the representatives of the Farhuni clan, Iyad and Ihab Farhuni (both sons of Tawfiq), did not express any regret about the murder, nor did they assume any responsibility for it. On the contrary, they accused the victimized clan of starting the dispute (with Dr. Salman's alleged insult to Tawfiq) and refused to start the Sulha process until they received a commitment from the Salman family to intercede with the state's prosecution in order to try to assist the detained Farhunis.

The Sulha Committee dismissed out of hand these demands. This is a stock response. The Sulha Committee as a rule does not accept dictates or even implied conditions by either disputant – particularly not the perpetrator's side. In Khneifes' words: 'They did not understand that this was illegal, and even more so, there was no way in the world we [the *Jaha*] would have agreed to a 'demand' by them – any demand'.[4]

For three months, the dignitaries continued to meet and negotiate with the representatives of the Farhuni clan – about once every two weeks – without any progress. The situation, according to Khneifes, was becoming quite explosive, and the committee and village leaders feared yet another attack by the Farhuni family on the Salman clan out of frustration at not getting what they wanted.

In an attempt to avert further escalation, and with the realization that both the Sulha Committee and the village dignitaries had little leverage with the Farhuni clan, an idea was floated to bring into the process *another* third-party intervener – this time in the form of a purported leading drug dealer, Zeid Abu Shret, from the village of Hura in southern Israel, who was thought to have significant influence over the Farhuni family through their alleged illegal, drug-related activities. Abu Shret gladly seized this opportunity to participate in a positive communal effort

Figure 8.2 The killer's family approaching the Sulha site

at dispute resolution and to do it in the company of the community's most distinguished peace makers.

Although the inclusion of a criminal in a Sulha process is rather uncommon, it is by no means an unheard-of occurrence and, according to the Sulha Committee members, their attitude when approaching a dispute is that of 'whatever works' – as long as it is not in contravention of the Shari'a – Islam's legal code.

What did the victim's clan do/say?

The members of the victim's clan were terrified of the Farhunis and eager to begin and conclude a Sulha settlement that would lower the flames of the conflict. They would have agreed to just about any condition put to them by the Farhunis and, according to Khneifes, the Sulha Committee had to restrain them from showing excessive eagerness for concluding the dispute.

Apparently, aside from fearing the wrath of the Farhunis, the Salmans also feared that one of their members would take it upon himself to exact retribution, further exacerbating the dispute.

How did the Sulha process start?

With Abu Shret's intervention, the Farhunis agreed to launch the process. As we have seen, the signing of a Tafweeth is the first ritualistic act required to 'formally' initiate a Sulha process. In this dispute, the Tafweeth was signed at Salim's home, with the Sulha Committee represented by Khneifes, Abu M'bada and Hatib; also present were Salim, Abu Shret and Iyad and Ihab Farhuni.

The signing of a Tafweeth was followed immediately by the Farhunis' payment of an Atwa (a token of goodwill) – an act symbolizing the conclusion of the preliminary stages of the Sulha. The Salmans accepted the Atwa but refused the money ('Atwa Tsharaf'). The Sulha process had thus formally started.

Was there a Hudna? How long? How many times was it extended?

Once the Salman representatives signed the Tafweeth, the two sides immediately agreed on a formal Hudna, which was declared by the *Jaha* (now officially recognized by the disputants and known to the community), which visited the homes of the two clans to notify them about its start. The duration of the first formal Hudna was six months, and it was subsequently renewed seven times before the sides reached an agreement to terminate the dispute.

How did the Jaha's deliberations proceed?

Following the Hudna, the *Jaha* initiated a round of consultations with the disputing clans. It met regularly with Iyad and Iham, sons of the murderer, at the Farhuni clan's home. The *Jaha* met regularly with Faraj Salman, a prominent lawyer, as well as with the victim's brothers, Akram and As'ad, at the Salmans' home.

The *Jaha* met the Salman representatives several times. Traditionally, the victim's family is quite aggravated by the loss of a relative and by the gross offense on its honour, and the *Jaha* must usually work hard to convince it to agree to reconciliation. In this particular case, by contrast, the situation was somewhat reversed: the Salmans, fearing another attack by the Farhunis, pressed for a quick settlement and were willing to accommodate the perpetrator clan. The Farhunis, on the other hand, were supposed to fear a retaliatory attack by the Salmans,

180 *Sulha case study*

but they were not afraid at all; on the contrary, they projected a very aggressive posture, accusing the members of the Salman clan of provoking the dispute and implying that they might attack again to save their honour and avenge the arrest of their father and brother.

The members of the *Jaha* thus found themselves trying to reformat an 'inverted' process – whereby the victim's clan assumed alleged responsibility for the conflict

Figure 8.3 Victim's brother returns the blood money

and the perpetrator's family viewed itself as the victim – that could have resulted in a verdict forcing the victims to compensate the perpetrators and apologize to them, practically denying the Sulha its greatest prize, which is the restoration of the (real) victimized clan's honour while getting the perpetrators to assume responsibility for their action without humiliating them and damaging their sense of honour as well.

It was here that Abu Shret's inclusion in the process bore fruit, as he was the only person capable of influencing the Farhunis. In Khneifes' words: 'He knew how to talk to them. This was the only way we could make any headway with these guys'.[5] Abu Shret started articulating the *Jaha*'s perspective to the Farhunis and eventually, through a combination of persuasion and cajoling, got them to accept the *Jaha*'s verdict, assume responsibility for the murder, offer blood money compensation and agree to publicly apologize for their father's and brother's crimes.

What tools did the Jaha use during the process?

The *Jaha* used a variety of tools during the process:

- It adopted an arbitrative posture as it, initially unsuccessfully, tried to convince the Farhunis to sign a Tafweeth, assume responsibility for their kins' crimes and offer Atwa to officially start the Sulha process.
- It assumed a meditative-evaluative role by portraying to the two clans the potential consequences of an unresolved dispute. In this case, they often had to restrain the victim's clan from taking too conciliatory steps in their eagerness to conclude an agreement.
- It used private caucus meetings to negotiate with each party without the presence of the other side. Such meetings created the right setting for venting (in this case, by both the victim and perpetrator clans). Furthermore, such meetings (where the other side is not present) allowed the *Jaha* to 'filter' disputants' positions and utterances, giving the *Jaha* more control over the exchange of narratives between the disputing clans.
- It identified its own inability to move the Farhunis along a reconciliation path and took the unusual step of inviting a drug dealer into the *Jaha*, converted some of its own honour into a functional ability to advocate, communicate and, when needed, coerce the Farhuni clan into a recognition and an admission of its role in the process (the perpetrator's role). That move gave the *Jaha* a substantial (and very necessary) leverage over the Farhunis because in the internal drug-dealing hierarchy, the invited drug dealer was superior to the Farhuni clan members and thus could coerce them into behaving in ways that helped facilitate an agreement.

The Sulha ceremony

The Sulha ceremony took place in the village of A'eblin on 21 February 2009, almost four years after the eruption of the conflict.

182 *Sulha case study*

Figure 8.4 Christian clergy ties a knot in the Sulha flag

Before the ceremony, a respected Muslim family (Hatib), whose grandfather was a local Sulha maker, invited dignitaries from the village, as well as the *Jaha* members, for a preliminary meal and strategy session. The meal was served at the family's home in A'eblin by the male members of the host family. Guests included Christian and Muslim religious leaders, as well as civil dignitaries (e.g. prominent businessmen, municipal leaders and local politicians) and Christian, Druze and Muslims from A'eblin and from neighbouring villages and towns.[6]

The occasion of the meal was used, as it most always is, by the *Jaha* members to discuss, plan, write down and rehearse the sequence of events planned for the upcoming ceremony. An action plan was agreed upon in writing; individual *Jaha* members were assigned roles (e.g. bring the victim's clan, bring the perpetrator's clan, prepare the hall where the ceremony was about to take place).

Following the meal, which took place in the early afternoon, a retinue of dignitaries left in a motorcade for the home of the head of the Salman clan. Once there, they positioned themselves in a reception line along the driveway and greeted the members of the Salman family as they descended from the house led by a Christian priest.

The members of the Salman family, which included several brothers of the slain physician as well as cousins and uncles, shook hands with the waiting dignitaries and the *Jaha* members. After a brief welcoming ceremony, a member of the *Jaha* produced the Sulha flag (*Rayah*), which included a simple wooden pole and a large white linen sheet. Another *Jaha* member explained to the victim's brother that he was about to tie a knot of reconciliation in the flag and showed him how to do it. The brother of the victim tied the first knot in the Sulha flag, making it into a symbol of forgiveness and protection for the members of the Farhuni clan participating in the ceremony.

With the first knot tied in the *Rayah*, the dignitaries' motorcade formed again and left for the village church at the top of a hill. Having left their cars once more, the dignitaries, the *Jaha* members and some village residents formed a semicircle around the Sulha flag and waited for the representatives of the Farhuni clan to appear. They arrived by car several minutes later, also accompanied by *Jaha* members, arranged themselves behind the *Rayah* (which at this point was handed to the leader of the Farhuni clan) and a procession led by the Sulha flag started making its way by foot from the parking area, about 200 metres below the church, towards the church's compound.[7]

In the meantime, members of the Salman clan, having arrived separately at the church accompanied by several *Jaha* members, were already arranged in a reception line at the entrance to the church's auxiliary building. When the Farhuni representatives arrived, the hand-shaking ritual, one of the Sulha's core elements, took place. There was visible tension as the two families met for the first time since the eruption of the conflict and shook hands. Nobody smiled, but everybody was cordial as each member of the murderers' clan shook the hand of each member of the victim's clan. They exchanged formal greetings but otherwise spoke very little. Throughout the process, members of the *Jaha* were close at hand to make sure the ritual proceeded smoothly and nobody lost his nerve. There were, of course, no women in sight.

Despite the fact that the disputing clans were Christian, the Sulha ceremony was conducted by Sheikh Abdallah Hatib, a Muslim imam (religious leader) from one the village's mosques. In retrospect, members of the *Jaha* commented that it was a mistake to use an imam for a Sulha ceremony at a church between two

Christian families. According to them, the reasons for this decision had to do with internal village politics.

The church's auxiliary hall was full to capacity, with some 200 people, Christians and Muslims from the village and from adjacent and far-away villages. Hundreds of additional spectators remained outside the building and around the church's perimeter fence. This was another expression of the communal nature of the conflict and its resolution. According to Khneifes, the audience gave credibility to the agreement by witnessing its signing and at the same time made sure that the agreement actually took place, because although the community at large was not a formal side to the conflict, it had a strong vested interest in the maintenance of peaceful coexistence, which in this instance was directly dependent on the successful culmination of the ritual that took place in front of them.

The imam explained to the congregation what was going to take place and why. He praised both families for having the honour and courage to let bygones be bygones and move to resolving such a painful conflict and invited the victim's brother to speak. The latter spoke about the pain of losing his brother, about the uselessness of random violence and about the need to bring such conflicts to an end before more innocents pay a price. A *Jaha* member then handed to the victim's brother a brown leather briefcase containing NIS 300,000 (c. £55,000) in cash. The brother did not even open the briefcase. Holding it, he declared that the Salman family did not need the money, that no money in the world would bring back his dead brother and that the family decided to give the blood money (*Diya*) in its entirety back to the Farhuni family. He handed the briefcase back. The audience applauded the gesture, signalling approval of the Salmans' demonstrated sense of honour and their willingness to forgo a large sum of compensation in favour of symbolism that increased their communal status.

The next stage in the ceremony included the public tying of knots in the Sulha flag by Christian and Muslim religious leaders, civil leaders from A'ebelin and neighbouring villages and all members of the Sulha Committee. Each dignitary made a short speech after tying the knot, praising the disputing clans and the community for having the courage, honour and fortitude to see the reconciliation process through to a favourable conclusion.

At the end of the process, the entire white sheet was tied around the *Rayah* poll in a series of about fifteen tight knots. In fact, because there were more dignitaries than available length of linen, the *Jaha* member in charge of administering the ritual started untying the knots after they were made and after the dignitary left the area so as to make the last yard of linen available for the next dignitary. Following the tying of the Sulha knot, each dignitary was directed by a *Jaha* member to a side table next to the podium, where he signed the Sulha agreement in full view of the watching audience.

Throughout the process, the families of the killer and the victim sat with expressionless faces, avoiding eye contact with each other and watching the proceedings.

The ritual ended with a mandatory ceremonial seeping of a bitter cup of coffee offered at the door to the members of the victim's clan as they were leaving the hall. It was raining hard, including hail and a strong wind, so many participants raced for their cars, which were parked at the foot of the hill about a hundred yards away.

Notes

1 The description of events in this case study is based on personal observations of the author, as well as multiple interviews with two senior Sulha makers who participated in every stage of the dispute: Faraj Khneifes and Ibrahim M'bada Naum (Abu M'bada). The author did not attend every, or even most, of the events described here, as they spanned several years and included dozens of separate meetings and consultations.
2 Author interview with Khneifes, 5 July 2012.
3 *Ibid.*
4 *Ibid.*
5 *Ibid.*
6 Personal observation by the author.
7 See picture of procession in Figure 8.2.

Conclusions

This exploration set out to examine, describe and explain how the ubiquitous Muslim/Arab customary justice practice of Sulha works within the Arab population of northern Israel. The study did not limit itself to an examination of the public Sulha ceremony, which marks the end of the process. Instead, it explored each of the Sulha's seven stages, in detail and in depth, using interviews, surveys, questionnaires, analysis of existing literature, informants' insights and, for the first time, participant observations by the author from within the most confidential moments of the process, such as the initiation of the Sulha process by the perpetrator's clan, the recruitment of the victim's clan, the internal negotiations of the *Jaha* with the disputants' representatives and internal *Jaha* deliberations.

Findings and new insights

This research effort generated multiple new insights into the Sulha process. Most notably it:

- Demonstrated how the *Jaha* recruits, guides, instructs, cajoles, coerces and at times almost physically drags the disputing clans' representatives through the Sulha process, taking concrete actions and using task-specific tools from a relatively wide toolbox of mediation and arbitration techniques – all geared toward transformation from a desire for revenge to a willingness to forgive.
- Showed through the findings of a survey administered to members of several victims' clans, combined with testimonies of interviewees, informants, Sulha practitioners and the author's personal observations of numerous Sulha meetings, that the gradual reduction in the perception of damage to victimized clans' sense of honour is expressed by a monotonic, statistically significant altering of these clans' perspectives regarding the best way to respond to the perceived offence against them.
- Underlined the possible link between the Prophet Mohammad's preference of Sulha to other mediation/arbitration techniques and this practice's central place in Muslim/Arab jurisprudence.
- Located and described for the first time the specific use by Sulha interveners of a mix of mediation and arbitration tools designed to help restore the

honour of the victim's clan and facilitate its shift from a desire for revenge to a willingness to forgive.
- Developed a new conceptual framework – re-integrative honouring concept (RHC) – for the understanding of the Sulha (and, for that matter, of Muslim/Arab conflict resolution mechanisms).
- Underscored the tentative, conflictual yet symbiotic relationship between the Sulha and Israel's formal legal system that has helped preserve the place and functionality of each system, both separately and together.
- Identified the essential differences and similarities between Western ADR practices and relevant Sulha elements and their implication for conflict resolution/management in both societies.
- Provided the first examination of gender relations within Sulha, demonstrating that, notwithstanding their formal exclusion from the process, women exert a significant impact on the Sulha.

All these findings confirm the proposed thesis: that the Sulha's power lies in its logical and chronological progression, in which each stage plays a small but crucial role in enabling the attitudinal change and its attendant behaviour. No less importantly, these findings resolve the core question of this book by showing that the Sulha works by leveraging its unique historical and theological posture within both Islam and the Muslim/Arab community of northern Israel, together with its ambiguous yet symbiotic relationship with Israel's formal legal system, to bring to bear a finely timed and orchestrated set of mediation and arbitration tools designed to help the *Jaha* facilitate a transition in the victimized clan's sense of honour to a degree that will enable it to replace its cultural prerogative of honour restoration through revenge with another honour-restoring path: that of forgiveness and reconciliation, a path that is clearly preferred by the community and is conducive to its general well-being. This transformation is achieved with the informal, yet significant, participation of the disputing clans' women, who exert substantial influence on the process despite their formal exclusion.

Possible directions for future research

> '...every answer, given according to the fundamental laws of experience, gives birth to a new question, just as much requiring an answer...'
>
> Immanuel Kant

While constituting the most comprehensive exploration of Sulha to date, the exploratory process conducted in this book uncovered a number of questions and unknowns that merit further examination:

- How can a Shari'a-based practice serve Muslim, Christian and Druze Arabs? In northern Israel, and in many other places in the Muslim/Arab world, Muslims and non-Muslims use the Shari'a-based Sulha process to resolve

- inter- and intraclan disputes. Such an Islam-based, cooperative, interfaith conflict resolution effort may well be considered a welcomed synergy; but it may also be seen as yet another demonstration of Islam's supremacist control over ethnic and religious minorities within its area of hegemony (cultural or political).
- The place of 'priming' in Sulha. Priming is an implicit type of memory effect in which exposure to a preplanned stimulus creates special sensitivity, which in turn generates a specific response (both in memory and action) to a later stimulus. It is considered implicit because it does not involve, nor require, explicit recollection of previous experience.[1] Priming is seen as an independent mechanism, which closely interacts with other memory systems, outside of conscious awareness, and affects the decision-making process.[2]

  It may be that re-integrative honouring is predicated on a form of priming, in which positive priming serves to accelerate forgiveness and negative priming slows down the willingness to forgive, thus accelerating the desire to avenge. The vehicle for this effect is the manipulation of honour perception in the victim's clan carried out by the *Jaha* (e.g. increased honour perception primes for forgiveness, and decreased honour perception primes for revenge).[3]
- The possible effects of understanding Muslim/Arab dispute resolution practices on Muslim/Western negotiations. The exploration of Muslim/Arab conflict management/resolution practices highlights major differences between such practices and their equivalent Western counterparts. It is reasonable to assume that when two such different practices meet around the negotiating table, the underlying differences in philosophies and in application will affect both the way the disputants see the issues on hand and the strategies, tactics and mechanisms they employ in their attempt to negotiate settlements to disputes. Future research is needed to examine areas where the divergence between Muslim/Arab and Western dispute resolution practices may hinder proper communication and progress, as well as suggest possible mechanisms to mitigate the effect of such differences on the practice and progress of relevant negotiations.

As the lives of northern Israel's Arabs and their clans evolve and change, and because the fortunes of Sulha and clans are inextricably bound together, both culturally and functionally, it is likely that in the coming years and decades, the place, function and interrelations between and amongst the clans and the Sulha process will also continue to evolve and change.

To that end, and because of the significant inter-relations between clans and the Sulha process, it is reasonable to assume that if and when the place of the clan changes significantly within northern Israel's Arab community (e.g. if its dominant position within the local culture declines), so will the place of Sulha change accordingly. Such changes will undoubtedly reflect on the relations among and between the various parts of the Arab community, as well as their interactions with Israel's society in general and the country's formal legal system in particular.

Ongoing research and analysis of the place of Sulha within these continuing changes is, therefore, necessary and useful, and it is the hope of the author that qualified local and international scholars will continue to conduct such research to enrich our understanding of Muslim/Arab dispute resolution practices.

Notes

1 Moshe Bar, 'Conscious and Non-Conscious Processing of Visual Object Identity', in Y. Rosetti & A. Revonsuo (eds.), *Dissociations: Interaction Between Dissociable Conscious and Nonconscious Processing* (Amsterdam: John Benjamins, 2000), p. 153.
2 Daniel Kahaneman, *Thinking Fast and Slow* (New York: Farrar, Straus and Giroux, 2011). See also Larry L. Jacoby, 'Perceptual Enhancement: Persistent Effects of An Experience', *Journal of Experimental Psychology: Learning, Memory, and Cognition*, Vol. 9 (1983), pp. 21–38.
3 Endel Tulving & Daniel L. Schacter, 'Priming and Human Memory Systems', Science, Vol. 247, No. 4940 (1990), pp. 301–6.

Appendices: Appendix A
Sample Sulha agreement

This appendix includes a photograph of a real Sulha agreement (Sulha agreements are public-domain documents), as well as an English translation of the original document.

Sample Sulha agreement: English translation

In the Name of Allah The Merciful

Allah Said: "Believers are brothers, therefore make peace between your brethren, for they will see Allah, and maybe he will take mercy on all of you. For right he was, Allah, the Great."

Taking note of the killing of the late Nasser Nur Suliman, on the date of 23.7.2005, and the arrest of Mr. Tawfiq Elias Farouni.

And taking note of the intervention of the respectable Sulha Committee, to include Mr. Taha Abed El Halim, and Chaled Taha from Kafar Kana, and the gentlemen Ali Fuad Diab, and Hamid Awad Matmara, and Mr. Ahmed Jarbuni from Arabe, and the gentlemen Fathi Hatib and Abed Alla Hativ, and the priest, father Awad Awad, and Sheikh Hassan Haider from A'eblin, and the gentlemen Faraj Khneifes and Ibrahim Naum from Shefa'amer, and the Sheikh Ali Abu Sabit; it was agreed that:

1. When family Suliman and family Farouni partook in the Sulha (reconciliation), it is considered to be a charter with Allah, and a binding promise that the respectable conciliation comes in the place of the conflict and the hateful disagreements.
2. The reconciliation between the two families took place on Saturday, 21.2.2009, in A'eblin.
3. Family Farouni paid, as per the decision of the respectable Sulha Committee, and handed the blood money over to the family of the late Nasser Nur Suliman, without declaring a value, and that as per request from the respectable family.
4. Both sides hereby forgo all civil and Sharia'h and acceptable rights, and no side will have any additional claims from the other side.
5. Everybody bears witness that the conciliation is binding for all the present and the absent, those in this country and abroad, those in their mother's womb, and those in this country and abroad, those in their mother's uterus, and those who are still sperm with their father.

192 *Appendix A: sample sulha agreement*

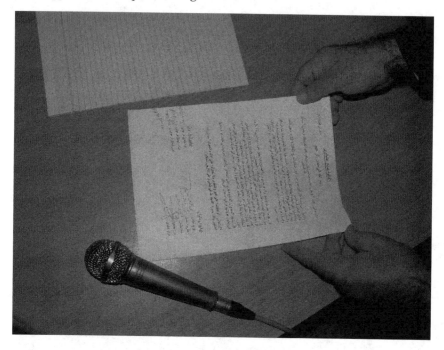

Figure A.1 Photograph of a Sulha agreement

Allah said: "cooperate for the sake of good and the faithful, and do not cooperate in search of sin and hostility." Allah the magnificent is right.

Signatures of the Suliman Family
Faraj Suliman
Acrame Suliman
Asad Suliman

Nur Suliman
Nizar Suliman

Signatures of the Farouni Family
I'ad Towfiq Farouni
Ihab Towfiq Farouni
Anwar Towfiq Farouni

The Respectable Sulha Committee
The Sheikh Taha Abed Al Halim – Kfar Manda
The Sheikh Chaled Taha – Kfar Manda
The Sheikh Ali Fuad Diab – Tamra
The Sheikh Chamid Awad – Tamra
The Sheikh Ahmed Jarbuni – Arabe
The Sheikh Fathi Hatib – A'eblin
The Sheikh Abed Alla Hativ – A'eblin

The Sheikh Abed Alla Hativ – A'eblin
The Father Awad Awad – A'eblin
The Sheikh Hassan Haider – A'eblin
The Sheikh Ibrahim Naum – Shefa'amer
The Sheikh Faraj Khneifes – Shefa'amer
The Sheikh Ali Abu Sabit
The Sheikh Ali Natour – Alrina
The Sheikh Araf Chamdan – Kfar Khana
The Sheikh Maghed Ouwouda – Kfar Khana
The Sheikh Sadki Dahamshe – Kfar Khana
Ibrahim Yasser Abed Al Chaleq
Gamal Tarbia

Appendix B
Victim's clan questionnaire

Disputant revenge, forgiveness and honour assessment)

الثأر المختلف عليه، المسامحة وتقييم الشرف

Please mark your answer on the scale of 1–5 below each question.

يرجى وضع علامة إجابتك على مقياس من 1–5 في اسفل كل سؤال

Immediately after the start of the conflict, you felt your clan's honour was hurt badly (1c).

بعد بداية النزاع مباشرة، شعرت بأن شرف عشيرتك قد أوذي بشدة.

Strongly Disagree	Disagree	Neutral	Agree	Strongly Agree
غير موافق بشدة	غير موافق	محايد	موافق	موافق بشدة
1	2	3	4	5

After you agreed to the Atwa and hudna, you felt you still wanted to take revenge (4a).

بعدما وافقت على دفع عطوة وهدنة، شعرت بأنك لا زلت ترغب في الأخذ بالثأر.

Strongly Disagree	Disagree	Neutral	Agree	Strongly Agree
غير موافق بشدة	غير موافق	محايد	موافق	موافق بشدة
1	2	3	4	5

After participating in the Sulha ceremony, you felt you still wanted to take revenge (7a).

بعد المشاركة في مراسم الصلحة، شعرت بأنك لا زلت ترغب في الأخذ بالثأر.

Strongly Disagree	Disagree	Neutral	Agree	Strongly Agree
غير موافق بشدة	غير موافق	محايد	موافق	موافق بشدة
1	2	3	4	5

Appendix B: victim's clan questionnaire

When the Jaha came to talk with you for the first time after the conflict started, you felt you still wanted to take revenge (2a).

.عندما جاءت الجاهة للحديث معك لأول مرة بعد بداية النزاع، شعرت بأنك ما زلت ترغب في الأخذ بالثأر

Strongly Disagree	Disagree	Neutral	Agree	Strongly Agree
غير موافق بشدة	غير موافق	محايد	موافق	موافق بشدة
1	2	3	4	5

When the Jaha came to talk with you for the first time after the conflict started, you felt your clan's honour was hurt badly (2c).

.عندما جاءت الجاهة للحديث معك لأول مرة بعد بداية النزاع، شعرت بأن شرف عشيرتك قد أوذي بشدة

Strongly Disagree	Disagree	Neutral	Agree	Strongly Agree
غير موافق بشدة	غير موافق	محايد	موافق	موافق بشدة
1	2	3	4	5

After reaching a Sulha agreement, you felt you still wanted to take revenge (6a).

.بعد التوصل لاتفاق الصلحة، شعرت بأنك لا زلت ترغب في الأخذ بالثأر

Strongly Disagree	Disagree	Neutral	Agree	Strongly Agree
غير موافق بشدة	غير موافق	محايد	موافق	موافق بشدة
1	2	3	4	5

Immediately after the start of the conflict, you were very angry and wanted to take revenge (1a).

.بعد بداية النزاع مباشرة، كنت غاضبا جدا وأردت الأخذ بالثأر

Strongly Disagree	Disagree	Neutral	Agree	Strongly Agree
غير موافق بشدة	غير موافق	محايد	موافق	موافق بشدة
1	2	3	4	5

When the Jaha came to talk with you for the first time after the conflict started, you were willing to forgive the perpetrator's clan (2b).

.عندما جاءت الجاهة للحديث معك لأول مرة بعد بداية النزاع، كنت على استعداد لمسامحة عشيرة الجاني

Strongly Disagree	Disagree	Neutral	Agree	Strongly Agree
غير موافق بشدة	غير موافق	محايد	موافق	موافق بشدة
1	2	3	4	5

Appendix B: victim's clan questionnaire

When you signed the* Tafweeth, *you felt you still wanted to take revenge (3a).

.عندما وقعت على التفويض، شعرت بأنك لا زلت ترغب في الأخذ بالثأر

Strongly Disagree	Disagree	Neutral	Agree	Strongly Agree
غير موافق بشدة	غير موافق	محايد	موافق	موافق بشدة
1	2	3	4	5

After reaching a Sulha agreement, you still felt your clan's honour was hurt badly (6c).

.بعد التوصل لاتفاق الصلحة، لا زلت تشعر بأن شرف عشيرتك قد أوذي بشدة

Strongly Disagree	Disagree	Neutral	Agree	Strongly Agree
غير موافق بشدة	غير موافق	محايد	موافق	موافق بشدة
1	2	3	4	5

After you agreed to the Atwa and* hudna, *you were willing to forgive the perpetrator's clan (4b).

.بعدما وافقت على دفع عطوة وهدنة، كنت على استعداد لمسامحة عشيرة الجاني

Strongly Disagree	Disagree	Neutral	Agree	Strongly Agree
غير موافق بشدة	غير موافق	محايد	موافق	موافق بشدة
1	2	3	4	5

After you agreed to the Atwa and* hudna, *you still felt your clan's honour was hurt badly (4c).

.بعدما وافقت على دفع عطوة وهدنة، لا زلت تشعر بأن شرف عشيرتك قد أوذي بشدة

Strongly Disagree	Disagree	Neutral	Agree	Strongly Agree
غير موافق بشدة	غير موافق	محايد	موافق	موافق بشدة
1	2	3	4	5

When you signed the* Tafweeth, *you were willing to forgive the perpetrator's clan (3b).

.عندما وقعت على التفويض، كنت على استعداد لمسامحة عشيرة الجاني

Strongly Disagree	Disagree	Neutral	Agree	Strongly Agree
غير موافق بشدة	غير موافق	محايد	موافق	موافق بشدة
1	2	3	4	5

After meeting the Jaha several times, you felt you still wanted to take revenge (5a).

.بعد الاجتماع مع الجاهة عدة مرات، شعرت بأنك لا زلت ترغب في الأخذ بالثأر

Strongly Disagree	Disagree	Neutral	Agree	Strongly Agree
غير موافق بشدة	غير موافق	محايد	موافق	موافق بشدة
1	2	3	4	5

After meeting the Jaha several times, you still felt your clan's honour was hurt badly (5c).

.بعد الاجتماع مع الجاهة عدة مرات، لا زلت تشعر بأن شرف عشيرتك قد أوذي بشدة

Strongly Disagree	Disagree	Neutral	Agree	Strongly Agree
غير موافق بشدة	غير موافق	محايد	موافق	موافق بشدة
1	2	3	4	5

After participating in the Sulha ceremony, you still felt your clan's honour was hurt badly (7c).

.بعد المشاركة في مراسم الصلحة، لا زلت تشعر بأن شرف عشيرتك قد أوذي بشدة

Strongly Disagree	Disagree	Neutral	Agree	Strongly Agree
غير موافق بشدة	غير موافق	محايد	موافق	موافق بشدة
1	2	3	4	5

After reaching a Sulha agreement, you were willing to forgive the perpetrator's clan (6b).

.بعد التوصل لاتفاق الصلحة، كنت على استعداد لمسامحة عشيرة الجاني

Strongly Disagree	Disagree	Neutral	Agree	Strongly Agree
غير موافق بشدة	غير موافق	محايد	موافق	موافق بشدة
1	2	3	4	5

When you signed the Tafweeth, *you still felt your clan's honour was hurt badly (3c).*

.عندما وقعت على التفويض، لا زلت تشعر بأن شرف عشيرتك قد أوذي بشدة

Strongly Disagree	Disagree	Neutral	Agree	Strongly Agree
غير موافق بشدة	غير موافق	محايد	موافق	موافق بشدة
1	2	3	4	5

Appendix B: victim's clan questionnaire

After participating in the Sulha ceremony, you were willing to forgive the perpetrator's clan (7b).

بعد المشاركة في مراسم الصلحة، كنت على استعداد لمسامحة عشيرة الجاني.

Strongly Disagree	Disagree	Neutral	Agree	Strongly Agree
غير موافق بشدة	غير موافق	محايد	موافق	موافق بشدة
1	2	3	4	5

Immediately after the start of the conflict, you were willing to forgive the killer's clan (1b).

بعد بداية النزاع مباشرة، كنت على استعداد لمسامحة عشيرة القاتل.

Strongly Disagree	Disagree	Neutral	Agree	Strongly Agree
غير موافق بشدة	غير موافق	محايد	موافق	موافق بشدة
1	2	3	4	5

After meeting the Jaha several times, you were willing to forgive the perpetrator's clan (5b).

بعد الاجتماع مع الجاهة عدة مرات، كنت على استعداد لمسامحة عشيرة الجاني.

Strongly Disagree	Disagree	Neutral	Agree	Strongly Agree
غير موافق بشدة	غير موافق	محايد	موافق	موافق بشدة
1	2	3	4	5

Appendix C
Maps

Figure C.1 General map of Israel

Credit: Mycolors | Dreamstime.com — State of Israel – Vector Map Photo

Figure C.2 Map of research region (northern Israel)

Credit: Mycolors | Dreamstime.com — State Of Israel – Vector Map Photo

Bibliography

Primary sources

Interviews

Author interviews with Faraj Khneifes, member of the Sulha Committee of northern Israel's Arab community: 21 July 2007, 14 June 2009, 15 July 2011, 5 July 2012.

Author interview with Ibrahim M'bada Naum (Abu M'bada), member of the Sulha Committee of northern Israel's Arab community, 13 November 2011.

Author interview with Elias Jabbour, member of the Sulha Committee of northern Israel's Arab community, 4 March 2009.

Author interview with Sulha practitioner Sheikh Mahmud Abu Saaluk, 12 July 2007.

Author interview with Sheikh Abu Riad Ali Shtewe, member of the Sulha Committee of northern Israel's Arab community, 16 October 2012.

Author interview with Dr. Musa Abu Ramadan, an expert on Islamic law from the Academic Center, Carmel, and Bar Ilan University, Israel, 11 February 2011.

Author interview with Sheikh Ihye Abdel Rani (Abu Muhammad), head of the Sulha Committee of northern Israel's Arab community, 16 October 2012.

Author interview with Lawyer and Imam, Abdul Wahab, Shefa'amer, Israel, 27 July 2011.

Author interview (on 6 November 2011) with one of the leaders of a clan whose member was killed in a clash with one of Nazareth's main clans (interviewed on condition of anonymity).

Author interview (on 12 July 2011) with a member of a clan in Dir al-Assad, whose nephew was murdered in 2007 (interviewed on condition of anonymity).

Author interview with a woman, 3 June 2009 (interviewed on condition of anonymity).

Author interview with Fairouz Yassin, Arabe resident and educator, 5 June 2009.

Author interview with District Judge, Aharon Aminof, 15 July 2007.

Author interview with retired Israeli Supreme Court Justice, Sheikh Abdel Rahman Zuabi, 12 July 2007.

Anonymous, semi-structured, interviews with 85 women (33 Druze, 28 Christian, 24 Muslim) and 108 men (35 Druze, 35 Christian, 38 Muslim). Interviews were conducted during the summers of 2006, 2007, and 2008 in towns and villages in northern Israel, including: Haifa, Nazareth, Acre, Sachnin, Shefa'amer, Rame, Dir al-Assad, A'eblin, Nachef, Kafar Yassif, Daliat al-Karmel, isfiya.

Participation in Sulha ceremonies

Sulha in A'eblin (Christian-Christian), 21 February 2009 (Farhuni and Salman clans).
Sulha in A'eblin (Muslim-Muslim), 18 January 2013 (Marisat and Shakran clans).
Sulha in Shefa'amer (Druze-Christian), 13 July 2010 (Druze and Christian clans).
Sulha in Shefa'amer (Druze-Druze), 28 February 2009 (Abu Raed and Wehebe clans).
Sulha in Nazareth (Muslim-Muslim), 26 March 2011 (Salaam and Faisal clans).
Sulha in Dir al Assad (Muslim-Muslim), 9 August 2010 (Assadi and Moussa clans).
Sulha in Kafar Kana (Muslim-Muslim), 17 December 2011 (Hatib clan).
Sulha in Fureidis (Muslim-Muslim), 17 March 2012 (Abu D'ib and Abu Saleh clans).
Sulha in Kabul (Muslim-Muslim), 20 March 2008 (Rian and Hamud clan).

Participation in Jaha deliberations and meetings with disputing clans

Nazareth (Multiple meetings)*
A'eblin (Multiple meetings)
Nahef (Multiple meetings)
Shefa'amer (Multiple meetings)
Dir al-Assad (Multiple meetings)
Reine (Multiple meetings)
Kafar Kana (Multiple meetings)

*Note: Multiple in this section means more than five meetings. In Shefa'amer, the author participated in dozens of meetings, and in Nahef in more than ten meetings.

Sulha documents

Sample Sulha Agreement – Photo of Original Document
Sample Sulha Agreement – English Translation

Document collections

Taqdin Elyon (Israeli Supreme Court Law Reports, online service), www.takdin.co.il/searchg/וויילעה20%טפשממה20%תיבב.html
The American Bar Association and American Arbitration Association and Association for Conflict Resolution, 'Model Standards of Conduct, 2005', www.mediate.com/articles/model_standards_of_conflict.cfm

Secondary sources

Abdal-Haqq, Irshad, 'Islamic Law – An Overview of Its Origin and Elements', *Journal of Islamic Law and Culture*, Vol. 7, No. 1 (2002), pp. 27–82.
Abdulrahim, Walid, *Arbitration Under the Lebanese Law* (online book), https://sites.google.com/site/walidabdulrahim/home/my-miscellaneous-studies-in-english/5-arbitration-under-the-l
Abel, Richard L., 'The Rise of Capitalism and Transformation of Disputing: From Confrontation Over Honor to Competition for Property', *UCLA Law Review*, Vol. 27 (1979), pp. 223–55.

Abramson, Harold I., *Mediation Representation – Advocating in a Problem-Solving Process* (Louisville: NITA, 2004).

Abu Baker, Khawla, ' "Career Women" or "Working Women"? Change Versus Stability for Young Palestinian Women in Israel', *Journal of Israeli History*, Vol. 2, No. 1–2 (2002), pp. 85–109.

Abu Nimer, Mohammad, 'Conflict Resolution Approaches: Western and Middle Eastern Lessons and Possibilities', *American Journal of Economics and Sociology*, Vol. 55, No. 1 (1996), pp. 35–52.

Agar, Michael, *The Professional Stranger: An Informal Introduction to Ethnography* (San Diego: Academic Press, 1996).

Ahmed, Eliza, Harris, Nathan, Braithwaite, John and Braithwaite, Valerie, *Shame Management Through Reintegration* (Melbourne: Cambridge University Press, 2001).

Akbar, Ahmed S., *Islam Under Siege: Living Dangerously in a Post-Honour World* (Cambridge: Polity Press, 2003).

al-Fadhel, Faisal M.A., 'Party Autonomy and the Role of the Courts in Saudi Arbitration Law', Thesis Submitted for the Degree of Doctor of Philosophy in Law at Queen Mary College, University of London, 2010.

Alsheikh, Essam, 'Distinction Between the Concepts Mediation, Conciliation, Sulh and Arbitration in Shari'a Law', *Arab Law Quarterly*, Vol. 25 (2011), pp. 367–400.

Anderson, Norman and Bullock, Merry, *Forgiveness, A Sampling of Research Results* (Washington, DC: American Psychological Association, Office of International Affairs, 2006).

Arendt, Hannah, *The Human Condition* (Chicago: University of Chicago press, 1975).

Ariely, Dan, *The Upside of Irrationality* (New York: Harper Collins, 2010).

Atran Man, Scott, 'Hamula Organisation and Masha'a Tenure in Palestine', *New Series*, Vol. 21, No. 2 (1986), pp. 271–95.

Ayoub, Victor, 'Conflict Resolution and Social Reorganization in a Lebanese Village', *Human Organization*, Vol. 24, No. 1 (1965), pp. 11–7.

Bannerman, Patrick J., *Islam in Perspective, A Guide to Islamic Society, Politics and Law* (New York: Routledge, 1988)

Bar, Moshe, 'Conscious and Non-Conscious Processing of Visual Object Identity', in Y. Rosetti and A. Revonsuo (eds.), *Dissociations: Interaction Between Dissociable Conscious and Nonconscious Processing* (Amsterdam: John Benjamins, 2000).

Barakat, Halim, *The Arab World: Society, Culture and State* (Berkeley: University of California Press, 1993).

Barrett, Jeromme and Barrett, Joseph, *A History of Alternative Dispute Resolution* (San Francisco: Jossey-Bass, 2004).

Barzily, Gad, 'Arabs? Only in Singular', *Mishpat Nosaf* (Hebrew), Vol. 1 (2001), pp. 55–63.

Batrice, Yvette, *al-Mar'a al-Filastiniyya fi Isra'il: Waqi wa-Tahaddiyat (The Palestinian woman in Israel: Reality and Challenges)* (Haifa: Self-Published, 2000).

Bellah, Robert N., Madsen, Richard, Sullivan, William M. and Tipton, Steven M., *Habits of the Heart: Individualism and Commitment in America* (New York: Life Harper and Row, 1985).

Bensinger, Gad J., 'Criminal Justice in Israel', in Robert Freedman (ed.), *Crime and the Criminal Justice System in Israel: Assessing the Knowledge Base Toward the Twenty First Century* (Albany: SUNY Press, 1998).

Besnier, Niko, 'Language and Affect', *Annual Review of Anthropology*, Vol. 19 (1990), pp. 419–51.

Birzeit University Institute of Law, 'Informal Justice, Rule of Law and Dispute Resolution in Palestine, National Report on Field Research Results: 113' (2006), http://lawcenter.birzeit.edu/iol/en/project/outputfile/5/a391785614.pdf

Black-Michaud, Jacob, *Cohesive Force: Feud in the Mediterranean and the Middle East* (Oxford: Basil Blackwell, 1975).

Bonderman. David, 'Modernization and Changing Perceptions of Islamic Law', *Harvard Law Review*, Vol. 81, No. 6 (1967), pp. 1169–93.

Braithwaite, John, *Crime, Shame and Reintegration* (Cambridge: Cambridge University Press, 1989).

Brown, Bert R., 'The Effects of Need to Maintain Face on Interpersonal Bargaining', *Journal of Experimental Social Psychology*, Vol. 4 (1968), pp. 107–22.

Brown, Brene, *I Thought It Was Just Me (But It Isn't), Telling the Truth About Perfectionism, Inadequacy and Power* (New York: Gotham Books, 2007).

Buckley, Ross P., 'Cross-Cultural Commercial Negotiations', *Australian Dispute Resolution Journal*, Vol. 6 (1995), pp. 179–86.

Bush, Baruch R., 'The Dilemmas of Mediation Practice: A Study of Ethical Dilemmas and Policy Implications', *Journal of Dispute Resolution*, Vol. 1 (1994), pp. 384–437.

Bush, Baruch R. and Folger, Joseph P., *The Promise of Mediation: Responding to Conflict Through Empowerment and Recognition* (San Francisco: Jossey-Bass, 1994).

Bush, Darren and Massa, Salvatore, 'Rethinking the Potential Competition Doctrine', *Wisconsin Law Review*, Vol. 1035, No. 4 (2004), pp. 1036–124.

Campbell, Donald T., 'Ethnocentric and Other Altruistic Motives', in D. Levine (ed.), *Nebraska Symposium on Motivation* (Lincoln: University of Nebraska Press, 1965), pp. 283–311.

Carnevale, Peter and Pruitt, Dean, *Negotiating in Social Conflict* (Philadelphia: Open University Press, 1993).

Chesler, Phyllis, 'Worldwide Trends in Honour Killings', *Middle East Quarterly*, Vol. 7, No. 2 (2010), pp. 3–11.

Cloke, Kenneth, 'Revenge, Forgiveness, and the Magic of Mediation', *Conflict Resolution Quarterly*, Vol. 11, No. 1 (1993), pp. 67–78.

Cohen, Orna and Savaya, Rivka, 'Reasons for Divorce among Muslim Arabs in Israel', *European Societies*, Vol. 5, No. 3 (2003), pp. 303–25.

Cohen, Raymond, 'Language and Conflict Resolution: The Limits of English', *International Studies Review*, Vol. 3, No. 1 (2001), pp. 25–51.

Coulson, Noel, J., *A History of Islamic Law* (Edinburgh: Edinburgh University Press, 1978).

Coulson, Noel, J., *Commercial Law in Gulf States: The Islamic Legal Tradition* (London: Graham and Trotman, 1984).

Daly, Martin and Wilson, Margo, *Homicide* (New York: Aldine de Gruyter, 1988).

Darwin, Charles, *The Descent of Man, and Selection in Relation to Sex* (Chicago: University of Chicago Press, 1952; originally published in 1871).

Dawisha, Adeed, 'Power, Participation, and Legitimacy in the Arab World', *World Policy Journal*, Vol. 3, No. 3 (1986), pp. 517–34.

de Silva, David A., *Honor, Patronage, Kinship and Purity: Unlocking New Testament Culture* (Downers Grove, IL: Inter Varsity Press, 2000).

Definition of "Tort", Cornell University Law School, *Public Access Law Dictionary*, www.law.cornell.edu/wex/index.php/Tort

Deutsch, Morton, *The Resolution of Conflict* (New Haven: Yale University Press, 1973).

Dodd, Peter, 'Family Honor and the Forces of Change in Arab Society', *International Journal of Middle East Studies*, Vol. 4, No. 1 (1973), pp. 40–54.

Elliott, John H., 'Disgraced Yet Graced. The Gospel According to 1 Peter in the Key of Honor and Shame', *Biblical Theology Bulletin*, Vol. 24 (1994), pp. 166–78.

Elster, John, 'Norms of Revenge', *Ethics*, Vol. 100 (1990), pp. 862–85.
Elwert, Georg, Feuchtwang, Stephan and Neubert, Dieter (eds.), *Dynamics of Violence: Processes of Escalation and De-Escalation in Violent Group Conflicts* (Berlin: Duncker and Humblot, 1999).
Esses, Victoria, Jackson, Lynne, Dovido, John and Hodson, Gordon, 'Instrumental Relations Among Groups: Group Competition, Conflict and Prejudice', in John Dovido, Peter Glick and Laurie Budman (eds.), *On the Nature of Prejudice, Fifty Years After Allport* (Malden, MA: Blackwell Publishing, 2005), 227–244.
Feldner, Yotam, ' "Honor" Murders – Why the Perps Get Off Easy', *Middle East Quarterly*, Vol. 7, No. 4 (2000), pp. 41–50.
Fetterman, David, *Ethnography: Step By Step*, 2nd ed. (Newbury Park: Sage Publications, 1998).
Fisher, Roger and Ury, William, *Getting to Yes* (New York: Penguin, 1991).
Freedman, Lawrence R. and Prigoff, Michael L., 'Confidentiality in Mediation: The Need for Protection', *Ohio State Journal on Conflict Resolution*, Vol. 2, No. 1 (1986), pp. 37–46.
Freilich, Morris, *Marginal Natives: Anthropologists at Work* (New York: Harper and Row, 1970).
Gellman, Mneesha and Vuinovich, Mandi, 'From Sulha to Salaam: Connecting Local Knowledge With International Negotiations for Lasting Peace in Palestine/Israel', *Conflict Resolution Quarterly*, Vol. 26, No. 2 (2008), pp. 127–48.
Giacaman, Rita, Jad, Islah and Johnson, Penny, 'For the Common Good? Gender and Social Citizenship in Palestine', in S. Joseph and S. Slyomovics (eds.), *Women and Power in the Middle East* (Philadelphia: University of Pennsylvania Press, 2001).
Gibson, Kevin, Leigh, Thompson and Bazerman, Max H., 'Shortcomings of Neutrality in Mediation: Solutions Based on Rationality', *Negotiation Journal*, Vol. 12, No. 1 (1996), pp. 69–80.
Giddens, Anthony, *Modernity and Self-Identity: Self and Society in the Modern Age* (Palo Alto: Stanford University Press, 1991).
Ginat, Joseph, *Women in Muslim Rural Society: Status and Role in Family and Community* (New Brunswick: Transaction Books, 1982).
Ginat, Joseph, *Blood Disputes Among Bedouin and Rural Arabs in Israel: Revenge, Mediation, Outcasting and Family Honour* (Pittsburgh: University of Pittsburgh Press, 1987).
Goitein, Shelomo D., 'The Birth-Hour of Muslim Law', *Muslim World*, Vol. 50, No. 1 (1960), pp. 23–9.
Golann, Dwight, 'Variations in Mediation: How-and Why-Legal Mediators Change Styles in the Course of a Case', *Journal of Dispute Resolution*, No. 1 (2000), pp. 41–63.
Goldziher, Ignacz, 'The Principles of Law in Islam', in H.S. Williams (ed.), *The Historians' History of the World* (New York: Hooper and Jackson, 1908), pp. 294–298.
Gorkin, Michael, *Three Mothers, Three Daughters: Palestinian Women's Stories* (Berkeley: University of California Press, 1996).
Greco, Anthony P., 'ADR and a Smile: Neo-Colonialism and the West's Newest Export in Africa', *Pepperdine Dispute Resolution Law Journal*, Vol. 10, No. 3 (2010), pp. 649–76.
Greenhalgh, Leonard, 'SMR Forum: Managing Conflict', *Sloan Management Review* Vol. 27 (1986), pp. 45–51.
Grillio, Trina, 'Respecting the Struggle: Following the Parties' Lead', *Conflict Resolution Quarterly*, Vol. 13, No. 4 (1996), pp. 279–86.
Guillaume, Alfred, *The Life of Muhammad – A Translation of Ishaq's Sirat Rasul Allah* (Oxford: Oxford University Press, 1955)

Haj, Samira, 'Palestinian Women and Patriarchal Relations', *Signs: Journal of Women in Culture and Society*, Vol. 17, No. 4 (1992), pp. 761–78.

Hakeem, Farrukh B., Haberfeld, Maria R. and Verma, Arvind, *Policing Muslim Communities: Comparative and International Context* (New York: Springer, 2012).

Hallaq, Wael, B., *A History of Islamic Legal Theories: an Introduction to Sunni Usul al-Fiqh* (Cambridge: Cambridge University Press, 1997).

Hallaq, Wael B., *The Origins and Evolution of Islamic Law* (Cambridge: Cambridge University Press. 2005).

Hamlin, Alan P., 'Rational Revenge', *Ethics*, Vol. 101, No. 2 (1991), pp. 374–81.

Harrington, Christine, *Shadow Justice: The Ideology and Institutionalization of Alternatives to Court* (Westport, CT: Greenwood Press, 1985).

Harris, Nathan and Maruna, Shadd, 'Shame, Shaming and Restorative Justice: A Critical Appraisal', in Dennis Sullivan and Larry Tiff (eds.), *Handbook of Restorative Justice* (New York: Routledge, 2006).

Hasan, Manar, 'The Politics of Honor: Patriarchy, the State and the Murder of Women in the Name of Family Honor', *Journal of Israeli History: Politics, Society, Culture*, Vol. 21 (2002), pp. 1–37.

Hashim Kamali, Muhammad, *Principles of Islamic Jurisprudence* (Britain: Islamic Texts Society, 2006).

Hatch, Elvin, 'Theories of Social Honour', *American Anthropologist*, Vol. 91, No. 2 (1989), pp. 341–53.

Herrman, Margaret S. (ed.), *The Blackwell Handbook of Mediation – Bridging Theory, Research and Practice* (Oxford: Blackwell Publishing, 2006), pp. 237–38.

Hersi, Rahma, 'A Value Oriented Legal Theory for Muslim Countries in the 21st Century: A Comparative Study of Both Islamic Law and Common Law Systems', Cornell Law School Inter-University Graduate Student Conference Papers, Paper 29 (2009), http://scholarship.law.cornell.edu/cgi/viewcontent.cgi?article=1057&context=lps_clacp

Hertz-Lazarowitz, Rachel and Shapira, Tamar, 'Muslim Women's Life Stories: Building Leadership', *Anthropology and Education Quarterly*, Vol. 36, No. 2 (2005), pp. 51–67.

Hollands, Ramon, Rahwan, Iyad, Dignum, Frank and Soneberg, Liz, 'An Empirical Study of Interest-Based Negotiation', *Autonomous Agents and Multi-Agent Systems*, Vol. 22, No. 2 (2011), pp. 249–88.

Honeyman, Christopher, 'Confidential, More or Less', *Dispute Resolution Journal*, Vol. 5, No. 12 (1998), pp. 12–4.

Hornsey, Matthew J., 'Social Identity Theory and Self-categorization Theory: A Historical Review', *Social and Personality Psychology Compass*, Vol. 2, No. 1 (2008), pp. 204–22, www.apa.org/international/resources/forgiveness.pdf

Hughes, Scott, 'A Closer Look: The Case for a Mediation Privilege Still Has Not Been Made', *Dispute Resolution Magazine*, Vol. 5, No. 2 (1998), pp. 14–6.

Hyder, Gulam, 'Dispute Management: An Islamic Perspective', *Arbitrator and Mediator*, Vol. 22, No. 3 (2003), pp. 1–11.

Impunity for Domestic Violence: 'Honour Killings' Cannot Continue – UN official', UN News Center (4 March 2010), www.un.org/apps/news/story.asp?NewsID=33971#.UQ50JaXoRNk.

Iqbal, Walid, 'Dialogue and the Practices of Law and Spiritual Values: Courts, Lawyering, and ADR Glimpses into the Islamic Tradition', *Fordham Urban Law Journal*, Vol. 28, No. 4 (2001), pp. 991–1087.

Irani, George, 'Islamic Mediation Techniques for Middle East Conflicts', *Middle East Review of International Affairs* (MERIA), Vol. 3, No. 2 (1999), pp. 1–17.

Irani, George and Funk, Nathan, 'Rituals of Reconciliation – Arab-Islamic Perspectives', *Arab Studies Quarterly*, Vol. 20, No. 4 (1998), pp. 53–69.

Islam, Zahidul, 'Provision of Alternative Dispute Resolution Process in Islam', *Journal of Business and Management* (IOSR-JBM), Vol. 6, No. 3 (2012), pp. 31–6.

Jabbour, Elias, *Sulha – Palestinian Traditional Peacemaking Process* (Montreat, NC: House of Hope Publications, 1993).

Jackson, Jay W., 'Realistic Group Conflict Theory: A Review and Evaluation of the Theoretical and Empirical Literature', *Psychological Record*, Vol. 43, No. 3 (1993), pp. 395–415.

Jacoby, Larry L., 'Perceptual Enhancement: Persistent Effects of an Experience', *Journal of Experimental Psychology: Learning, Memory, and Cognition*, Vol. 9 (1983), pp. 21–38.

János, Jany, 'The Four Sources of Law in Zoroastrian and Islamic Jurisprudence', *Islamic Law and Society*, Vol. 12, No. 3 (2005), pp. 291–332.

John, Braithwaite, 'Restorative Justice and De-Professionalization', *The Good Society*, Vol. 13, No. 1 (2004), pp. 28–31.

Jones, Edward, 'The Rocky Road from Acts to Dispositions', *American Psychology*, Vol. 34 (1979), pp. 107–17.

Jones, Tricia S. and Bodtker, Andrea, 'Mediating With Heart in Mind: Addressing Emotion in Mediation Practice', *Negotiation Journal*, Vol. 17, No. 3 (2001), pp. 207–44.

Kahaneman, Daniel, *Thinking Fast and Slow* (New York: Farrar, Straus and Giroux, 2011).

Karl, David J., 'Islamic Law in Saudi Arabia: What Foreign Attorneys Should Know', *George Washington Journal of International Law and Economy*, Vol. 25 (1991), pp. 131–70.

Karsh, Efraim, *Islamic Imperialism: A History* (London: Yale University Press, 2006).

Kelley, Harold H., 'Attribution Theory in Social Psychology', in David Levine (ed.), *Nebraska Symposium on Motivation* (Lincoln: University of Nebraska Press, 1967), pp. 192–238.

Kelley, Harold H. and Thibaut, John W., *Interpersonal Relations: A Theory of Interdependence* (New York: Wiley-Interscience, 1978).

Khadduri, Majid, 'Nature and Sources of Islamic Law', *George Washington Law Review*, Vol. 22, No. 3 (1953), pp. 3–23.

Khadduri, Majid, 'Sulh', in
C. E. Bosworth, P. J. Bearman, Th. Bianquis, E. van Donzel and W. P. Heinrichs (eds.), *The Encyclopedia of Islam* (Leiden: Brill, 1997), Vol. 9, pp. 845–46.

Khadduri, Majid and Liebesny, Herbert, *Law in the Middle East* (Washington, DC: The Middle East Institute, 1955).

Khan, Ali, 'Commentary on the Constitution of Medina', in Hisham M. Ramadan (ed.), *Understanding Islamic Law* (New York: AltaMira Press, 2006), pp. 205–206.

Kim, Hee Joo and Gerber, Jurg, 'Evaluating the Process of a Restorative Justice Conference: an Examination of Factors that Lead to Re-Integrative Shaming', *Asia Pacific Journal of Police and Criminal Justice*, Vol. 8, No. 2 (2010), pp. 1–20.

Kim, Sung Hee, Smith, Richard, H. and Brigham, Nancy L., 'Effects of Power Imbalance and the Presence of Third Parties on Reactions to Harm: Upward and Downward Revenge', *Personality and Social Psychology Bulletin*, Vol. 24 (1998), pp. 353–61.

King-Irani, Laurie, 'Rituals of Forgiveness and Processes of Empowerment in Lebanon', in William I. Zartman (ed.), *Traditional Cures for Modern Conflicts* (Boulder: Lynne Rienner, 2000), Chapter 8.

Kressel, Gideon, 'Shame and Gender', *Anthropological Quarterly*, Vol. 65, No. 1 (1992), pp. 34–46.

Kurzban, Robert, DeScioli, Peter and O'Brien, Erin, 'Audience Effects on Moralistic Punishment', *Evolution and Human Behavior*, Vol. 28 (2007), pp. 75–84.

Landry, Sherry, 'Med-Arb: Mediation With a Bite and an Effective ADR Model', *Defense Counsel Journal*, Vol. 63, No. 2 (1996), pp. 263–69.

Lang, Sharon, 'Sulha Peacemaking and the Politics of Persuasion', *Journal of Palestine Studies*, Vol. 31, No. 3 (2002), pp. 52–66.

Lederach, John Paul, *Preparing for Peace: Conflict Transformation Across Cultures* (Syracuse: Syracuse University Press, 1995).

Levine, Linda, 'Reconstructing Memory for Emotions', *Journal of Experimental Psychology: General*, Vol. 126, No. 2 (1997), pp. 165–77.

Levinson, David, 'The Human Relations Area Files', *Reference Services Review*, Vol. 17, No. 3 (1989), pp. 83–90.

Levy, Reuven, *The Social Structure of Islam* (Cambridge: Cambridge University Press, 1969).

Levy-Weiner, Naomi, 'I am Like a Bird That Hasn't Flown Yet: Life Stories of Druze Women Who Pursued Higher Education', PhD Thesis, Hebrew University of Jerusalem, 2003.

Lewis, Bernard, 'Islam and Liberal Democracy: A Historical Overview', *Journal of Democracy*, Vol. 7, No.2 (1996), pp. 52–63.

Lewis, Bernard, *The Arabs in History* (Oxford: Oxford University Press, 2002)

Likert, Rensis, 'A Technique for the Measurement of Attitudes', *Archives of Psychology*, Vol. 140 (1932), pp. 1–55.

Love, Lela, 'Top Ten Reasons Why Mediators Should Not Evaluate, *Florida Law Review*, Vol. 24 (1997), pp. 937–48.

Lovleen, Gupta, 'Regulating the Regulator: The Need for a Super Regulator', *International Journal of Business Economics and Management Research*, Vol. 2, No. 4 (2011), pp. 223–31.

Maghen, Ze'ev, 'Dead Tradition: Joseph Schacht and the Origins of Popular Practice', *Islamic Law and Society*, Vol. 10, No. 3 (2003), pp. 276–347.

Mahmassani, Hani, S., *The Philosophy of Jurisprudence in Islam*, trans. by Farhat J. Ziadeh (Leiden: Brill, 1961).

Margoliouth, David S., 'Omar's Instructions to the Kadi', *Journal of the Royal Asiatic Society of Great Britain and Ireland* Vol. 42, No. 2 (1910), pp. 307–26.

Maslow, Abraham H., 'A Theory of Human Motivation', *Psychological Review*, Vol. 50, No. 4 (1943), pp. 370–96.

Matz, David, 'Notes Towards a Mediator's Theory of Mediation' (1996), (unpublished Paper, on File With Author).

McCorkle, Suzanne, 'The Murky World of Mediation Ethics: Neutrality, Impartiality, and Conflict of Interest in State Codes of Conduct', *Conflict Resolution Quarterly*, Vol. 23, No. 2 (2005), pp. 165–83.

McCullough, Michael E., 'Forgiveness as Human Strength: Theory, Measurement, and Links to Well-Being', *Journal of Social and Clinical Psychology*, Vol. 19, No. 1 (2000), pp. 43–55.

McCullough, Michael E., *Beyond Revenge: The Evolution of the Forgiveness Instinct* (San Francisco: Jossey-Bass, A Wiley Imprint, 2007).

Merry, Sally, 'Mediation in Nonindustrial Societies', in K. Kressel and D. Pruitt (eds.), *Mediation Research* (San Francisco: Jossey-Bass Publishers, 1989), pp. 68–90.

Montville, Joseph V., 'Psychoanalytic Enlightenment and the Greening of Diplomacy', in Vamik D. Volkan, Joseph V. Montville and Demetrius A. Julius (eds.), *The Psychodynamics of International Relations* (Lexington: Lexington Books, 1991).

Moore, Christopher W., 'The Caucus: Private Meetings That Promote Settlement', *Conflict Resolution Quarterly*, Vol. 1987, No. 16 (1987), pp. 87–101.

Motzki, Harald, 'Review of *The Origins of Islamic Law: The Qur'an, the Muwatta' and Madinan Amal*, by Yasin Dutton', *Journal of Law and Religion*, Vol. 15, No. 1/2 (2000–01), pp. 369–73.

Motzki, Harald, *The Origins of Islamic Jurisprudence: Meccan Fiqh before the Classical Schools*, translated by Marion H. Katz (Leiden: Brill Academic Publisher, 2002).

Moursi Badr, Gamal, 'Islamic Law: Its Relation to Other Legal Systems', *American Journal of Comparative Law*, Vol. 26, No. 2 (1978), pp. 187–98.

Nathan, Susan, *The Other Side of Israel: My Journey Across the Jewish/Arab Divide* (New York: Random House, 2005).

Nisbett, Richard E. and Cohen, Dov, *Culture of Honour: The Psychology of Violence in the South* (Boulder: Westview 1996).

Nolan-Haley, Jacqueline M., *Alternative Dispute Resolution in a* Nutshell, 4th ed. (St. Paul, MN: West Wadsworth, 2008).

Othman, Aida, '"And Amicable Settlement Is Best": Sulh and Dispute Resolution in Islamic Law', *Arab Law Quarterly*, Vol. 21, No. 2 (2007), pp. 64–90.

Otterbein, Keith and Otterbein, Charlotte, 'An Eye for an Eye, a Tooth for a Tooth: A Cross Cultural Study of Feuding', *American Anthropologist*, Vol. 67, No. 6 (1965), pp. 1470–82.

Parkes, Colin M., 'Psychiatric Problems Following Bereavement by Murder or Manslaughter', *British Journal of Psychiatry*, Vol. 162 (1993), pp. 49–54.

Parrinder, Geoffrey, 'And is it True?' *Religious Studies*, Vol. 8, No. 1 (1972), pp. 15–27.

Pely, Doron, 'When Honor Trumps Basic Needs: The Role of Honor in Deadly Disputes Within Israel's Arab Community', *Negotiation Journal*, Vol. 27, No. 2 (2011a), pp. 205–25.

Pely, Doron, 'Women in Sulha — Excluded yet Influential: Examining Women's Formal and Informal Role in Traditional Conflict Resolution, Within the Patriarchal Culture of Northern Israel's Arab Community', *International Journal of Conflict Management*, Vol. 22, No.1 (2011b), pp. 89–104.

Posner, Richard, *Law and Literature* (Cambridge: Harvard University Press, 1988).

Pruitt, Dean G., 'Process and Outcome in Community Mediation', *Negotiation Journal*, Vol. 11, No. 4 (1995), pp. 365–77.

Qleibo, Ali H., 'Tribal Methods of Conflict Resolution: The Palestinian Model: Atwa or Sulh Asha'iry', in Jay Rothman (ed.), *Practicing Conflict Resolution in Divided Societies*, Policy Studies, No. 46 (Jerusalem, Leonard Davis Institute, 1993), pp. 57–9.

Ramahi, Aseel, 'Sulh: A Crucial Part of Islamic Arbitration', London School of Economics and Political Science Law Department, LSE Law, Society and Economy Working Papers 12/2008.

Rashid, Syed Khalid, 'Alternative Dispute Resolution in the Context of Islamic Law', *The Vindobona Journal of International Commercial Law and Arbitration*, Vol. 8, No. 1(2004), pp. 95–118.

Rice, Paul R., 'Mediation and Arbitration as a Civil Alternative to the Criminal Justice System—An Overview and Legal Analysis', *American University Law Review*, Vol. 29 (1979–80), pp. 17–82.

Rifkin, Janet, Millen, Jonathan and Cobb, Sara, 'Toward a New Discourse for Mediation: A Critique of Neutrality', *Conflict Resolution Quarterly*, Vol. 9, No. 2 (1991), pp. 151–64.

Rippin, Andrew, *Muslims: Their Religious Beliefs and Practices* (London: Routledge, 2005).

Riskin, Leonard L., 'Mediator Orientations, Strategies and Techniques', *Alternatives to the High Cost of Litigation*, Vol. 12, No. 9 (1994), pp. 111–14.

Roehl, Janice and Cook, Royer, 'Issues in Mediation: Rhetoric and Reality Revisited', *Journal of Social Issues*, Vol. 41, No. 2 (1985), pp. 161–78.

Roman, Patricia C., *Provincial and Islamic Law: The Origins of the Islamic Patronate* (Cambridge: Cambridge University Press, 1987).

Ross, Lee, 'The Intuitive Psychologist and His Shortcomings: Distortion in the Attribution Process', in Leonard Berkowitz (ed.), *Advances in Experimental Psychology* (New York: Academic Press, 1977), pp. 173–220.

Rubin, Barry, 'Pan-Arab Nationalism: The Ideological Dream as Compelling Force', *Journal of Contemporary History*, Vol. 26, No. 3/4 (1991), pp. 535–51.

Rubin, Jeffrey, Dean, Pruitt and Sung, Hee Kim, *Social Conflict: Escalation, Stalemate and Settlement*, 2nd ed. (New York: McGraw-Hill, 1994).

Ruggi, Suzanne, 'Commodifying Honor in Female Sexuality: Honor Killings in Palestine', in 'Power and Sexuality in the Middle East', *Middle East Report*, Vol. 28, No. 206 (1998), pp. 12–5.

Rye, Mark S., Loiacono, Dawn M., Folck, Chad D., Olszewski, Brandon T., Heim, Todd A. and Madia, Benjamin P., 'Evaluation of The Psychometric Properties of Two Forgiveness Scales', *Current Psychology*, Vol. 20, No. 3 (2001), pp. 260–77.

Sa'ar, Amalia, 'Contradictory Location: Assessing the Position of Palestinian Women Citizens of Israel', *Journal Of Middle East Women's Studies*, Vol. 3, No. 3 (2007), pp. 45–74.

Sa'ar, Amalia and Yahia-Younis, Taghreed, 'Masculinity in Crisis: The Case of Palestinians in Israel', *British Journal of Middle Eastern Studies*, Vol. 35, No. 3 (2008), pp. 305–23.

Safa, Oussama, Conflict Resolution and Reconciliation in the Arab World: The Work of Civil Society Organisations in Lebanon and Morocco', Berghof Research Center for Constructive Conflict Management, www.berghof-handbook.net/documents/publications/safa_handbook.pdf

Sahih al-Bukhari, Vol.3, English translation by Muhammad Muhsin Khan (Beirut: Dar al-Arabia, n.d).

Said, Abdul Aziz, Funk, Nathan and Kadayifci, Ayse, *Peace and Conflict Resolution in Islam: Precepts and Practice* (Lanham: University Press of America, 2001).

Saleh, Samir, *Commercial Arbitration in the Arab Middle East* (Portland: Hart Publishing, 2006),

Salem, Paul, 'A Critique of Western Conflict Resolution from a Non-Western Perspective', *Negotiation Journal*, Vol. 9, No. 4 (October 1993), pp. 361–369.

Sandole, Dennis J.D., 'Traditional Approaches to Conflict Management: Short-Term Gains vs. Long-Term Costs', *Current Research on Peace and Violence*, Vol. 9, No. 3 (1986), pp. 119–24.

Sanna, Lawrence and Chang, Edward (eds.), *Judgement Over Time: The Interplay of Thoughts, Feelings and Behaviours* (Oxford: Oxford University Press, 2006).

Sayen, George, 'Arbitration, Conciliation, and the Islamic Legal Tradition in Saudi Arabia', *University of Pennsylvania Journal of International Business Law*, Vol. 9, No. 2 (1987), pp. 211–27.

Schacht, Joseph, 'Foreign Elements in Ancient Islamic Law', *Journal of Comparative Law and International Law*, Vol. 32, Nos. 3/4 (1950), pp. 9–17.

Schacht, Joseph, 'The Origins of Muhammadan Jurisprudence', *Journal of Comparative Legislation and International Law*, Third Series, Vol. 33, Nos. 3/4 (1951), pp. 113–14.

Schacht, Joseph, *An Introduction to Islamic Law* (Oxford: Oxford University Press, 1983).

Schneider, Jane, 'Of Vigilance and Virgins: Honor, Shame and Access to Resources in Mediterranean Societies', *Ethnology*, Vol. 10, No. 1 (1971), pp. 1–24.

Schnell, Izhak, 'Urban Restructuring in Israeli Arabs Settlements', *Middle Eastern Studies*, Vol. 30, No. 2 (1994), pp. 330–50.

Schnell, Izhak and Sofer, Michael, 'Embedding Entrepreneurship in Social Structure: Israeli-Arab Entrepreneurship', *International Journal of Urban and Regional Research*, Vol. 27, No. 2 (2003), pp. 300–18.

Shapiro, Ron, 'It's Sulha Time', *Hapraklit* (Hebrew), Vol. 48, No. 2 (2006), pp. 433–58.

Silbey, Susan S. and Sally, Merry E., 'Mediator Settlement Strategies', *Law and Policy Quarterly*, Vol. 8, No. 1 (1986), pp. 7–32.

Sills, David L., *International Encyclopaedia of the Social Sciences*, 18 Vols. (New York: Macmillan and Free Press, 1968).

Sites, Paul, *Control: The Basis of Social Order* (New York: Dunellen Publishing Company, 1972).

Smith, Daniel, 'The Rewards of Allah', *Journal of Peace Research*, Vol. 26, No. 4 (1989), pp. 385–98.

Smith, Jane, 'Women, Religion and Social Change in Early Islam', in Elison Findly and Yvonne Haddad (eds.), *Women, Religion, and Social Change* (Albany: State University of New York Press, 1985), pp. 19–37.

Staub, Ervin, 'Constructive Rather Than Harmful Forgiveness, Reconciliation, Ways to Promote Them After Genocide and Mass Killing', in Everett Worthington (ed.), *Handbook of Forgiveness* (New York: Routledge, 2005).

Stempel, Jeffrey W., 'Reflections on Judicial ADR and the Multi-Door Courthouse at Twenty: Fait Accompli, Failed Overture, or Fledgling Adulthood', *Ohio State Journal on Dispute Resolution*, Vol. 11, No. 2 (1996), pp. 297–395.

Stets, Jan E. and Burke, Peter J., 'Identity Theory and Social Identity Theory', *Social Psychology Quarterly*, Vol. 63, No. 3 (2000), pp. 224–37.

Stuckless, Noreen and Goranson, Richard, 'The Vengeance Scale: Development of a Measure of Attitudes Toward Revenge', *Journal of Social Behavior and Personality*, Vol. 7, No. 1, (1992), pp. 25–42.

Stulberg, Joseph B., 'Facilitative Versus Evaluative Mediator Orientations: Piercing the "Grid" Lock', *Florida State University Law Review*, Vol. 24 (1997), pp. 985–1003.

Suad, Joseph, 'Gender and Family in the Arab World', in S. Sabbagh (ed.), *Arab Women Between Defiance and Restraint* (New York: Olive-Branch Press, 1996), pp. 194–201.

Susan Sprecher, 'Social Exchange Theories and Sexuality', *Journal of Sex Research*, Vol. 35, No. 1 (1998), pp. 32–43.

Subkoviak, Michael J., Enright, Robert D., Wu, Ching-Ru, Gassin, Elisabeth A., Freedman, Suzanne, Olson, Leanne M. and Sarinopoulos, Issidoros, 'Measuring Interpersonal Forgiveness in Late Adolescence and Middle Adulthood', *Journal of Adolescence*, Vol. 18 (1995), pp. 641–55.

Tahir-ul-Qadri, Muhammad, *The Constitution of Medina: 63 Constitutional Articles* (London: Minhaj-ul-Quran Publications, 2012).

Tajfel, Henri and Turner, John C., 'An Integrative Theory of Intergroup Conflict', in Stephen Worchel and William G. Austin (eds.), *The Social Psychology of Intergroup Relations* (Monterey, CA: Brooks-Cole, 1979), pp. 33–47.

Tetlock, Philip, 'Accountability: A Social Check on the Fundamental Attribution Error', *Social Psychology Quarterly*, Vol. 48, No. 3 (1985), pp. 227–36.

Tsafrir, Nurit, 'Arab Customary Law in Israel: Sulha Agreements and Israeli Courts', *Islamic Law and Society*, Vol. 1, No. 13 (2006), pp. 76–98.

Tulving, Endel and Schacter, Daniel L., 'Priming and Human Memory Systems', *Science*, Vol. 247, No. 4940 (1990), pp. 301–6.

Van Boven, Leaf, Gilovich, Thomas and Husted Medvec, Victoria, 'The Illusion of Transparency in Negotiations', *Negotiation Journal*, Vol. 19, No. 2 (2003), pp. 117–31.

Van Maanen, John, *Tales of the Field: On Writing Ethnography* (Chicago: University of Chicago Press, 1988).

Van Vliet, Jessica, 'Shame and Resilience in Adulthood: A Grounded Theory Study', *Journal of Counselling Psychology*, Vol. 55, No. 2 (2008), pp. 233–45.

Vesey-Fitzgerald, Seymour G., 'The Alleged Debt of Islamic Law to Roman Law', *The Law Quarterly Review*, Vol. 67, No. 265 (1951), pp. 81–102.

Walgrave, Lode and Aertsen, Ivo, 'Reintegrative Shaming and Restorative Justice', *European Journal on Criminal Policy and Research*, Vol. 4, No. 4 (1996), pp. 67–85.

Warren, Edgar L. and Bernstein, Irving, 'The Arbitration Process', *Southern Economic Journal*, Vol. 17, No. 1 (1950), pp. 16–32.

Warrick, Catherine, 'The Vanishing Victim: Criminal Law and Gender in Jordan', *Law and Society Review*, Vol. 39, No. 2 (2005), pp. 315–48.

Watt, William M., 'The Dating of the Qur'an: A Review of Richard Bell's Theories', *Journal of the Royal Asiatic Society* (New Series), Vol. 89, Nos. 1/2 (1957), pp. 46–56.

Watt, William M., *Muhammad: Prophet and Statesman* (Oxford: Oxford University Press, 1961).

Watt, William M., *Islam and the Integration of Society* (London: Routledge, 2001), p. 5.

Wegner, Judith, R., 'Islamic and Talmudic Jurisprudence: The Four Roots of Islamic Law and their Talmudic Counterparts', *American Journal of Legal History*, Vol. 26, No. 1 (1982), pp. 25–71.

Wheeler, Brandon M., *Applying the Canon in Islam: The Authorization and Maintenance of Interpretive Reasoning in Hanafi Scholarship* (Albany: State University of New York Press, 1996).

Whitehead, Tony, 'Basic Classical Ethnographic Research Methods: Secondary Data Analysis, Fieldwork, Observation/Participant Observation, and Informal and Semi Structured Interviewing', Ethnographically Informed Community and Cultural Assessment Research Systems (EICCARS) Working Paper Series Source, 2005, www.cusag.umd.edu/documents/WorkingPapers/ClassicalEthnoMethods.pdf,

Wikan, Umi, 'Shame and Honour: A Contestable Pair', *New Series*, Vol. 19, No. 4 (1984), pp. 635–52.

Zahraa, Mahdi and Hak, Nora, 'Tahkim (Arbitration) in Islamic Law Within the Context of Family Disputes', *Arab Law Quarterly*, Vol. 20, No. 1 (2006), pp. 2–42.

Index

Abraham 42, 51, 206
Abramson 151, 201
Abu-Nimer 7, 8, 9, 51, 53, 55, 68, 72, 74, 136, 138, 150
acceptance 12, 15, 16, 28, 96, 97, 98, 114, 115, 117, 121, 124, 135, 163, 165, 166, 167, 169
accommodate 3, 15, 44, 85, 87, 90, 91, 92, 106, 133, 158, 159, 179
accused 146, 157, 177
acknowledge 2, 5, 77, 82, 94, 98, 112, 138, 148, 176
adherents 11, 14, 15, 16, 25, 95,
adjudication 19, 25, 28, 139, 141, 153, 168
adulthood 53, 74, 151, 209, 210
advantage 16, 44, 142, 149
advocate 17, 139, 155, 171, 181
A'ebelin 184
A'eblin 174, 176, 177, 181, 182, 183, 191, 192, 199, 200
agencies 15, 128
aggressive 85, 92, 101, 143, 180
aggressor 16, 62, 67
agnate 43, 57, 129
agreement 1, 2, 3, 6, 8, 9, 15, 22, 23, 24, 28, 65, 77, 79, 82, 84, 90, 91, 93, 95, 96, 98, 99, 100, 101, 105, 106, 107, 108, 109, 110, 111, 113, 114, 115, 116, 120, 127, 131, 132, 133, 134, 135, 136, 141, 143, 144, 145, 146, 147, 149, 154, 155, 156, 157, 158, 159, 160, 161, 162, 163, 165, 166, 167, 168, 169, 170, 179, 181, 184, 191, 192, 194, 195, 196, 200, 209
Aharon 169, 173, 199
Ahmad 15, 173
Ahmed 33, 53, 72, 158, 191, 192, 201
Aida 8, 207
Alah 9, 16, 17, 18, 22, 25, 26, 28, 29, 30, 31, 154, 191, 192, 203, 209
Alfred 30, 203

Ali 8, 9, 22, 23, 33, 91, 128, 136, 137, 172, 191, 192, 199, 205, 207
Alrina 192
Alsheikh 16, 32, 201
Altamira 33, 205
Altruistic 51, 202
Amalia 58, 72, 136, 208
ambivalent 89, 95, 98, 104, 118, 153
amicable 8, 22, 26, 101, 207
Aminof 169, 173, 199
Anas 15
Anderson 201
Andrea 152, 205
Andrew 32, 207
anonymous 85, 137, 199
anthropologist 2, 7, 9, 35, 39, 50, 56, 58, 72, 73, 139, 203, 204, 207
apology 5, 68, 69, 114, 124, 181
Appel-Danon 157
appellant 156, 160
appellate 154, 168
Arabe 134, 191, 192, 199
Arabia 10, 15, 17, 18, 19, 23, 30, 32, 34, 54, 126, 150, 205, 208
al-Arabia 208
Arabian 13, 15, 17, 21, 58
Arabs 1, 2, 8, 33, 54, 56, 70, 72, 74, 128, 129, 130, 136, 137, 138, 140, 162, 170, 171, 172, 173, 187, 188, 201, 202, 203, 206, 209
arbiter 17, 18, 27, 29
arbitral 15, 16, 21
arbitrate 9, 10, 15, 16, 17, 19, 20, 21, 22, 23, 24, 30, 31, 81, 90, 107, 139, 144, 145, 149, 159, 204
argue 38, 39, 40, 47, 59, 78, 133
argument 11, 13, 18, 38, 40, 45, 59, 61, 64, 65, 92, 100, 105, 107, 134, 138, 145, 155, 159, 161, 167, 168
Ariely 51, 56, 62, 64, 72, 73, 201

Index

Armand 156
armed 82, 85
arrange 23, 87, 89, 95, 114, 137, 155, 171, 183
arrest 133, 157, 158, 176, 180, 191
assassin 23, 135
assault 2, 29, 48, 76, 155, 158, 176
assumption 14, 28, 36, 37, 44, 49, 78, 79, 83, 88, 97, 124, 138, 139, 150, 157, 170
atonement 28
attack 1, 4, 27, 44, 48, 64, 65, 66, 81, 82, 90, 96, 129, 131, 133, 156, 176, 177, 179, 180
attitudes 4, 5, 13, 24, 25, 26, 36, 47, 48, 49, 58, 60, 73, 78, 90, 94, 98, 106, 118, 121, 123, 124, 134, 138, 161, 168, 169, 206, 209
attribution 45, 52, 205, 208, 209
Atwa 9, 71, 80, 95, 96, 97, 98, 99, 107, 108, 119, 126, 131, 179, 181, 193, 195, 207
audience 64, 74, 184, 206
authority 1, 12, 13, 21, 22, 23, 26, 27, 28, 32, 37, 38, 80, 86, 90, 91, 129, 137, 144, 160, 161, 170
authors 71, 148, 150
autonomous 151, 204
autonomy 33, 154, 161, 201
auxiliary 183, 184
avenge 1, 2, 5, 25, 41, 44, 46, 49, 55, 60, 63, 65, 70, 76, 77, 79, 80, 81, 83, 84, 85, 86, 88, 90, 94, 98, 104, 105, 110, 111, 118, 119, 120, 121, 122, 123, 124, 129, 133, 176, 180, 188
Ayoub 2, 8, 201

Barakat 51, 52, 72, 201
bargain 73, 102, 115, 132, 162, 163, 164, 165, 167, 168, 202
Baruch 140, 151, 152, 202
Barzily 170, 171, 173, 201
Bedouin 72, 137, 150, 152, 156, 203
behaviour 11, 24, 43, 44, 45, 46, 47, 48, 58, 62, 65, 66, 67, 69, 70, 76, 100, 102, 123, 132, 155, 156, 169, 187
belligerent 3, 65, 71, 115, 135, 160
belonging 43, 44, 45, 83, 125
benefit 28, 61, 66, 140
bereavement 73, 207
blood 5, 21, 25, 40, 44, 57, 62, 65, 66, 72, 81, 96, 106, 113, 129, 135, 137, 143, 154, 172, 180, 181, 184, 191, 203; blood-related 39

Braithwaite 9, 47, 48, 52, 53, 201, 202, 205
brothers 25, 57, 132, 179, 183, 191
al-Bukhari 34, 208

calculated 62, 100, 118, 120, 121, 122, 123
caucus 3, 46, 97, 99, 102, 107, 142, 145, 146, 152, 181, 207
ceremony 1, 4, 5, 6, 7, 8, 68, 69, 77, 80, 108, 110, 111, 112, 113, 114, 115, 116, 117, 118, 120, 125, 127, 132, 135, 137, 148, 174, 181, 182, 183, 184, 186, 193, 196, 197
Chamdan 192
choreographed 70
chose 8, 15, 16, 21, 85, 113, 175
chronological 31, 49, 123, 187
clans 1, 3, 5, 6, 7, 8, 21, 25, 37, 40, 41, 42, 45, 46, 50, 52, 55, 56, 60, 66, 68, 71, 73, 77, 79, 82, 83, 90, 91, 92, 95, 97, 99, 101, 103, 107, 108, 112, 113, 116, 125, 126, 127, 132, 133, 135, 136, 140, 141, 142, 146, 149, 156, 157, 162, 173, 176, 179, 181, 183, 184, 186, 187, 188, 199, 200
clash 40, 73, 199
coerce 16, 22, 81, 82, 90, 115, 116, 127, 143, 181
co-exist 11, 21
collaboration 39, 41, 101, 161
communal 2, 5, 11, 23, 26, 27, 37, 39, 41, 47, 61, 67, 70, 71, 77, 85, 92, 108, 111, 112, 114, 116, 117, 135, 136, 141, 160, 172, 177, 184
compensation 27, 68, 106, 154, 158, 159, 160, 169, 181, 184
competition 17, 35, 41, 42, 51, 56, 58, 72, 73, 140, 200, 202, 203
complications 90, 91, 99, 146
compound 46, 85, 95, 112, 113, 115, 183
condition 42, 47, 60, 64, 67, 73, 74, 125, 126, 127, 131, 134, 137, 179, 199, 201
conflict 1, 3, 4, 5, 6, 7, 8, 9, 11, 17, 20, 22, 24, 26, 28, 29, 30, 31, 33, 34, 35, 36, 37, 38, 39, 40, 41, 42, 43, 44, 45, 46, 48, 49, 50, 51, 53, 55, 56, 57, 58, 60, 63, 65, 66, 67, 68, 69, 70, 71, 72, 73, 74, 76, 77, 80, 82, 83, 84, 85, 86, 87, 88, 89, 91, 93, 94, 96, 97, 98, 101, 103, 105, 106, 108, 112, 115, 116, 117, 119, 120, 123, 125, 126, 127, 128, 129, 131, 134, 135, 136, 138, 139, 140, 141, 143, 145, 147, 148, 150, 151, 152, 159, 160, 161, 170, 172, 179,

180, 181, 183, 184, 187, 188, 191, 193, 194, 197, 200, 201, 202, 203, 205, 206, 207, 208, 209
congregation 114, 184
conscious 131, 188, 189, 201
consent 9, 16, 20, 22, 23, 24
consequences 66, 136, 143, 181
contestable 72, 151, 210
counter-revenge 1, 42, 142
court 1, 2, 15, 16, 23, 24, 28, 34, 133, 144, 145, 146, 153, 154, 155, 156, 157, 158, 159, 160, 161, 162, 163, 164, 165, 166, 167, 168, 169, 171, 173, 174, 199, 200, 204
criminal 47, 52, 72, 137, 152, 154, 155, 156, 159, 160, 162, 172, 173, 174, 178, 201, 205, 207, 210
culture 2, 9, 28, 32, 36, 37, 38, 48, 51, 55, 57, 60, 62, 68, 72, 74, 128, 129, 143, 154, 156, 158, 169, 188, 200, 201, 202, 204, 207
customary 1, 2, 9, 10, 11, 12, 13, 17, 18, 19, 21, 23, 25, 28, 47, 49, 54, 55, 76, 80, 128, 144, 146, 150, 152, 161, 168, 172, 173, 186, 209
customs 25, 27, 54, 55, 59, 128

Dahamshe 192
Daniel 3, 9, 189, 205, 209
David 9, 18, 31, 32, 34, 51, 52, 55, 72, 73, 151, 202, 203, 205, 206, 209
decisions 3, 9, 17, 21, 31, 143, 147, 153, 157, 159, 161, 162, 163, 164, 165, 166, 167, 168, 169, 171, 172, 176
de-escalation 50, 203
defendant 26, 145, 146, 155, 156, 157, 158, 159
delegation 134, 148
deliberate 85, 99, 100, 101, 105, 106, 133, 136, 137, 146, 147, 179, 186, 200
demand 54, 81, 90, 110, 120, 124, 159, 177
de-professionalization 52, 205
desire 2, 5, 25, 38, 49, 55, 60, 62, 63, 71, 76, 77, 78, 79, 80, 81, 83, 84, 85, 88, 89, 90, 92, 94, 98, 104, 105, 110, 111, 118, 119, 120, 121, 122, 123, 124, 136, 145, 148, 149, 154, 186, 187, 188
detention 133, 137, 146, 157, 158, 161, 163, 164, 165, 166, 167, 168, 170, 173, 176
determination 11, 32, 92, 100, 107, 136, 155
dignitary 92, 115, 177, 184

dignity 5, 47, 56, 59, 68, 69, 70, 95
diplomacy 3, 50, 206
direct 12, 19, 20, 25, 27, 43, 65, 68, 130, 140, 148, 155, 156, 170
disagree 3, 78, 118, 191, 193, 194, 195, 196, 197
discussions 46, 89, 90, 107, 111, 119, 126, 145
disease 63, 64, 67, 156
disgrace 53, 58, 202
dishonoured 56, 81, 84, 99, 124
disputant 2, 3, 4, 5, 7, 8, 9, 11, 16, 20, 21, 22, 23, 24, 25, 26, 28, 35, 36, 39, 40, 41, 42, 43, 44, 45, 46, 47, 49, 50, 56, 59, 60, 67, 68, 70, 71, 76, 77, 78, 80, 82, 84, 90, 91, 92, 93, 96, 99, 100, 101, 102, 105, 106, 107, 108, 109, 110, 111, 112, 113, 114, 115, 120, 125, 126, 127, 129, 132, 133, 134, 135, 137, 139, 140, 141, 142, 143, 144, 145, 146, 147, 148, 149, 153, 156, 157, 169, 174, 177, 179, 181, 186, 188, 193
disputes 1, 11, 17, 19, 20, 22, 23, 24, 26, 28, 29, 33, 52, 56, 58, 59, 60, 68, 70, 72, 76, 77, 100, 124, 137, 149, 150, 161, 171, 172, 176, 188, 203, 207, 210
disregard 43, 95
disrespect 84, 90
disrupted 21, 39, 130, 131, 136
dissociable 189, 201
divide 9, 12, 42, 72, 125, 162, 207
divine 12, 13, 15, 17, 18, 31
Diya 100, 106, 107, 108, 113, 114, 126, 184
Dodd 52, 58, 72, 202
Donald 41, 51, 74, 202
Donzel 205
Druze 1, 8, 128, 136, 140, 143, 159, 171, 172, 183, 187, 199, 200, 206
Duncker 50, 203
Dunellen 51, 209
Dwight 141, 151, 203

Edgar 152, 210
Edmund 7
Edward 52, 73, 125, 205, 208
Efraim 21, 33, 205
Eiccars 9, 210
Eisenman 172
Elgabar 173
Elias 3, 7, 8, 41, 55, 80, 128, 148, 156, 191, 199, 205
Eliezer 155

214 *Index*

Elisabeth 74, 209
Elison 136, 209
Eliza 53, 201
Elkahar 173
Elliott 48, 53, 202
Elsatar 173
Elster 52, 63, 70, 73, 75, 203
Elvin 72, 204
Elwert 50, 203
Elyakim 154
emotion 5, 64, 67, 78, 82, 97, 113, 121, 134, 139, 147, 152, 205, 206
empathy 100, 101
Ervin 74, 209
escalation 39, 50, 65, 71, 177, 203, 208
ethics 11, 52, 54, 73, 140, 152, 203, 204, 206
ethnocentric 51, 202
exile 82, 110, 129, 130, 131, 135

facilitate 1, 2, 3, 4, 5, 9, 11, 20, 24, 25, 27, 48, 49, 57, 60, 68, 76, 79, 85, 86, 99, 100, 124, 125, 135, 139, 141, 142, 143, 181, 187
failure 21, 28, 101
Fairouz 134, 137, 199
families 2, 34, 37, 39, 58, 69, 71, 82, 96, 99, 108, 113, 129, 131, 134, 135, 140, 148, 154, 155, 156, 157, 160, 169, 183, 184, 191
Faraj 1, 7, 45, 75, 79, 81, 95, 100, 101, 103, 106, 133, 135, 150, 179, 185, 191, 192, 199
Feldner 57, 72, 203
female 43, 57, 72, 126, 128, 130, 131, 133, 135, 137, 176, 208
fester 2, 23
feud 40, 62, 74, 109, 156, 202
feuding 21, 66, 73, 156, 207
al-Filastiniyya 136, 201
final 3, 4, 9, 21, 23, 27, 28, 93, 96, 105, 110, 112, 113, 114, 115, 161, 162
findings 7, 83, 89, 94, 98, 118, 123, 124, 171, 186, 187
al-Fiqh 31, 204
folkloristic 4, 56, 57, 143
followers 14, 21
food 42, 43, 69
forcing 98, 168, 181
forgive 2, 3, 5, 25, 41, 49, 55, 60, 67, 68, 69, 76, 77, 78, 79, 80, 82, 83, 84, 87, 88, 89, 90, 92, 94, 95, 96, 98, 99, 100, 102, 104, 105, 109, 110, 111, 116, 118, 119, 120, 121, 122, 123, 124, 154, 186, 187, 188, 194, 195, 196, 197
forgiveness 2, 4, 5, 6, 7, 9, 40, 48, 49, 54, 55, 56, 59, 60, 61, 63, 66, 67, 68, 69, 70, 71, 73, 74, 76, 77, 78, 79, 80, 81, 83, 84, 85, 87, 89, 90, 92, 93, 94, 95, 96, 97, 98, 99, 100, 101, 102, 103, 104, 107, 108, 109, 110, 111, 112, 113, 114, 116, 117, 118, 119, 120, 121, 123, 124, 125, 140, 148, 170, 183, 187, 188, 193, 201, 202, 204, 205, 206, 208, 209
formally 89, 90, 93, 99, 129, 133, 134, 139, 142, 144, 156, 179
fornication 28, 33
foundation 18, 48, 49, 50, 58, 60, 61, 63, 64, 68, 69, 70, 77, 98, 101, 140, 153
founding 10, 13, 17, 18, 21, 101
framing 21, 56
Freedman 74, 145, 152, 172, 201, 203, 209
frustration 85, 88, 89, 92, 96, 129, 132, 140, 142, 143, 147, 177
Fuad 191, 192
Fuaz 158, 173
functional 12, 31, 35, 38, 55, 57, 60, 79, 91, 92, 114, 138, 139, 141, 150, 161, 169, 181
fundamental 45, 52, 187, 209
Funk 8, 9, 33, 34, 37, 47, 51, 52, 65, 74, 139, 140, 151, 172, 205, 208

gathering 112, 113
gesture 99, 101, 110, 111, 114, 117, 184
Giacaman 72, 203
Giddens 70, 74, 203
Gideon 72, 205
Gilovich 46, 52, 210
Ginat 72, 129, 136, 137, 172, 203
Giroux 189, 205
goals 6, 21, 35, 80, 143, 153
God 2, 10, 12, 15, 25, 28, 32, 55, 60, 84
Golann 141, 151, 203
Goldziher 32, 203
Goodwill 69, 95, 101, 111, 113, 114, 127, 131, 179
Goranson 61, 73, 209
Gordon 51, 203
Gorkin 136, 203
Gospel 53, 202
Gotham 53, 202
governance 154
Govier 63, 73
gratification 42, 100
Greenwood 34, 204

guilt 25, 48, 100, 106, 107, 157, 158, 159
Gulam 11, 31, 32, 33, 204
Gupta 140, 151, 206

Hakam 10, 16, 17, 21, 22, 23, 81
Hakeem 54, 71, 204
Halim 51, 191, 192, 201
hall 113, 183, 184
Hallaq 11, 12, 14, 31, 32, 204
Hamis 149, 150, 152
Hamlin 64, 73, 204
Hamula 8, 39, 44, 51, 66, 84, 132, 134, 156, 160, 201
Hanafi 15, 32, 210
Hanbal 15
Hanbali 15, 16
Hannah 66, 74, 201
Harold 51, 52, 151, 201, 205
Harrington 29, 34, 204
Hart 32, 208
Hasan 57, 72, 136, 204
Hassan 191, 192
Hatib 177, 179, 182, 183, 191, 192, 200
Hee 48, 50, 52, 73, 205, 208
Henri 51, 209
Herbert 32, 205
Herrman 151, 204
Hersi 33, 204
Hertz-Lazarowitz 137, 204
hierarchy 12, 23, 27, 28, 42, 44, 45, 140, 181
Hisham 33, 205
Hollands 151, 204
Honeyman 152, 204
honour 2, 3, 4, 5, 6, 7, 20, 25, 35, 40, 41, 42, 43, 44, 45, 46, 47, 48, 49, 50, 52, 54, 55, 56, 57, 58, 59, 60, 64, 65, 66, 68, 69, 70, 71, 72, 73, 74, 76, 77, 78, 79, 80, 81, 82, 83, 84, 85, 86, 87, 88, 89, 90, 91, 92, 93, 94, 95, 96, 97, 98, 99, 100, 101, 102, 103, 104, 106, 107, 108, 109, 110, 111, 112, 114, 115, 116, 117, 118, 119, 120, 121, 122, 123, 124, 125, 128, 129, 132, 136, 140, 143, 150, 151, 170, 179, 180, 181, 184, 186, 187, 188, 193, 194, 195, 196, 202, 203, 204, 207, 210
honourable 55, 57, 70, 71, 98, 100, 110, 144, 155
honouring 5, 6, 35, 48, 49, 50, 55, 76, 77, 85, 99, 187, 188
honour-restoring 44, 76, 77, 85, 110, 187
Hudna 3, 80, 95, 96, 97, 98, 99, 103, 119, 126, 131, 133, 179, 193, 195

Hudud 19, 28, 33
humiliation 86, 88, 94, 104, 110

Ibrahim 8, 141, 177, 185, 191, 192, 199
idea 2, 24, 29, 36, 47, 114, 134, 177
identity 14, 24, 37, 39, 40, 43, 51, 66, 138, 189, 201, 204, 209
ideology 34, 36, 140, 204
Ignacz 32, 203
Ihab 177, 179, 192
Ihye 31, 41, 65, 91, 199
Ijtihad 12, 16
Imam 15, 16, 33, 183, 184, 199
impact 5, 11, 13, 40, 56, 58, 59, 64, 76, 84, 94, 98, 103, 104, 107, 119, 128, 129, 130, 131, 135, 187
impartial 139, 148, 149, 151, 152, 206
implementation 18, 55, 80, 90, 98, 108
impose 63, 82, 140, 144
inclusion 142, 155, 162, 168, 169, 178, 181
al-Indi 130
indigenous 36, 38, 46, 47, 49
indirect 27, 65, 135, 136
individual-focused 40
individualism 48, 56, 139, 150, 173, 201
individualistic 27, 140
individual-oriented 70
inevitable 93, 97, 140
inflicted 2, 64, 99, 160
influence 4, 6, 13, 14, 22, 45, 59, 91, 128, 129, 131, 133, 134, 135, 136, 146, 155, 157, 159, 161, 168, 176, 177, 187
informal 6, 7, 9, 17, 18, 19, 37, 48, 71, 75, 90, 129, 131, 134, 135, 136, 137, 140, 144, 157, 158, 159, 162, 169, 171, 176, 187, 201, 207, 210
informant 7, 83, 84, 94, 98, 103, 104, 110, 117, 118, 124, 125, 127, 133, 135, 137, 162, 186
infraction 2, 16, 33, 64, 66, 80, 106, 107, 113, 154, 174, 176
injustice 4, 47, 99, 143
instinct 44, 71, 73, 206
instrumental 20, 51, 61, 203
insult 42, 81, 89, 94, 107, 177
integration 30, 70, 210
integrative 48, 51, 74, 139, 209
interclan 21, 27, 28, 40, 58, 68, 116, 129, 136, 160, 168, 169, 173, 176
interdependence 39, 42, 51, 205
interest 20, 23, 27, 35, 36, 39, 41, 42, 48, 92, 114, 139, 140, 152, 160, 171, 172, 176, 184, 206

216 *Index*

interest-based 139, 151, 204
intergroup 39, 41, 42, 51, 66, 209
internal 22, 38, 69, 105, 129, 147, 181, 184, 186
interpersonal 2, 27, 40, 51, 73, 74, 138, 202, 205, 209
intervener 5, 6, 12, 17, 19, 20, 21, 22, 24, 27, 28, 29, 30, 41, 45, 46, 49, 60, 68, 70, 81, 84, 90, 91, 95, 99, 100, 103, 106, 114, 129, 139, 141, 142, 143, 144, 146, 148, 149, 150, 153, 177, 186
intervention 39, 55, 95, 149, 154, 179, 191
interview 7, 8, 31, 33, 34, 51, 52, 73, 74, 75, 79, 84, 99, 125, 126, 127, 130, 133, 136, 137, 146, 151, 152, 172, 173, 185, 199
interviewee 77, 78, 79, 82, 84, 86, 88, 89, 92, 94, 95, 96, 98, 99, 102, 104, 109, 110, 111, 116, 117, 118, 124, 135, 186
intractable 140, 141
intuitive 35, 52, 208
investigation 80, 176
Iqbal 34, 204
irrational 51, 60, 62, 63, 64, 72, 73, 139, 201
irrevocable 16, 81, 144
Irshad 32, 200
Islam 2, 3, 6, 7, 8, 9, 10, 11, 12, 13, 14, 15, 16, 17, 18, 19, 20, 21, 22, 23, 24, 25, 27, 28, 29, 30, 31, 32, 33, 34, 37, 50, 51, 54, 55, 59, 60, 71, 72, 90, 126, 136, 139, 140, 172, 187, 199, 200, 201, 202, 203, 204, 205, 206, 207, 208, 209, 210
Ivo 48, 52, 210
Iyad 151, 177, 179, 204
Izhak 74, 209

Jabbour 3, 7, 8, 9, 34, 41, 51, 52, 55, 68, 72, 73, 74, 80, 81, 125, 126, 127, 129, 136, 137, 148, 150, 151, 152, 156, 172, 173, 199, 205
Jacob 74, 202
Jacoby 189, 205
Jacqueline 152, 207
Jad 72, 203
Jaha 3, 4, 5, 7, 24, 26, 34, 41, 46, 52, 80, 81, 82, 85, 86, 87, 88, 89, 90, 91, 92, 93, 94, 95, 96, 97, 98, 99, 100, 101, 102, 103, 104, 105, 106, 107, 108, 109, 110, 111, 112, 113, 115, 119, 123, 124, 125, 126, 127, 129, 131, 132, 133, 134, 135, 136, 137, 142, 143, 144, 145, 146, 147, 148, 149, 152, 174, 177, 179, 180, 181, 182, 183, 184, 186, 187, 188, 194, 196, 197, 200
Jane 34, 50, 53, 136, 208, 209
Janet 148, 152, 207
János 33, 205
Jany 33, 205
Jaxornk 73, 204
Jeffrey 50, 151, 208, 209
Jeromme 150, 201
Jessica 48, 53, 210
Jews 9, 14, 15, 21, 36, 37, 72, 161, 162, 170, 171, 172, 173, 207
Jonathan 152, 207
Jones 52, 152, 205
Joo 48, 52, 205
Jordan 15, 28, 72, 150, 210
Jossey-Bass 73, 150, 151, 201, 202, 206
Judaism 14, 15
judge 15, 16, 19, 24, 32, 100, 145, 146, 154, 157, 158, 159, 160, 167, 168, 169, 173, 199
judicial 17, 19, 20, 151, 153, 158, 162, 171, 176, 209
judiciary 153, 154, 161, 169, 171
jurisprudence 10, 11, 12, 13, 14, 15, 18, 19, 20, 21, 25, 28, 31, 32, 33, 72, 140, 186, 204, 205, 206, 207, 208, 210
jurists 12, 13, 16, 18, 31
justice 1, 2, 5, 9, 10, 12, 13, 17, 18, 20, 21, 23, 24, 25, 26, 27, 28, 34, 37, 39, 47, 48, 49, 52, 56, 60, 65, 71, 75, 76, 80, 107, 108, 128, 139, 144, 145, 150, 152, 154, 155, 156, 158, 160, 161, 172, 186, 199, 201, 204, 205, 207, 210

Kadayifci 8, 9, 34, 172, 208
Kahaneman 189, 205
Kamali 55, 72, 204
Katz 31, 207
Keith 62, 73, 207
Kelley 51, 52, 205
Kenneth 73, 172, 202
al-Khabar 19
Khadduri 7, 13, 31, 32, 205
Khalid 30, 207
Khan 33, 34, 205, 208
al-Khattab 29
Khneifes 1, 7, 8, 32, 34, 45, 52, 75, 79, 81, 91, 95, 100, 103, 106, 125, 126, 133, 135, 137, 142, 143, 150, 151, 152, 159, 172, 173, 176, 177, 179, 181, 184, 185, 191, 192, 199
killer 85, 126, 184

killing 43, 44, 52, 57, 58, 59, 72, 73, 74, 80, 82, 86, 98, 107, 128, 129, 130, 143, 176, 191, 202, 204, 208, 209
King-Irani 9, 205
kinship 72, 202
Kressel 72, 73, 151, 205, 206
Kurzban 74, 206

land 13, 26, 41, 56, 59, 144, 153, 154, 172
Landry 34, 206
Laurie 9, 51, 203, 205
law 1, 2, 8, 9, 11, 12, 13, 14, 15, 16, 17, 18, 19, 20, 24, 25, 28, 29, 30, 31, 32, 33, 34, 54, 59, 72, 73, 75, 90, 126, 133, 138, 140, 141, 143, 144, 147, 151, 152, 153, 154, 159, 160, 170, 172, 173, 199, 200, 201, 202, 203, 204, 205, 206, 207, 208, 209, 210
leaders 27, 29, 37, 56, 73, 87, 92, 97, 101, 113, 114, 124, 136, 140, 176, 177, 182, 183, 184, 199
leadership 66, 91, 112, 131, 137, 170, 204
Lebanese 8, 33, 200, 201
Lebanon 9, 15, 16, 28, 51, 150, 205, 208
Lederach 50, 206
legal 1, 2, 6, 11, 12, 13, 14, 15, 16, 17, 18, 19, 20, 21, 22, 23, 26, 28, 29, 30, 31, 33, 43, 55, 57, 62, 70, 80, 133, 140, 144, 145, 146, 152, 153, 154, 155, 157, 159, 160, 161, 167, 168, 169, 170, 171, 172, 174, 178, 187, 188, 202, 204, 207, 208, 210
legislation 14, 18, 140, 153, 154, 169, 170, 172, 208
legitimate 16, 17, 22, 25, 44, 76, 147, 155
leniency 157, 162
leverage 3, 21, 101, 107, 145, 159, 176, 177, 181
Levine 51, 52, 78, 125, 202, 205, 206
Levinson 73, 206
Levy 54, 71, 206
Levy-Weiner 136, 206
Lewis 7, 19, 22, 30, 33, 206
Lexington 50, 52, 206
liability 100, 106
liberal 30, 61, 94, 99, 206
Liebesny 32, 205
lies 37, 50, 187
limited 3, 17, 19, 28, 41, 42, 68, 92, 99, 142
linkage 17, 19, 22, 128, 155
Loiacono 124, 208
Louisville 151, 201

Lovleen 140, 151, 206
loyalty 27, 66, 129
lubricant 41
Lynne 9, 51, 203, 205

Macmillan 50, 209
Madia 124, 208
Madsen 150, 173, 201
Maghen 31, 32, 206
magnanimity 64, 81, 95, 112, 114, 117, 118
magnanimous 109, 114
Mahdi 33, 210
Mahmassani 32, 206
Mahmud 137, 149, 150, 152, 199
Majid 7, 13, 31, 32, 205
makers 4, 27, 29, 60, 76, 82, 85, 95, 99, 102, 105, 106, 111, 113, 127, 131, 133, 135, 142, 172, 178, 185
Malden 51, 203
male 43, 44, 57, 96, 126, 129, 130, 131, 132, 133, 134, 135, 137, 148, 176, 182
Maliki 15, 16
management 1, 4, 9, 17, 31, 32, 33, 35, 38, 50, 51, 53, 60, 63, 129, 140, 151, 160, 161, 187, 188, 201, 203, 204, 205, 206, 207, 208
mandatory 23, 144, 184
Mandi 8, 203
Margaret 151, 204
Margo 62, 73, 202
Margoliouth 34, 206
Maria 54, 71, 204
Marion 31, 207
Maruna 5, 9, 204
masculinity 72, 208
Maslow 43, 51, 206
Masrawa 155, 173
Matthew 51, 204
Matz 151, 152, 206
M'bada 8, 26, 34, 96, 107, 115, 125, 126, 127, 129, 137, 141, 142, 143, 144, 145, 147, 148, 151, 152, 179, 185, 199
McCorkle 152, 206
McCullough 63, 64, 65, 66, 67, 68, 73, 74, 76, 124, 206
measure 22, 59, 63, 69, 73, 78, 79, 82, 85, 86, 92, 93, 96, 102, 109, 116, 161, 209
Mecca 10, 21
Mechafafa 106
Med-Arb 29, 30, 34, 206
median 78, 83, 87, 92, 97, 102, 109, 116
mediation 2, 3, 4, 6, 9, 10, 17, 22, 24, 29, 30, 32, 34, 37, 49, 50, 51, 52, 72, 73, 76,

101, 108, 115, 136, 137, 138, 139, 140, 141, 142, 143, 144, 145, 146, 147, 148, 149, 150, 151, 152, 153, 172, 186, 187, 201, 202, 203, 204, 205, 206, 207, 208
mediator 31, 126, 145, 147, 148, 149, 151, 152, 204, 208, 209
Medina 10, 14, 17, 21, 22, 33, 205, 209
Mejelle 28, 29, 34, 154, 172
mercy 25, 191
methods 3, 7, 9, 16, 36, 38, 69, 207, 210
Mezaraafe 106
minhag 14
minhaj 14
minority 16, 161, 169, 170, 171, 172
mixed 17, 22, 29, 30, 79, 91, 113, 167, 169
mixed-mode 22, 30
Mneesha 8, 126, 203
Mohammad 31, 201
monetary 95, 106, 113, 114, 159, 160
money 5, 25, 41, 56, 62, 71, 95, 99, 105, 106, 108, 113, 114, 117, 126, 127, 135, 179, 180, 181, 184, 191
Moshe 189, 201
mother 43, 57, 68, 111, 130, 134, 148
Motzki 31, 207
mourning 87, 88, 89, 96
Moursi 31, 207
Muhammad 4, 7, 8, 10, 12, 13, 14, 15, 16, 17, 18, 20, 21, 22, 23, 25, 26, 28, 29, 30, 31, 32, 33, 34, 54, 55, 72, 138, 173, 199, 203, 204, 208, 209, 210
Mumalacha 68, 115
murder 1, 2, 8, 29, 55, 57, 65, 72, 73, 84, 91, 95, 96, 100, 106, 137, 174, 176, 177, 179, 181, 204, 207
Muruwwa 54
Musafacha 68, 113, 125
Musalaha 141
Musamacha 68
Musayara 86, 89, 99, 123
Muslim 1, 2, 3, 6, 10, 11, 12, 13, 14, 15, 17, 18, 19, 20, 21, 23, 24, 26, 28, 30, 31, 32, 33, 35, 36, 38, 39, 41, 45, 49, 54, 55, 56, 57, 58, 60, 61, 63, 65, 68, 71, 76, 81, 96, 126, 128, 134, 136, 137, 138, 139, 140, 141, 143, 150, 154, 161, 167, 171, 173, 182, 183, 184, 186, 187, 188, 189, 199, 202, 203, 204
mutual 16, 19, 20, 22, 23, 113, 115, 139, 176
Muwatta 31, 207

Nancy 73, 205
Naomi 136, 206
narrative 3, 17, 18, 85, 136
nationalism 33, 37, 208
Naum 8, 107, 125, 126, 127, 137, 141, 145, 148, 151, 152, 177, 185, 191, 192, 199
negotiate 24, 46, 52, 101, 102, 104, 111, 124, 132, 135, 139, 140, 143, 145, 149, 150, 151, 152, 177, 181, 188, 203, 204, 205, 207, 208, 210
neighbours 14, 23, 65, 84, 141
neutral 9, 27, 46, 78, 88, 89, 94, 95, 98, 99, 104, 110, 117, 118, 139, 140, 141, 144, 148, 149, 150, 152, 193, 194, 195, 196, 197, 203, 206, 207
Niko 139, 151, 201
Nimer 4, 31, 72, 201
Nisbett 74, 207
Nolan-Haley 152, 207
nomadic 37, 65, 82
Nora 33, 210
normative 14, 15, 57, 58
Nurit 9, 146, 157, 209

O'Brien 74, 206
offence 43, 70, 76, 85, 100, 106, 114, 159, 186
offender 43, 48, 50, 65, 66, 69, 80, 82, 113, 124, 133, 146, 154, 170
offer 5, 20, 40, 47, 69, 95, 97, 100, 181
official 13, 23, 73, 81, 153, 154, 169, 170, 171, 172, 176, 204
Olson 74, 209
Olszewski 124, 208
opportunity 46, 47, 81, 95, 96, 97, 112, 115, 117, 133, 142, 147, 159, 162, 177
option 5, 30, 46, 70, 71, 76, 79, 85, 92, 96, 98, 101, 104, 110, 121, 148
order 3, 14, 21, 30, 41, 43, 44, 51, 54, 57, 60, 62, 65, 77, 79, 82, 92, 95, 100, 101, 112, 130, 132, 135, 142, 146, 158, 161, 177, 209
Orna 136, 202
Osama 174, 175, 176
Othman 8, 207
Otterbein 62, 73, 207
Oussama 38, 51, 57, 208

pagan 25
Palestine 2, 7, 8, 9, 16, 51, 72, 75, 124, 136, 152, 171, 172, 201, 203, 204, 205, 206, 207, 208
Parkes 63, 73, 207
parole 154, 157
participant 7, 9, 78, 90, 97, 108, 126, 131, 152, 184, 186, 210

patriarchy 9, 37, 58, 71, 72, 85, 128, 129, 130, 131, 132, 134, 136, 204, 207
Patricia 13, 31, 208
Patrick 33, 201
patronage 72, 86, 202
patron-client 37, 86
Paul 9, 36, 43, 50, 51, 138, 144, 152, 206, 207, 208, 209
payment 5, 25, 80, 95, 100, 106, 108, 119, 150, 160, 179
peace 1, 7, 8, 9, 16, 25, 26, 29, 33, 34, 36, 37, 50, 51, 52, 55, 59, 68, 86, 101, 103, 117, 120, 148, 154, 155, 156, 160, 171, 172, 173, 178, 184, 191, 203, 206, 208, 209
Penny 72, 203
perceived 3, 5, 21, 35, 38, 41, 43, 56, 57, 60, 64, 65, 66, 67, 70, 76, 85, 86, 94, 98, 129, 135, 144, 147, 156, 168, 186
perception 19, 41, 42, 49, 54, 56, 57, 59, 60, 77, 78, 79, 80, 83, 85, 88, 93, 94, 97, 103, 110, 111, 112, 114, 117, 119, 120, 121, 122, 123, 124, 138, 143, 146, 149, 172, 186, 188
period 11, 15, 18, 21, 34, 55, 61, 81, 96, 118, 126, 144
perpetrator 40, 42, 43, 47, 57, 65, 66, 77, 90, 95, 97, 99, 121, 126, 129, 140, 146, 156, 170, 179, 181
personal 3, 10, 12, 16, 25, 40, 54, 56, 59, 61, 62, 68, 71, 81, 91, 100, 111, 125, 126, 127, 137, 149, 160, 167, 171, 176, 185, 186
perspective 4, 12, 13, 14, 15, 23, 25, 27, 31, 33, 36, 39, 41, 43, 46, 49, 50, 51, 57, 58, 60, 62, 63, 64, 67, 68, 81, 108, 128, 133, 136, 139, 140, 141, 150, 151, 157, 159, 161, 174, 181, 201, 204, 208
plaintiff 26, 155, 158, 160
poetic 57, 145
police 52, 82, 113, 130, 144, 146, 156, 176, 205
political 2, 3, 7, 8, 10, 19, 21, 22, 27, 29, 33, 34, 35, 36, 37, 38, 40, 52, 56, 57, 59, 90, 129, 139, 141, 144, 149, 170, 188, 207
politics 7, 23, 33, 37, 72, 94, 136, 184, 201, 204, 206
popular 15, 23, 31, 37, 57, 62, 206
position 5, 16, 17, 18, 21, 22, 25, 29, 43, 47, 81, 86, 91, 100, 114, 134, 135, 136, 149, 156, 188, 208
Posner 61, 73, 207
powerful 17, 22, 48, 81, 86

practical 18, 19, 26, 38, 47, 57, 68, 71, 80, 82, 95, 98, 99, 111, 115, 133, 136, 149, 154
practice 4, 5, 8, 10, 11, 12, 15, 17, 18, 19, 20, 21, 22, 23, 25, 26, 27, 28, 29, 30, 31, 34, 38, 39, 44, 46, 47, 54, 55, 59, 61, 62, 64, 79, 82, 91, 101, 115, 129, 130, 131, 135, 138, 139, 145, 147, 148, 151, 152, 153, 160, 161, 171, 172, 186, 187, 188, 202, 204, 205, 206, 208
practitioner 1, 2, 3, 5, 6, 8, 11, 18, 26, 36, 38, 41, 42, 57, 60, 65, 80, 81, 85, 96, 102, 105, 126, 131, 132, 136, 137, 138, 139, 141, 145, 149, 150, 153, 154, 157, 162, 171, 186, 199
precedence 12, 26, 90, 100, 107, 134
preference 10, 12, 17, 22, 26, 28, 29, 158, 186
pre-islamic 11, 13, 17, 18, 19, 21, 25, 54, 59, 129
prejudice 51, 203
prestige 57
Prigoff 152, 203
primary 11, 12, 17, 21, 24, 29, 44, 77, 99, 167, 199
prime 18, 50, 103, 143
principles 11, 31, 32, 47, 72, 153, 203, 204
priority 43, 44, 59, 133, 170
problem-solving 151, 201
procedure 16, 19, 26, 28
process 1, 2, 3, 4, 5, 6, 7, 9, 11, 12, 13, 16, 20, 22, 23, 24, 25, 27, 28, 29, 30, 33, 34, 36, 41, 42, 44, 45, 46, 47, 48, 49, 50, 52, 57, 58, 60, 63, 65, 68, 69, 70, 71, 76, 77, 78, 79, 80, 81, 82, 84, 85, 86, 89, 90, 91, 92, 93, 94, 95, 96, 97, 98, 99, 100, 101, 102, 103, 104, 105, 107, 108, 109, 110, 112, 114, 115, 116, 118, 119, 120, 121, 122, 123, 124, 125, 126, 128, 129, 131, 132, 133, 134, 135, 136, 137, 138, 139, 140, 141, 142, 143, 144, 145, 146, 147, 148, 149, 151, 152, 153, 157, 159, 160, 162, 165, 167, 168, 169, 170, 171, 173, 174, 176, 177, 178, 179, 180, 181, 183, 184, 186, 187, 188, 201, 205, 207, 208, 210
procession 112, 183, 185
professional 7, 9, 37, 38, 107, 149, 201
progress 6, 43, 60, 92, 98, 102, 119, 132, 133, 177, 188
prominent 15, 25, 39, 55, 60, 64, 86, 154, 168, 179, 182
property 2, 29, 59, 72, 76, 125, 154, 156, 200

proportion 95, 104, 110, 162, 163
protect 112, 129, 146, 170
provision 28, 33, 34, 139, 205
proximity 83, 99, 112, 113, 134
Pruitt 46, 50, 52, 151, 202, 206, 207, 208
psychological 2, 43, 51, 56, 67, 74, 92, 141, 201, 205, 206
punishment 27, 42, 47, 55, 62, 64, 74, 85, 107, 146, 155, 156, 157, 168, 169, 206
purity 14, 72, 202

Qadi 16, 26, 28, 29, 154, 171
Qiyas 12, 15, 16
Qleibo 9, 207
qualitative 7, 76
quantitative 7, 161, 162, 164
questionnaire 60, 78, 79, 193
Qur'an 2, 8, 12, 13, 14, 15, 16, 17, 18, 23, 25, 29, 30, 31, 32, 33, 34, 55, 60, 68, 71, 73, 74, 207, 210

Rachel 137, 204
rage 85, 86, 88, 132
Rahma 33, 204
Rahman 1, 199
Rahwan 151, 204
Ramadan 2, 11, 31, 33, 199, 205
Ramahi 2, 4, 8, 9, 19, 22, 25, 27, 30, 31, 33, 34, 59, 73, 138, 150, 151, 207
Ramon 151, 204
random 9, 39, 72, 123, 163, 165, 166, 167, 168, 184, 207
Rani 31, 41, 51, 52, 65, 74, 91, 107, 125, 126, 199
rape 2, 29
Rashid 30, 207
rationale 35, 36, 78, 85, 86
Rayah 111, 112, 113, 115, 183, 184
Raymond 59, 66, 72, 114, 202
reasoning 15, 32, 145, 165, 210
reception 88, 112, 113, 183
recognition 2, 28, 59, 121, 147, 151, 153, 154, 161, 170, 181, 202
recompense 2, 25, 55
reconcile 34, 40, 69, 76, 79, 110, 124, 136, 141
redeem 65, 84
redress 4, 5, 62, 89
reduce 20, 26, 82, 85, 119, 129, 135, 142, 156
reframe 26, 46, 52, 99, 101, 111, 126, 142
regret 80, 114, 116, 157, 177
reintegrative 52, 210

relationship 5, 11, 12, 21, 42, 43, 47, 48, 69, 86, 135, 153, 156, 170, 171, 187
relatives 2, 83, 126, 129, 130, 132, 133, 134, 135, 156
relevance 29, 31, 35, 39, 41, 42, 49, 147
religion 3, 7, 10, 11, 12, 13, 16, 17, 18, 19, 21, 22, 27, 28, 31, 32, 34, 35, 37, 38, 55, 56, 60, 64, 67, 68, 101, 113, 114, 116, 129, 132, 135, 136, 140, 154, 170, 171, 182, 183, 184, 188, 207, 209
relocate 129, 134
repair 47, 112
representative 3, 20, 78, 79, 80, 81, 89, 90, 93, 95, 97, 99, 100, 107, 108, 111, 112, 113, 125, 129, 131, 132, 137, 142, 167, 172, 176, 177, 179, 183, 186
reputation 4, 65, 90, 91
research 3, 4, 5, 7, 9, 35, 46, 50, 51, 52, 74, 75, 77, 123, 126, 127, 150, 151, 170, 171, 186, 187, 188, 189, 198, 201, 204, 206, 208, 209, 210
resentment 20, 28, 135, 149
resilience 53, 210
resistance 63, 128
resolution 1, 3, 4, 5, 6, 7, 8, 9, 10, 11, 12, 16, 17, 18, 19, 20, 21, 22, 23, 26, 27, 28, 29, 30, 31, 33, 34, 35, 36, 37, 38, 39, 41, 42, 44, 45, 46, 48, 49, 50, 51, 53, 54, 55, 56, 57, 58, 59, 60, 61, 68, 70, 72, 73, 74, 75, 92, 99, 100, 101, 105, 117, 124, 127, 128, 129, 131, 136, 138, 139, 140, 143, 147, 148, 150, 151, 152, 158, 160, 161, 167, 169, 171, 172, 174, 178, 184, 187, 188, 189, 200, 201, 202, 203, 204, 205, 206, 207, 208, 209
resolve 1, 9, 11, 19, 22, 27, 28, 39, 43, 44, 66, 68, 92, 98, 103, 105, 154, 187
respect 4, 12, 13, 24, 28, 48, 59, 68, 77, 78, 81, 84, 86, 88, 93, 99, 100, 101, 108, 111, 114, 124, 125, 132, 146, 169
response 41, 60, 61, 66, 80, 105, 114, 158, 177, 188
responsibility 5, 16, 24, 25, 44, 66, 68, 80, 81, 95, 97, 100, 114, 120, 124, 129, 139, 154, 156, 157, 159, 160, 174, 176, 177, 180, 181
restoration 1, 2, 4, 5, 9, 39, 41, 44, 47, 48, 49, 50, 52, 55, 56, 60, 65, 70, 76, 80, 86, 92, 93, 94, 98, 100, 103, 108, 110, 181, 187, 204, 205, 210
retaliation 54, 62, 63, 64, 76, 80, 81, 85, 96, 98, 131, 133, 142, 147, 156, 161, 173, 179

retribution 66, 179
Reuven 54, 71, 206
revelation 12, 13, 15, 17, 18
reward 2, 25, 26, 27, 55
Richard 31, 61, 72, 73, 74, 150, 173, 200, 201, 205, 207, 209, 210
Rienner 9, 205
Rifaat 155, 173
Rifkin 148, 152, 207
rights 28, 69, 89, 106, 149, 169, 170, 191
ripeness 117
ritual 2, 3, 5, 8, 9, 14, 36, 37, 51, 52, 65, 68, 70, 74, 77, 78, 79, 85, 94, 95, 97, 102, 108, 111, 112, 113, 114, 115, 116, 125, 126, 132, 135, 137, 139, 148, 151, 153, 175, 183, 184, 205
rivalry 59, 66
Robert 74, 150, 172, 173, 201, 206, 209
Roehl 151, 208
Roger 151, 203
role 1, 4, 6, 9, 10, 21, 25, 33, 43, 52, 54, 56, 57, 58, 59, 66, 68, 70, 85, 95, 99, 107, 123, 127, 128, 129, 132, 135, 136, 139, 143, 153, 154, 155, 156, 167, 168, 169, 170, 181, 187, 201, 203, 207
roots 14, 18, 23, 25, 31, 58, 61, 69, 140, 210
Rothman 9, 207
Royer 151, 208
Rubin 23, 33, 50, 208
Ruggi 57, 72, 208
rule 1, 23, 25, 75, 100, 145, 177, 201
Rye 124, 208

Saaluk 137, 150, 152, 172, 173, 199
Sabbagh 72, 209
Sabit 191, 192
Sachnin 130, 199
Safa 38, 51, 57, 72, 208
safety 42, 43, 44, 45, 108, 112, 140, 171
salaam 7, 8, 9, 51, 52, 72, 73, 126, 200, 203
Saleh 32, 100, 150, 176, 200, 208
Salem 9, 36, 37, 50, 51, 138, 150, 151, 208
Salim 176, 177, 179
Sally 151, 152, 206, 209
Salman 174, 175, 176, 177, 179, 180, 183, 184, 200
Salvatore 73, 202
Samir 32, 208
Samira 58, 72, 204
sanction 48, 50, 70, 108
Sandole 50, 208

Sanna 78, 125, 208
Sara 152, 207
Sarinopoulos 74, 209
Savaya 136, 202
Sayen 22, 24, 26, 30, 32, 33, 34, 208
Sa'ar 58, 72, 136, 208
Schacht 13, 31, 32, 206, 208
Schacter 189, 209
schism 20, 22, 23
Schneider 50, 53, 208
Schnell 74, 209
Scott 39, 51, 152, 201, 204
self-confidence 93, 107, 119
sentence 154, 155, 156, 157, 159, 160, 161, 163, 164, 166, 167, 168, 169, 170, 173, 174
Seymour 13, 32, 210
Shadd 5, 9, 204
Shafi 16
shame 5, 9, 38, 47, 48, 50, 52, 53, 56, 58, 72, 73, 124, 147, 151, 201, 202, 204, 205, 208, 210
Shapiro 8, 9, 127, 160, 170, 172, 173, 209
Sharaf 4, 55, 85, 86
Shari'a 11, 12, 19, 22, 23, 25, 28, 31, 32, 134, 137, 140, 141, 154, 171, 172, 178, 201
Sharon 4, 7, 55, 85, 206
Sheikh 1, 8, 27, 31, 41, 51, 52, 65, 91, 100, 107, 126, 128, 136, 137, 146, 149, 150, 152, 177, 183, 191, 192, 199
Shelomo 32, 203
Shema 52
Sherry 34, 206
Shiite 16, 22, 23
Shret 177, 179, 181
Shtewe 8, 91, 125, 126, 128, 136, 137, 146, 152, 199
Siege 72, 201
Silbey 152, 209
Silva 55, 72, 202
Slyomovics 72, 203
Smith 3, 4, 9, 34, 73, 136, 205, 209
Sofer 74, 209
solidarity 2, 37, 70
solution 20, 22, 26, 28, 44, 48, 64, 94, 101, 105, 107, 111, 139, 141, 144, 147, 149, 161
Soneberg 151, 204
stalemate 3, 50, 208
state 7, 10, 12, 21, 24, 27, 32, 34, 37, 51, 54, 56, 70, 72, 77, 78, 79, 83, 101, 104, 110, 111, 121, 126, 128, 136, 141, 144,

146, 151, 152, 153, 154, 158, 170, 171, 172, 173, 176, 198, 201, 203, 204, 206, 209, 210
statistics 7, 82, 83, 87, 92, 96, 97, 102, 109, 116, 119
Staub 74, 209
Stephan 50, 203
Stephen 51, 140, 209
stuck 37, 73, 102, 103, 209
Suad 72, 209
sub-koviak 74
substitute 76, 149, 155, 156, 157, 158, 161
success 6, 41, 58, 120
suffering 63, 64, 84, 86, 113, 132, 175
sulh 1, 2, 7, 8, 9, 17, 22, 24, 26, 27, 30, 31, 32, 33, 34, 65, 71, 73, 150, 151, 201, 205, 207
Sulha 1, 2, 3, 4, 5, 6, 7, 8, 9, 10, 11, 12, 16, 17, 18, 19, 22, 24, 25, 26, 27, 28, 29, 30, 31, 34, 35, 39, 40, 41, 42, 44, 45, 46, 47, 48, 49, 50, 51, 52, 54, 55, 56, 57, 58, 59, 60, 65, 66, 68, 69, 70, 71, 72, 73, 74, 75, 76, 77, 78, 79, 80, 81, 82, 84, 85, 86, 88, 89, 90, 91, 92, 93, 95, 96, 98, 99, 100, 101, 102, 103, 105, 106, 107, 108, 109, 110, 111, 112, 113, 114, 115, 116, 117, 118, 120, 121, 122, 123, 124, 125, 126, 127, 128, 129, 130, 131, 132, 133, 134, 135, 136, 137, 138, 139, 141, 142, 143, 144, 145, 146, 147, 148, 149, 150, 151, 152, 153, 154, 155, 156, 157, 158, 159, 160, 161, 162, 163, 164, 165, 166, 167, 168, 169, 170, 171, 172, 173, 174, 175, 176, 177, 178, 179, 181, 182, 183, 184, 185, 186, 187, 188, 189, 191, 192, 193, 194, 195, 196, 197, 199, 200, 203, 205, 206, 207, 209
Suliman 191, 192
Sullivan 9, 150, 173, 201, 204
Sung 50, 73, 205, 208
Sunna 12, 13, 15, 16, 18, 23
Sunni 8, 15, 22, 23, 31, 204
Sura 25
Susan 3, 9, 51, 66, 152, 207, 209
Suzanne 57, 72, 74, 152, 206, 208, 209
Syed 30, 207
symbolic 82, 95, 108, 111, 115, 127

Taawir 106, 107
taboo 134, 136, 150
Tafweeth 30, 80, 81, 89, 90, 92, 93, 94, 95, 108, 115, 119, 121, 123, 131, 132, 142, 144, 179, 181, 195, 196

Taghreed 58, 72, 208
Taha 191, 192
Tahkim 10, 16, 17, 18, 19, 20, 21, 22, 23, 24, 33, 81, 210
Taifel 39, 51, 66, 74
Takdin 162, 200
Tamar 137, 204
Taqdin 172, 173, 200
Tarhil 82, 125, 129
task-specific 6, 11, 60, 76, 186
Tawfiq 174, 176, 177, 191
techniques 34, 38, 50, 51, 72, 136, 143, 151, 172, 186, 204, 208
tendency 45, 69, 78, 92, 130, 168
tensions 70, 113, 160
tentative 94, 135, 187
terminate 141, 179
testimony 107, 167
theological 10, 13, 55, 60, 187
Thibaut 51, 205
Thomas 46, 52, 210
Thompson 152, 203
threat 46, 62, 100, 131, 133, 144
token 95, 131, 179
toolbox 20, 25, 186
tort 154, 172, 202
tradition 1, 3, 7, 8, 9, 11, 12, 14, 19, 21, 25, 30, 31, 32, 33, 34, 36, 37, 38, 50, 58, 65, 66, 68, 71, 85, 96, 100, 106, 107, 128, 134, 135, 137, 145, 153, 156, 161, 176, 202, 204, 205, 206, 207, 208
transformation 2, 5, 24, 49, 50, 60, 72, 77, 79, 80, 94, 98, 105, 106, 110, 111, 115, 147, 186, 187, 200, 206
treatment 4, 17, 22, 57, 58, 86
tribal 9, 13, 14, 17, 20, 21, 23, 25, 27, 54, 61, 71, 140, 144, 176, 207
truce 3, 6, 80, 82, 90, 95, 99, 131, 133
Tsafrir 9, 146, 152, 157, 161, 172, 173, 209
Tsharaf 95, 179
Turner 39, 51, 66, 74, 209

ubiquitous 1, 6, 10, 19, 28, 76, 138, 186
unanimous 12, 105
universal 15, 23, 36, 49, 63, 66
Ury 151, 203

Valerie 53, 201
value 25, 26, 27, 33, 34, 36, 38, 41, 47, 49, 55, 56, 57, 59, 68, 69, 83, 88, 128, 129, 138, 139, 140, 157, 191, 204
Vasey-Fitzgerald 13

vengeance 63, 64, 65, 73, 81, 85, 209
vent 85, 86, 88, 89, 131, 132, 135, 136, 139, 144, 147, 148, 181
verdict 6, 16, 21, 23, 28, 80, 81, 105, 106, 107, 108, 113, 119, 142, 144, 146, 147, 155, 158, 160, 162, 164, 165, 167, 181
Vesey-Fitzgerald 32, 210
victim 2, 5, 40, 42, 43, 48, 50, 60, 62, 64, 65, 72, 76, 84, 97, 99, 100, 106, 108, 113, 114, 126, 140, 154, 155, 156, 169, 170, 181, 183, 184, 210
violence 1, 43, 50, 58, 73, 74, 82, 100, 106, 142, 156, 169, 170, 184, 203, 204, 207, 208
virtue 7, 37, 44, 54, 60, 92, 113
Vliet 48, 53, 210
Volkan 50, 206
voluntary 9, 20, 22, 27, 141, 142, 144, 151
Vuinovich 1, 4, 8, 9, 47, 51, 52, 59, 70, 72, 73, 75, 126, 203
vulnerable 63, 65

Wadsworth 152, 207
Wael 11, 12, 31, 204
Wahab 33, 199
Wahabi 173
Walgrave 48, 52, 210
Walid 20, 33, 34, 200, 204
Warren 152, 210
Warrick 57, 72, 210
wasta 86
weakness 4, 98
Wegner 31, 32, 210
Wehebe 200

widow 134, 135
Wikan 56, 72, 151, 210
William 9, 30, 31, 32, 51, 150, 151, 173, 201, 203, 205, 209, 210
willingness 2, 5, 7, 25, 49, 55, 60, 68, 76, 77, 78, 79, 80, 81, 83, 84, 88, 89, 90, 94, 95, 98, 101, 104, 105, 107, 110, 111, 112, 114, 116, 118, 119, 120, 121, 122, 123, 124, 184, 186, 187, 188
Wilson 62, 73, 202
witness 44, 64, 65, 68, 99, 101, 105, 113, 114, 129, 133, 134, 146, 174, 191
women 5, 6, 9, 11, 25, 34, 57, 58, 59, 72, 85, 87, 89, 106, 113, 128, 129, 130, 131, 132, 133, 134, 135, 136, 137, 148, 183, 187, 199, 201, 203, 204, 206, 207, 208, 209
Worchel 51, 209
Writ 23, 30, 81, 90, 115, 131, 142

Yahia-Younis 58, 72, 208
Yassin 134, 137, 199
Yotam 57, 72, 203
Yuval 172
Yvette 136, 201
Yvonne 136, 209

Zahidul 24, 29, 30, 33, 205
Zahraa 33, 210
Zaidi 16
Zartman 9, 205
Ze'ev 31, 206
Zoroastrian 33, 205